"I was surprised to learn how sad Tommy's childhood was yet not surprised at his free-spirited friendliness to all. Tommy's been a friend for many years and I'm glad to have shared in many of his adventures. This book will be enjoyed by New Englanders who follow running and by everyone who has ever met Tommy Leonard and discovered his truly big heart and contributions to American Distance running.

—**Billy Rodgers, Author, *Marathoning* and 4 time winner, Boston and NYC Marathons**

"Tommy is the Patron Saint of Feel Good. Kathleen Cleary has created a rich and endearing portrait of the man who first makes you smile and then has you walking away convinced you are the most special person on earth. It's a gift he is blessed with. Reading his life story will be enjoyed by friends and strangers alike."

—**Billy Harbilas, Director, Holyoke Elks Talking Turkey 10K**

"Kathleen Cleary's storied and entertaining chronicle of Tommy Leonard's life describes one man's passion for life, the sport of running, and its people. Tommy's many experiences along the road he has chosen to run during his lifetime will make you laugh and cry. A wonderful tribute to a man who has given so much heart, soul, encouragement, song and verse to runners everywhere."

—**Joan Benoit Samuelson, Author, *Running Tide* and Gold Medallist of First Olympic Marathon for Women, 1984**

"I've known Tommy Leonard for almost 40 years and never knew the aching details of his childhood. Kathleen Cleary portrays his cheerless childhood in compelling fashion. It puts new light on his grit and determination to make things happen later in life while maintaining such a positive outlook.

"Tommy's story is thicker than the "Cheers Bar Guide." For anyone who is taking a bartender course, do yourself a favor and spend a few hours with Tommy while he is on the bar. You'll learn more about what it takes to be a great barman than just mixing drinks. Tommy is truly "America's Host."

—Eddie Doyle, Sr. Barman/Manager, "Cheers" and "Bull & Finch Pub" at the Hampshire House, Boston

If This Is Heaven, I Am Going to Be a Good Boy.

If This Is Heaven, I Am Going to Be a Good Boy.

The Tommy Leonard Story

Kathleen Cleary

Foreword by Doug Brown
Epigraph by Senator John F. Kerry

iUniverse, Inc.
New York Lincoln Shanghai

If This Is Heaven, I Am Going to Be a Good Boy.
The Tommy Leonard Story

iUniverse books may be ordered through booksellers or by contacting:

iUniverse
2021 Pine Lake Road, Suite 100
Lincoln, NE 68512
www.iuniverse.com
1-800-Authors (1-800-288-4677)

ISBN-13: 978-0-595-35698-0 (pbk)
ISBN-13: 978-0-595-80175-6 (ebk)
ISBN-10: 0-595-35698-2 (pbk)
ISBN-10: 0-595-80175-7 (ebk)

Printed in the United States of America

To Francis X. and Eleanor Tierney,
With gratitude for putting me on the right path
And

To Major John Archbold

In memory of one of the Marines' finest
—Tommy Leonard

To Michael,
With gratitude for understanding that "life without dreams would be intolerable."
—Kathleen Cleary

Tom Leonard is the genuine article. I was introduced to a bartender, and didn't realize I was beginning one of those friendships you're lucky to find. He's the real deal. He instinctively knows when something is just the "right thing to do" and fearlessly, doggedly makes sure it gets done. Whenever I was fortunate enough to spend any time with Tommy I always walked away shaking my head with a smile on my face. A cold beer always tasted better when served up by Tommy Leonard because of the conversation that accompanied it.

—Massachusetts Senator John F. Kerry

Contents

Foreword

By Doug Brown (Tommy's nineteen-year colleague at the stick of the Eliot Lounge)

Everyone who has ever met Thomas Francis Leonard has a "Tommy story." Now, with the publication of this tremendous book by Kathleen Cleary, the privilege has been extended to those unfortunate few who haven't yet met him. The stories-heartfelt, hilarious, and everything in between-make this book a great read for both longtime friends and strangers yet to be greeted with one of T.L.'s signature lines, such as "Holy cow! So you're from Grand Rapids! Do you know Greg Meyer?"

Having known the man personally for three decades now, I was amazed by what I didn't know. Each stage of Tommy's life has been researched carefully and portrayed thoughtfully by Kathleen as she found people, documents, and photos from the last seventy-five years. What develops as you read through the life of *Tommy Leonard*—who was *also* known as *Leonard*, Rainbow, T.L., The Guru, and dozens of other (mostly printable) nicknames—is a rich and endearing portrait of the man. The honesty and vibrancy of his life shine through these anecdotes and tales.

I have a few personal tales to add, if I may:

I'm not positive of the exact year (probably 1980 or 1981), but the events are fairly clear in my memory. Tommy had been going on and on about this little race in his hometown that was held over Thanksgiving weekend, the Talking Turkey 10K, or some such nonsense. Most of the Eliot patrons would urge Tommy on once he started to get excited, just to see how fast and how far he would spin out of control. They would ask question after question about the intricacies of a Talking Turkey road race: "Who's going to be there?" "What's the course like?" And on and on until I blurted out that my town also had a road race on the Sunday of Thanksgiving weekend. Well, before I knew what hit me, Tommy had invited himself down to my parents' house and asked if I could pick him up at the Stamford railroad station on Saturday evening.

At dinner that Saturday night, my mother served a New Zealand leg of lamb. Whether it triggered in Tommy's mind thoughts of the proud running tradition of that fair country or whether the lamb actually was that delicious is hard to say. I do know, however, that over the years, whenever my mother and Tommy met, the lamb was a prominent part of the conversation. "That was the best New Zealand leg of lamb I've ever tasted, Mrs. Brown," he would say. My mom would blush and deflect the praise, but I know she secretly loved seeing how much T.L. appreciated it. Tommy may never have tasted New Zealand leg of lamb before or since, and I suspect my mother knew that, too, but it didn't matter. It was their personal connection.

Later that night, we found other connections. Tommy knew that my dad had served in the Marines during World War II and had been in Guam guarding Japanese POWs. Looking back, I'm ashamed to say that I didn't know much else about his service days because he just never talked about them. Halfway through dinner Tommy quietly asked my dad about the war and where he had been posted. My father replied, "Originally, I guarded the brig in Portsmouth, New Hampshire." With that, Tommy just about tipped over the dining room table, jumping up in his seat with a "Holy geez, so did I!" And they were both off and running. Determining that they were at the naval prison about ten years apart, both as guards, they traded stories and compared notes on what appeared to have been a memorable time in their lives. My mother retreated to the kitchen, soon followed by my sister, while I sat there enjoying one tale after another, learning things about my father's life that I had never known.

Later that evening, during a little tour of some of the local pubs that I had promised him, Tommy was holding forth at Mullane's Mug, a now-defunct (aren't all the great ones?) tavern in Chappaqua, New York. I moved slightly away from the group and stoodby the doorway, watching this great scene of laughter and friendship among people who had been strangers just an hour earlier. A friend of mine entered the front door, surveyed the raucous scene, and, pointing to T.L., asked, "Who's that guy?" I replied that it was "T.L., my friend from Boston." He did a double-take and said, "Christ, Brownie. He's old enough to be your father!" And on this night, I could only nod and smile.

The next morning, we went to the Greeley 10K as spectators. We walked a quarter-mile from the house to a vantage point at the bottom of a steep hill, where the course flattened and led to a gradual but fast downhill mile to the finish line. It was a gorgeous late-fall day—perfect for running. The first runner came screaming down the hill and passed us in full flight with no one else in sight, heading for home. Ten seconds later, two more runners appeared, neck and neck. As they passed us, one guy said, "Hey, Tommy! Whadda ya doin' here?" I had friends, neighbors, high school teammates, and coaches out there, and I cheered a little louder and called out names as they cruised by. Then another "Hey, Tommy! Where you goin' after the race?" until it seemed every other runner was calling out his name. It was relentless. By the time one of my old girlfriends ran by and asked, "Who's that standing next to Tommy Leonard?" I had had enough.

Tommy never seeks the spotlight; the spotlight simply finds him wherever he is. As this book will aptly convey, Tommy Leonard is a man of many passions. One morning I was privy to a moment when two of his passions literally bumped heads. Clearly, T.L. has a passion for running. It began as an early interest in track and field and cross-country, and grew into participation in, and a fascination with, the world of marathoning. T.L. also has a great respect for history and traditions of all kinds. At marathon time each year, many international runners would make their way to the Eliot Lounge, either before or after the race. In the late 1970s and early 1980s, many of these visitors were Japanese. Tommy could often be seen greeting the runners, their coaches and trainers, and the assorted journalists. Keeping his feet together, elbows tucked to his sides, and palms clasped together, chest high, pointing skyward, Tommy would bow again and again, saying, "So glad to meet you!" over and over. It was a sort of geisha-girl curtsy that he had personalized, and everyone enjoyed viewing the spectacle time and again.

The morning in question was the Wednesday following the 1990 Boston Athletic Association Marathon. I was waiting for deliveries when Tommy arrived with his newspapers, coffee, and sweetie cake. The bar wouldn't open for another four hours or more. Tommy was puttering behind the bar when the front door swung open and two men walked in. Tommy moved slowly from behind the bar and met the two in the middle of the room. A gentleman in a BAA blazer said, "Mr. Ikaanga heard about you and the Eliot and he wanted to meet you." Of course, Tommy knew immediately who Mr. Ikaanga was. I watched from the corner as Tommy assumed the position, said he was honored, and started to bow. And bow. And bow some more, until Ikaanga, looking somewhat confused, started to do the same. As this continued, the inevitable occurred and they bumped heads. There was a second of startled silence, and then they both began laughing and shaking hands. The three men sat for twenty minutes in the otherwise empty bar, sharing stories and more laughs. As the two guests prepared to leave, the BAA rep asked Tommy to pose with Ikaanga. Standing in front of the running wall, Tommy draped his arm around the shoulder of the five-foot two-inch Ikaanga (who had just finished second in Boston for the third straight year), and somewhere in this great big world there is a picture of a smiling Tommy Leonard and a beaming Juma Ikaanga celebrating a brand-new friendship.

Hundreds—no, thousands—of photos have been taken throughout Tommy's life, some of which you'll see in the upcoming pages. There is one photo that I hold dear. Tommy did not take it, nor is he in it, but he once owned it, loaned it to a "gallery" for a while, and finally presented it to me.

The Eliot had closed its doors for good at 2 AM Sunday, September 29, 1996. OK, maybe a few of us stayed an extra hour or two. Or five. The place was empty all day Sunday. No one—not the owners, staff, or anyone else—wanted to start the inevitable dismantling of our longtime clubhouse. I think even the rats in the back alley of the hotel took that Sunday off out of respect. Now it was Monday, late morning, and the mourning was suspended because there was work to be done. Someone had bought the big-screen TV, and it took about seven of us to wrestle it down from its perch on the far wall. T.L. and I divvied up the cassette collection that had been the Eliot's background music for years. Tommy got Vera Lynn, Joni James, and "The Twenty Greatest College Fight Songs." I got Squeeze, Bruce Cockburn, John Hiatt, and all the other unpopular stuff I had foisted upon regulars and patient co-workers.

College banners that had covered the ceiling were torn down, and we choked on the dust. And then came the hard part, the running wall. Now, as anyone who has ever seen me knows, I am not a runner. This wall, however, had become a part of me and everyone else who had ever worked at the lounge. We had Windexed the pictures, re-glassed the frames, re-hung the photos, painted and puttied—you name it. The wall, started by T.L. in 1974 with a donated (of course!) picture, had become the keystone of the Eliot Lounge. It was famous in and of itself. Just ask Juma Ikaanga.

Slowly, picture by picture, the wall came down. Frames were placed in newspaper or bubble-wrap, and as each photo was boxed, the stories were told. Where did this come from? Who gave us that one? Each photo not only served as a depiction of a moment in time, but had a life story all its own. Optimistically, we offered scenarios: Tommy saying that when I opened my own bar I could have any picture I wanted, and me saying that he could parlay this into his next job. Who wouldn't hire Tommy Leonard and his world-class, road-running photo collection?

At the time of the closing, there was a lot of interest in finding a new location for the bar. Perhaps even somewhere along the marathon route. Find a decent-sized space, get a liquor license, re-create the Eliot. Easy, right? Some thought so. Tommy and I also hoped so, but we knew different.

As we were unscrewing the pictures from the two massive columns that framed the old bar, T.L. turned and handed me a small-framed photo. "I'd like you to have this" is all he said. This photo had originally hung on the columns when Don Akin was the owner. Tommy had been back a full year with the new ownership before he had it re-hung. I guess he wanted to be sure it would be safe. There are five men in the black-and-white shot. Left to right, their names are Bernie Carbo, Rick Wise, Ferguson Jenkins, Jim Willoughby, and Bill Lee. They were known as the "Buffalo Heads" back in the late 1970s, and existed as a band of brothers who played baseball for a living but didn't always see eye-to-eye with their manager, Don Zimmer. Jenkins, a Canadian, had explained that in his country, the buffalo was considered the dumbest of all beasts. Thus, the Buffalo Head Gang was created as a tribute to their skipper. To our good fortune, this group would sometimes convene at the lounge to enjoy a beverage or two—during the off-season only, of course. In the picture, the Red Sox uniforms are worn proudly and Mr. Carbo, the only position player in the group, is holding a bat. Fergie Jenkins had inscribed the photo and given it to Bill Lee. Bill had given it to Tommy as a token of friendship, and now, Tommy was sharing this gift with me.

I thanked him then, probably inadequately. I thank him again now. I especially would like to thank Kathleen Cleary for writing this book, this depiction of an extraordinary life led by a simple man, and for letting me be a small part of the effort.

The term "simple man" is not used lightly. It is used with respect and love. What Thomas Francis Leonard has achieved in life is monumental. Most men don't have the ability or capacity to give as generously, care as deeply, laugh as heartily, or make such a difference in people's lives. Tommy always has done that. And more. We are all the richer.

Preface

It was the summer of 1999 during the Falmouth Road Race weekend when I first approached Tommy Leonard with the idea of doing a book on his life. We were standing outside the Quarterdeck Restaurant in Falmouth, where he now tends bar. His response was that many people had told him he should have a book written about his life, and he would be "honored" to have me write the story. By that summer, I had known Tommy for almost twenty years, although we had gotten to know each other more intimately in the months after the Eliot Lounge closed in 1996.

That period of Tommy's life was a sort of limbo. He was trying to navigate through a personal "no-man's land," with little sense of where he was going or what he should do next, after twenty-four years as one of Boston's most personable and genuine bartenders. At the time, my husband, Michael, and I owned the Cork 'n Hearth Restaurant, in the Berkshires of western Massachusetts. Aware of Tommy's dilemma, we invited him to live at our house and bartend at our place. Tommy has a deep love of the natural beauty of the Berkshires, and he took up the offer with enthusiasm and gratitude.

Our boys were ten, twelve, and fourteen at the time. In addition to running the restaurant and selling local real estate, I was writing personal essays about family life, which were published in our local paper. Tom really enjoyed reading them. He would make copies of the essays and send them off to people he knew. We were very comfortable having Tom live with us, and he seemed quite at ease both in our home and as our employee.

I felt it was the fact that he was so comfortable with both my writing and my family that influenced him to agree to the idea of this book. However, knowing how much Tom dislikes the limelight, I wondered if by agreeing he was digging himself into one of his frequently visited holes where he says something kind to avoid hurting your feelings, but deep inside does not really want to make a commitment. It was no surprise to me, therefore, when it

proved difficult to pin him down to a time to get started. I had become familiar with his habit of disappearing even from events being held in his honor.
Finally, he told one of our friends, Margie Mitchell, who was working with
him at the Quarterdeck, that he was having nightmares about his childhood,
and wasn't sure he wanted to revisit those memories.

I decided to lay low and let Tommy come to terms with the demons of his
past. I let him know that when he was ready, I would be ready. If that day
never arrived, we would continue with our friendship and my life would
remain enriched, like thousands of others', because this wonderful man had
touched it.

A year after we first discussed doing this book, I was once again in Falmouth for the road race and a wedding. Tommy and I didn't discuss the book
at all. A couple of weeks later, I attended the state Realtors Association conference in Falmouth with my broker, MaryJo Piretti Miller. Years earlier,
MaryJo and I had discovered that we shared a connection with Tommy
Leonard. Her college roommate was Tommy's foster sister, Susan, who was
the biological daughter of Tommy's foster parents. We stopped at the Quarterdeck at about 5:30. I knew Tom's shift would have just ended and he would
be sitting on the opposite side of the bar, having a brew. I was determined to
talk to him about the book. Tommy deflected the conversation away from the
book a couple of times, until MaryJo suggested that it would be a wonderful
gift for his father, Frank Tierney, who was still alive at the time and had been
so instrumental in helping Tommy put his life on the right track. Tommy was
sold, and the next morning we did our first interview.

Jeff Fumorala, who was bartending at the QD that evening, made a casual
remark to MaryJo, which I felt captured the essence of why so many, many
people seek out Tommy's company.

"He's good for the ego, isn't he?" he said.

Acknowledgments

This book was developed through a series of interviews, phone calls, and email communications, as well as research of the extensive list of newspaper and magazine articles and books in which Tommy Leonard has been profiled, quoted, or mentioned, or has otherwise had an impact. In fact, I owe a debt of gratitude to Tommy's great friend, the late Joe Concannon of the Boston Globe, who captured so many of Tommy's priceless and colorful quotes which are used liberally in this book with the permission of the Globe.

I have spent many hours with Tommy and am both grateful for and awed by his incredibly acute memory. I'd like to thank the many people whom I interviewed for their time, good humor, wonderful stories, and encouragement. They are acknowledged in the bibliography, and many are mentioned throughout the story. The most enjoyable part of creating this work was speaking with the vast array of folks included in Tommy's mammoth treasure trove of friendships.

The book cover was designed with the help of graphic artist Sally Rohan, to whom I am deeply grateful. Both the Village Printer in Falmouth and the Photo Shop in Pittsfield assisted with scanning the photos into the proper format.

Falmouth Race co-director Rich Sherman provided a terrific source of information and factual accuracy for the Falmouth Road Race section, and has offered a great deal of support in helping me to market the book during road race weekend.

Eddie Doyle also provided a great deal of information both for the Charities chapter and on the development of his friendship with Tommy. He and Tom Kershaw, of the Hampshire House, also have been very supportive with the marketing of the book.

I'd also like to thank our friends in Falmouth for their support and encouragement, terrific meals, and gracious accommodations over the past four and a half years: Richard and Anne Prior, Scott Williamson and Marjorie Mitchell, Ed and Pat Pas, and Bill and Sylvette McCabe.

There is a very special group of women friends in my life who reunited thirty years after our high school graduation. They have bolstered my spirits, filled my life with laughter and joy, and inspired my creativity with their support and encouragement. So, to the "Divas," thank you for being there.

My husband, Michael, and I purchased our small business, The Lamplighter, in the Berkshires six months after I began work on this book, and I was convinced I would never have the time or energy to see the project to completion. Therefore, it is with the deepest gratitude that I thank Michael for his endless support. For many, many months I left Michael and our salesperson, Lois DeWitt, to mind the store at least two days and often three days *a* week so that I could focus on the research and writing of this book.

I would also like to thank our sons, Dan, Kevin, and Niall, as well as my mom, Peg Bulger, for their support and encouragement.

Ten percent of the sales for this book will be contributed to a retirement trust for Tommy Leonard. Therefore, I thank everyone who purchases this book for helping to create this fund.

The background photo on the back cover of the book, featuring the Nobska Lighthouse and the Falmouth Road Race, was taken by Don Borowski, of Mashpee, Massachusetts.

The names of foster families in the first three chapters have been changed to protect the privacy of the individuals.

1

The Shurtleff Mission

The Starting Line

"I'm always chasing rainbows."

—Tommy Leonard

Raucous laughter and friendly banter punctuated the air as guest after guest stepped to the podium to both "roast" and thank the guest of honor. The assembled crowd was marked by their diversity in ages, careers, backgrounds, and interests. The group was composed of journalists, sports writers, politicians, TV news anchors, media personalities, radio executives, runners and other athletes (Olympians and lesser-knowns), former Marines, FBI agents, policemen, physicians, business owners, executives, bartenders, restaurateurs, students, sports managers, race organizers, coaches, teachers, and friends—all of whom had come together out of love.

The unifying force in the room was the man they had come to honor, the man whose quarter-century career behind the stick at the Eliot Lounge in Boston was coming to an end, causing a lot of sadness and reminiscence. The event, dubbed "The Tommy Leonard Wicked Awesome Hampshire House Happening," gave those present the opportunity to thank the one man who had had a significant impact on all of them. Whether Tommy had influenced them to tend to their health and fitness, encouraged them through the trials and tribulations of running or professional careers, entertained them with his never-ending zest and passion for life and people, bolstered them when they were feeling down, delighted them with his zany ideas and events, or humbled them with his selflessness and thoughtfulness toward the little guy, all the men and women present knew that their lives had been touched by someone extraordinarily special.

As Tommy listened to the accolades and gentle jokes about his bartending skills, he reflected on the life that had brought him to this moment, surrounded by so many, many wonderful friends. His passion for running had taken him around the globe, his stint in the Marines had given him pride and discipline, his career as a bartender had provided a never-ending prism that reflected life's many interesting and diverse facets. A rainbow of joy enveloped him.

He took the podium to thank those present. Scanning the crowd and speaking from his heart, he said, "If this is Heaven, I am going to be a good boy." But his thoughts were on a cold winter day fifty-six years earlier.

Friday was six-year-old Tommy Leonard's favorite day. On Fridays, his father, Edward Arthur Leonard—known as "Artie" to the grown-ups in Tommy's life—would come home from his job at the Boston and Albany Railroad in West Springfield, Massachusetts, with a paycheck.

"Come on, Tommy, let's go get your friends," he'd say, and they would leave their small flat at 3 Greenwood Street in the North End of Springfield, Massachusetts (where many of the Irish settled in the late 1800s and early 1900s), gather all the kids in the neighborhood, and take them for an ice cream treat.

There was something different, however, about this Friday in March of 1940. Tommy's mother, Elizabeth McCarthy Leonard, known as "Lizzie," seemed quiet and sad as she told Tommy and his four-year-old sister, Grace, to put all of their belongings in the brown paper sacks she offered them. Her eyes seemed watery as she promised, "I will come to visit you soon." Why was she talking like that? Where were they going? Born in the heart of the Depression, Tommy and his sister were born into a home rich in love but little else. Their father's health had been failing and the resources they had were few. Tommy felt confused as his father led them to the bus. The three rode in silence through the driving snow to the Shurtleff Mission on Franklin Street in Westfield, Massachusetts.

Tommy Leonard stayed close to his father's side while the adults talked in the parlor of the large, three-story house. The house felt strange, dark, and ominous to young Tom. Opened in December 1899 by Reverend David

Shurtleff, the Shurtleff Mission was a home whose purpose was to "care for the children of the poor and destitute and foster in their minds the spirit and teachings of the gospel, adopting such measures as may seem best to rescue all children from vice and immorality and bring them under the influence of the Christian religion undenominational." It was a painful but not uncommon sacrifice for parents during the Depression to bring their children to such institutions, where they knew they would be fed and sheltered and given a chance at life.

Tommy's father took a seat while the matron led Tommy and Grace down a long hall to the dining room. They were brought pancakes on blue and white china plates with an Oriental pattern of a bridge over water. As he sat and looked at his pancakes, Tommy knew that his father's chair would be empty when he got up. Tears dropped onto his plate and swirled in the syrup like a river. This was going to be his new home, and he could feel family life as he knew it coming apart.

Tommy did not like the feeling one bit. Excusing himself from the dining room, he took a look at his father's empty chair and went into the large playroom at the back of the house. Assessing his situation with his intense hazel eyes, Tom lifted a window, clutched his paper bag of worldly possessions, jumped into a bank of snow up to his hips, and took off running. Thus Thomas Francis Leonard embarked on his first run, at the age of six, demonstrating the budding of a determined spirit to make things happen that would show itself time and time again throughout his life. Thus also began a quest to find a home and family he could call his own.

A young couple saw the young boy walking in the snow, clutching a paper bag. They picked him up and brought him to the police. Tom was escorted back to the Shurtleff Mission to begin his new life in the "Whip City"—Westfield, Massachusetts.

His mother and father came to visit Tom periodically. Within his first year at the mission Tom's aunt and uncle, Madeline and Charlie St. Francis, came to see him, too. They took Tommy outside for a walk around the house and pointed to the sky. "Your Dad has gone to Heaven, Tommy," they told him. "He is with God now." Tommy was crushed; his hope of returning to his home and mother in Springfield was disappearing.

Tommy's father, born on July 5, 1878, was the son of Edward Leonard, a saloon keeper from Ireland, and Ellen Connelly, from Saugus, Massachusetts. Educated almost to the eighth grade, Tommy's father loved children and dancing and having a good time. He was handsome and personable, a veteran of the Spanish-American War. He was very fond of the drink. Everybody loved to be around Artie Leonard. He died on November 30, 1940, at the age of sixty-two. His wife, Elizabeth, was forty-three at the time of his death. Although he would grow up without his father, Tommy Leonard grew to be remarkably like him.

After Tommy's father passed away, his mother moved into a tiny flat at 32 Mattoon Street in Springfield. The landlord gave her a break, charging only $3.00 a week for rent. She would live in that flat until her death in 1951.

Over the next five years, Tommy adapted to life at the mission. There were typically thirteen to fifteen other children living at the home at one time. Boys shared a large bedroom lined with cots and bunk beds, and girls shared the other bedroom. The children were not allowed to wear shoes unless they were going to school or to church. They would walk to the Franklin Avenue School for grade school. The boys were given short pants, which Tommy found very embarrassing; the other kids at school would laugh at the boys from the mission, who had to wear short pants even in sixth grade. One day, Tommy found a wallet with $350 in the playground across the street. He returned the wallet to the owner, who was the proprietor of a local pub, and was given his first suit with long pants as a reward for his honesty.

The children were given chores to do—shovel the walk, mow the lawn, set the table. They were told that the well on the property was bottomless so that they would keep away from it. The children thought that if you fell into the well, you would just keep falling to the center of the earth.

Tommy remembers the first matron at the home as a kind lady. But the next matron to arrive created some real problems and confusion for Tommy. A strict disciplinarian, Edna Williams firmly believed that sparing the rod would spoil the child. Tommy's mischievous personality was apparent even when he was a young boy. Never malicious, Tommy Leonard was, in his own words, "always a bit of a rapscallion," but Mrs. Williams did not have much patience for mischief.

The children were not allowed to go off the property to play in the playground across the street. Yet Tommy would sometimes sneak over there to play with other children. When Mrs. Williams found out, she gave him bread and water for dinner and sent him to bed at 5 PM, while all the other children were still playing outside. If he picked flowers for the girls at the mission, or tried to flatter them with his sparkling hazel Irish eyes and expressions, she would stand him behind the door in her office and bang his head against the wall repeatedly.

Often, when he broke a rule of the house, Mrs. Williams would send him up into the dark and dusty attic to sleep on the cot. "There are ghosts and witches up here in this attic, young man!" she would tell him. "You think about your behavior while you spend the night with them." It was a very spooky and terrifying place for a young child. Tom would cry himself to sleep wondering what he had done that was so wrong to warrant being left, horrified, in the attic all night.

On the weekends, Mrs. Williams would show a completely different side of her personality and often would take Tom with her to visit her nieces and nephews. They would go to places like Bantam Lake in Connecticut and Laurel Lake in Massachusetts. Tommy enjoyed these trips tremendously. Mrs. Williams would be very kind and gracious to Tommy while they were visiting her family. It was very confusing to him to be treated so poorly during the week and yet so kindly on the weekends. He doesn't remember any other children at the mission being taken on these adventures. Mrs. Williams was the only active mother figure in his life, and her frequent change of temperament and behavior toward him left him feeling lost and confused.

One can only surmise that it was the philosophy of the day that one had to be very strict and somewhat abusive with the children to get them to behave properly. Mrs. Williams must have been employing her own interpretation of "adopting such measures as may seem best to rescue all children from vice and immorality," as described in the original documents for the home. However, she must have recognized Tommy's basic goodness and felt a fondness for him despite her harsh treatment.

The mission converted the children at the home to the Advent Christian Church. Tommy's mother would visit him on Sundays whenever possible, and she tried to discourage him from leaving the Catholic faith. Being young and living at the mission, Tommy went through the conversion as he was told, and he really enjoyed Reverend Northrup, the pastor of the Advent Christian Church. His son, David, was close to Tommy's age. When he was invited to dinner at the Northrup's house on Western Avenue, Tom really looked forward to being a guest in a real home.

Tommy does have some happy memories from his years at the mission. Each year the children were taken to a big Christmas party at the Masonic Temple. In the summer they would attend the Westfield YMCA day camp. "I figured out early on I wasn't going to be a carpenter of any kind," Tommy said. "My projects were always rough and haphazard and out of alignment." Another outlet away from the mission was Boy Scout Troop 109. Tommy loved sleeping in a cabin in the woods with the birds and animals all about. The children were also encouraged to play a musical instrument, and Tommy picked up the harmonica and ukulele. Like his father, Tommy had a genuine love for music and bands.

By 1945, Tommy was getting restless. He was almost twelve years old and was tired of being just another kid who was fed and clothed and put in a bed at night. He yearned for a real home and a family to love. He longed for an adult to whom he could talk and really express his feelings. Since moving into the mission, Tommy had never experienced the daily and genuine love, concern, and caring that he saw other children getting from their parents. He craved a relationship with someone who really cared.

April 12, 1945, the day Franklin D. Roosevelt died, was a half-day of school, and Tommy ran away from the mission. Reverend Northrup saw him walking along Route 202.

"Tommy, what are you doing out here on 202?" Reverend Northrup asked.

"Reverend, I just needed to take a walk. The President died today, you know," Tom replied.

"Yes, I know, Tom. It is a sad day for the nation. But I think we better get you back to the mission. I am sure they are worried sick about you."

Tommy cringed at the thought of returning to the mission, and feared how Mrs. Williams would express her "concern and worry." As they entered the house, Mrs. Williams acted very relieved and grateful that Tommy had returned.

"We are so grateful to you, Reverend, for bringing Tommy safely home," she said. "I hope it wasn't a bother when you have such a busy schedule. Thank you so much."

As soon as Reverend Northrup left, Mrs. Williams took Tommy into her office. Her demeanor changed, and she said, "Drop your pants, young man." She then took a WWI army belt and whipped his bare behind to teach him a lesson for running away. His sister, Grace, was forced to watch this beating and several more during the time they lived at the mission.

Some of the Leonard children's aunts and uncles stayed in touch with them and visited them at the mission. Times were difficult; people were just beginning to crawl out of the devastation of the Depression, and World War II was raging. Their aunt and uncle, Madeline Duffy Hansen and Neil Hansen, lived near the mission, at 19 Shepherd Street in Westfield. Madeline's grandmother, Mary Duffy, was Tommy's father's sister.

Neil and his wife were living in a two-bedroom house with their three children and Madeline's mother. Tommy would often run to their house and ask his uncle to help him leave the mission or to take him to see his relatives in Springfield. Neil was heartbroken that he didn't have the space or the money to take Tommy in. Neil was used to hardship; his own father had lost his home in the Depression. By the time Neil had built his family a house on Woodside Terrace in Westfield, it was 1949, and Tommy was gone from the mission. He would lose touch with his Uncle Neil for many years.

Another aunt and uncle, Leo and Grace Benhardt, would also visit Tom and Grace at the mission. Grace Benhardt was also Mary Duffy's granddaughter and Madeline Hansen's first cousin. During the summer of 1945, the Benhardts took Tom to their house at 1530 Plum Tree Road in Springfield, Massachusetts. Leo Benhardt was district fire chief at the Winchester Square Fire Station in Springfield. Grace and Leo had two daughters, Barbara and Alberta, who were fifteen and twenty-three years old in 1945. They lived in a true family neighborhood of Colonial, Cape Cod, and ranch-style homes. Many had fireplaces and welcoming bay windows. It was the kind of neighborhood that Tommy could only dream of living in. A neighborhood of homes with children who were loved and cared for, with bicycles and backyard picnics, Easter egg hunts and Fourth of July celebrations, toys under the Christmas tree, family dinners, baths, and bedtime stories.

For two glorious weeks, Tommy's cousins took him to many places he had never been—Riverside Park, Forest Park, swimming, picnicking, cycling. It was heaven on earth for this young boy who had grown up with strict rules and regulations, harsh discipline, and little joy. At the end of his stay, he cried all the way back to the mission.

His aunt and uncle were trying to figure out a way to keep Tommy at their home, and Barbara and Alberta were excited about the prospect of having a brother. However, his aunt and uncle did not want to separate Tommy from his sister, Grace, and they were simply not in a position to add two children to their household. They decided they just could not do it. It was a heartbreaking period for everybody.

On the Feast of the Assumption, August 15, 1945, Tommy celebrated his twelfth birthday. He was very unhappy back at the mission after his stay with the Benhardts, and he wrote them letters asking them to help him get away. Tommy was growing into a fiercely independent person who did not want to stay in one place for any length of time. He was beginning to feel like a caged animal. One afternoon he felt like he would pop out of his skin if he didn't get some freedom, and he decided to take matters into his own hands. He ran across the yard of the mission to Route 20 and, despite his bare feet, started running toward West Springfield. He was on his way to his aunt and uncle's house fifteen miles away in Springfield. Alternately walking and running, Tommy was determined to reach 1530 Plum Tree Road. The sky grew dark and heavy, and a thunderstorm broke, the sheets of rain soaking Tommy.

Standing outside a diner, Tommy noticed a wedding reception at the Knights of Columbus across the street. Some of the wedding guests noticed Tommy and encouraged him to take shelter in the reception hall until the storm broke. His bare feet were coal black, and his wet clothing stuck to his body. He did not care that people were staring at him; he was on his way to his aunt and uncle's house! He was going to be free from the mission!

When the rain stopped, Tommy walked across the North End Bridge and ran to State Street in Springfield. Tommy asked people how to get to Plum Tree Road, and a kind lady offered him a quarter to take the bus. "You will catch pneumonia out here with your bare feet and wet clothing, son," she said. Relieved and grateful, Tommy took the quarter and jumped on the bus.

When Tom jumped off at Plum Tree Road and watched the bus drive away, he realized that he was at the wrong end of the street. The sun was sinking quickly in the west, and his cousins' house was three and a half miles down the road. Fatigue was setting in as Tommy continued to walk. Two high-school-aged girls came along and helped Tommy hitch a ride. A man in a Hood Milk truck stopped and picked him up. He pulled out a flashlight, and together they searched for the mailbox with 1530 on it.

"There it is!" Tommy yelled as he jumped excitedly out of the truck. "Thanks, Mister!"

"Sure, kid," the driver said, smiling, and watched sadly as Tommy ran to the door.

Tommy knocked on the door and Aunt Grace opened it, exclaiming, "Oh, Tommy! There's an APB out for you! The state and city police are looking all over for you!" Tommy's heart sank as he realized he would have to go back to the mission.

He waited for the Springfield police to pick him up. They put him in a holding cell while they phoned the Shurtleff Mission. They then drove him to the West Springfield/Springfield line, where the West Springfield police cruiser picked him up. It was now about 2 AM, and Tommy was exhausted, wet, and dirty. He did not want to face Mrs. Williams.

"Oh, officers, we've been worried sick over this," Mrs. Williams said when Tommy returned. "Thank you so much for bringing Tommy home."

"It's a pleasure, ma'am," one of the officers replied. "The people of West-field and West Springfield appreciate the fine work you do with these young children."

As the officers turned and walked away, Tommy could feel his muscles tighten and his breath grow shallow. His heart was beating so hard he thought his chest would explode. Mrs. Williams dragged him into her office and took out her WWI army belt. Once again, she whipped his bare bottom and sent him upstairs. The next morning, he was given no breakfast and was sent out-side to mow the wet lawn with a rusty lawnmower in his sore bare feet, under a steamy sun.

Tommy vowed he would find a way out of the Shurtleff Mission. There was a family for him out there somewhere, and he was going to find it.

2

The Foster Homes

Stretching

"Life without dreams would be intolerable."
—Tommy's favorite quote, by Anatole France

At one point, there was some discussion at the Shurtleff Mission about whether Tommy should be put in a correctional facility. It was determined that although he could be brash and brazen and often demonstrated a fierce determination, he didn't show criminal tendencies, and so he was not moved from the mission.

Tommy had spoken about his unhappiness to Harris Moulton, his state-appointed volunteer guardian, who was president of the Woronoco Savings Bank. On October 1, 1945, Harris Moulton signed Tommy and Grace out of the Shurtleff Mission. It had been five and a half years since their father had left them there. Tommy was now twelve and Grace was ten years old.

Moulton had arranged for Tommy and Grace to move into a foster home with the Powers family, a few blocks down the street. Tommy's quest to find a family was taking a new twist. He was about to learn that this was not going to be an easy journey.

Tommy desperately wanted to believe that having some light-hearted fun was okay, and getting into trouble doesn't have to hurt. He knew deep in his heart that there was someone out there who actually would care about how he felt and about what the future might hold for him. Unfortunately, this first home was not going to be the place to see those dreams fulfilled.

Mr. Powers was a strict disciplinarian who ran a television repair service out of his working-class house. The Powers had three children of their own. In addition to Tom and Grace, there was another set of foster siblings as well as a couple of other foster children at the house. They slept in bunk beds in tiny bedrooms. Like Mrs. Williams, the Powers had little patience for practical jokes or mischievous behavior. There were rules to live by and little laughter or happiness in the home. Mr. and Mrs. Powers were hot-tempered. Tommy learned very quickly not to cross Mr. Powers. Most of the kids in the neighborhood were a bit frightened of him. Although Tommy was free of Mrs. Williams, he now lived under the stress of worrying what might befall him if he did something to irritate Mr. Powers. More than once, he suffered the consequences of upsetting Mr. Powers, and wound up with a beating.

Tom learned that not everyone who brings foster children into their home does so out of an altruistic desire to love and care for needy children. As wards of the state, Tommy and the other foster children represented extra income from the state, which paid a stipend to families willing to take in such children. He began to look at himself as just a number being maintained by the state.

There was no emotional attachment, no real effort to get to know the foster children. Tom remembers being fed raw hamburger meat and being told it was good for him. The foster children did not have their laundry taken care of very frequently, and they did not receive any new clothes from the stipend the family received from the state. Tommy had a paper route and would buy what clothes he could manage from his earnings.

He does credit the Powers family with encouraging him to return to the Catholic Church, however. He was re-baptized and then received his first Holy Communion at age twelve, with all the second-graders at St. Mary's Church. The Powers transferred him to St. Mary's from the Normal Training School in the middle of seventh grade. They also saw to it that the children did their homework each night, and Tommy achieved very good grades while under this discipline. As an eighth-grader, he remembers being in the top third of the class. He was proud of his abilities and happy at St. Mary's.

Sister Mary Fidelis thought that Tommy had the makings of a priest, and talked him into considering entering a seminary in Hartford, Connecticut, after his summer job picking tobacco. (Westfield has a long history of growing and curing tobacco and manufacturing tobacco products. For many years, tobacco finished a close second to whips in terms of the dollar volume of products shipped from Westfield to all parts of the world.) He became totally intrigued with the idea and told his friends he was going to be a priest. They'd come over to the Powers' home and say, "Oh, Father Leonard, come on out and play," and he'd retort, "No, I can't. I am saying the rosary." Mother Superior Thomasine sat Tommy down and said, "Son, I think you better finish high school before you make this important decision."

Shortly thereafter, Tommy set his eyes on lovely Eleanor Flynn, a freckle-faced beauty with green Irish eyes, and "all my priestly ambitions disappeared." He recalls practicing for Confirmation in St. Mary's Church in the eighth grade and making eyes at Eleanor as they were lining up. Sister Mary Fidelis, who Tommy describes as being built like Ray Nitschke, the middle linebacker for the Green Bay Packers, was playing the role of the bishop. She'd been watching Tommy and as he approached, she slapped his face so hard he can still hear the reverberation that echoed through the church and see the glare in her eyes.

Back in the classroom, the girls sat in the first three rows and the boys sat in the next three rows. Sister Mary Fidelis said, "Master Leonard, since you love girls so much, you are going to sit in the first seat in the first row right in front of my desk. We are going to call you Sally Leonard." And for the remainder of the year, she did. Tommy considered this the finest piece of punishment he had ever received. Sitting in the center of all the girls, his greatest challenge was trying to appear as if this was too much to bear.

"Father Carberry helped us put on minstrel shows as fundraisers for St. Mary's," Tommy remembers. "I loved singing in the chorus. Maybe I loved watching Mary Ann Korsnecki singing 'I told every little star just how wonderful you are'" (by Oscar Hammerstein and Jerome Kern).

While at St. Mary's school, Tom became friendly with a kid named Robbie Bolan. He told Robbie about life at the Powers house. "Why don't you come and live at our house?" Robbie suggested. "We have foster kids at our house. Mom would probably let you move in, too." Robbie convinced his mother to invite Tommy to live with them. By this time, Tommy had another state-appointed guardian, Bill Brown, who was a local attorney. Mr. Brown approved the transition paperwork, and Tommy was moved into the Bolans' house. Grace was transferred to a family named Sandville, and she and Tom would be separated for the next few years.

The Bolan family had two sons and a daughter, as well as a few foster children. Tommy discovered that life at the Bolans was not going to be very different from life at the Powerses. Mr. Bolan was quiet and very stern, and he would sometimes strike Tommy or the other kids. In his usual self-deprecating way, Tommy says, "I had my thorns and was no bargain to live with."

At age thirteen, while living at the Bolans' house, Tommy Leonard was introduced to what would eventually become his perpetual partner for life: beer. Mr. Bolan gave the boys a sip of his Ballantine Ale. Tommy liked the taste of it. By age fifteen *or* sixteen, Tommy would be drinking frequently with his buddies while trying to cope with his ever-changing living situation.

Tommy recalls that his summer job picking tobacco was hot, dirty, and unpleasant, and probably influenced him not to smoke. Then he heard Gil Dodds (America's premier miler in the 1940s) give a talk at Springfield Tech on the downfall of cigarettes, which convinced Tommy never to try them. In later years, Tommy would often be quoted saying things like, "Smoking cigarettes is as attractive as picking your nose." On the other hand, his catechism classes included a section on the evils of alcohol. "Obviously, I didn't pay much attention to the alcohol lesson," he says with a guffaw. "If I hadn't been a runner, I probably wouldn't be here today. Seriously, running has been my stabilizer."

After a few months at the Bolan house, another friend suggested that Tommy move into his house. The Stetsons lived on Clay Road in Westfield. Tommy made the move, hoping to find a better home life. Tommy remembers his friend's father as a somewhat depressed guy. Disappointed once again, Tommy continued to feel like he represented a check from the state to people who took him in, and he continued to long for an emotional connection with an adult. He was beginning to lose hope that he would ever find anyone who could be a loving parent figure to him.

Despite his inner sadness, Tommy Leonard was a light-hearted and impish Irish kid who made friends easily. He loved a good time and a good laugh. Most of his friends were not aware of how difficult his home life was. No one ever made him feel ostracized or made fun of him for living in foster homes.

Sometime during Tommy's freshman year in high school, it was determined that it would be best if he move out of the Stetsons' house. He definitely did not want to move back to the mission, so for a while the state arranged for him to live at Westfield Town Farm, which Tommy calls "an old man's home," on Russell Road. It was also known as the "poor farm." The residents of the poor farm were welfare recipients, typically aging alcoholics with no family to support them. They would work the farm in exchange for living accommodations.

Westfield's annual report included a "Report of the City Infirmary," which was the poor farm. The local vernacular was to refer to the residents as "inmates." For example, the city report for the year ending December 31, 1946, included the following information:

During the year 52 inmates were cared for, 35 men and 17 women. The largest number at one time being 37. There were 23 inmates at the home on December 31, 1946. During the year 30 inmates were discharged, viz: 2 to Sherborn, 2 to Belchertown, 6 care of the State, 4 deceased, 11 care of self, 1 Holyoke City Hospital, 2 Northampton Hospital and 2 A.W.O.L.

In addition to supplying the table during the summer with vegetables the following were produced:

- 484 bu. Field corn
- 3000 sweet corn
- 6000 lbs. Potatoes
- 10 bu. Beets
- 13 bu. Carrots
- 15 bu. Parsnips
- 20 bu. Rut. Turnips
- 800 lbs. Squash
- 3 ton cabbage
- 5 bu. Cucumbers
- 10 bu. Chard
- 40 bu. Tomatoes
- 15 bu. Wax beans
- 50 bu. Apples
- 5 bu. Peppers
- 400 lbs. Onions.

An ample supply of hay and alfalfa was raised for winter feeding, 700 quarts of vegetables were canned. Our hens produced 637 doz. eggs and provided meat for chicken dinners. The dairy herd produced 20,000 qts. Milk, which was served freely, the balance made into butter and cheese. The skimmed milk was fed to the hogs. The hogs produced 3,104 lbs. of pork, which was served fresh and made into hams, bacon, lard, sausage, etc.

Total expenditures for the year $12,057.17

It was truly no place for a fourteen- or fifteen-year-old child, and Tommy remembers it as an absolutely dreadful place to call home. He was paid $1.00 a day to pick weeds. The poor farm was located three or four miles out of town, and was the last place Tommy wanted to spend time. Meals were taken in a large hall, and the only company Tommy had were the old, senile, and raspy residents with whom he now shared his home. Everyone was lost in his own little world, and no one took any real interest in Tommy. Each resident had his or her own bedroom. Tommy felt isolated and depressed. His appearance was deteriorating as his clothes started to fall apart. He recalls his Uncle Leo visiting and saying, "What happened to you, Tommy? You look like a tramp."

Tommy would run into town each day to attend school and be with his friends. This was probably the real beginning of his development as a runner. Running was a necessity to escape his situation and to get where he had to go. Tommy loved to run, and he was running all over town years before anyone would ever consider running for fitness. He'd easily cover six miles in a day just getting to and from the poor farm.

It was a depressing and demoralizing point in his life. Interestingly, none of Tommy's high school friends were aware that he had ever lived at the poor farm. Tommy has never been one to wallow in self-pity, and this character trait apparently was quite strong very early in his life. Peter Butler, who is two years younger than Tommy, commented recently, "He was always making us laugh, and a good time was his trademark. For a kid who had such a difficult childhood, you'd expect he'd be a bit bitter, but he never once mentioned his upbringing."

It was during these periods of family hopping and living at the poor farm that Tommy's grades really started to suffer. While the teachers were giving their lessons, Tommy often would be thinking about where he had to go to sleep that night or to get his meals. He started to lose focus on school and began drinking with his friends more and more. He would grow up to regret that he didn't pay better attention to his schoolwork, but at the time, it was the least of his concerns. "I spent a lot of time in detention," he says. "I wasn't happy bouncing around to these different homes."

Tommy was beginning to lose hope of ever finding a real home and family, and he was fighting to hold on to his dreams.

3

The High School Years

The Warm-up

"He who has friends is rich."

—*A* trademark Tommy Leonard expression

There is a granite boulder in Westfield, Massachusetts, that was deposited by a glacier thousands of years ago. It is in Stanley Park, with a prayer engraved on its plaque, and it has come to be known as the Prayer Boulder. Stanley Park used to send copies of this prayer "to anyone anywhere upon request."

It epitomizes the philosophy by which Tommy Leonard would live his life, and perhaps reflects one of the reasons he would grow up to be so well loved. The prayer reads: O Lord, grant that each one who has to do with me today may be the happier for it. Let it be given me each hour today what I shall say, and grant me the wisdom of a loving heart that I may say the right thing rightly.

Help me to enter into the mind of everyone who talks with me, and keep me alive to the feelings of each one present. Give me a quick eye for little kindnesses that I may be ready in doing them and gracious in receiving them. Give me a quick perception of the feelings and needs of others, and make me eager hearted in helping them.

17

In tenth grade, Tommy transferred from St. Mary's School to Westfield High School because he wanted to play football and run track. He made friends easily and fell in with the athletes—football, basketball, and baseball players—as his closest friends.

Everyone had nicknames: John "Jiggs" Morrissey, Michael "Champ" Morris, Ann "Pinky" McGowan, Fred "Moe" Placzek, Dick "Blizzard" Barry, Bruno "Hoot" Fioroni, "Digger" Bates, Don "Foley," Vernon "Skippy" White, Dante "Moldy" Molta, George "Bardo" Kelleher, John "Spider-Legs" Killips, "Doc" Koziol, Lenny "Rusty" Warner. Only a couple went by their given names, such as Peter Butler and Eddie Bonnini.

Tommy was christened by his friends as "Rainbow" for his colorful and usually mismatched clothes, which became his signature. He could have so many different colors and patterns in one outfit that the name "Rainbow" stuck. And like a rainbow, his friends all described him as a "presence." You were definitely aware when he was around. Although many friends over the years would call him T, T.L., or Tommy, he will always be "Rainbow" to his high school friends.

Tommy had a couple of friends in high school—Mickey Treat and Skippy White—who had been at the Shurtleff Mission with him. "Skippy," who was Champ Morris's first cousin, was there only for a brief while, before his aunt, Florence Andrews, took him in. Mickey would grow up to work in a local paper mill and live in the same room of a boarding house for thirty-seven years. Skippy, however, eventually would move to California and become an agent for Willie Nelson and Kris Kristofferson. He married five times, and lived for a while on Rod Steiger's property. He overcame his own battles with drugs and alcohol, and became dearly loved by family and friends. He died in October 2001, and his online memorial refers to him as a "Writer, Poet, Road Manager, Best Friend, Dog Lover and Family Man who will be missed for his quick wit, charm, positive attitude, and ever-present sense of humor." Other than his sister, Grace, Tommy considers Skippy to be the one success story he is aware of from the mission, since several of the kids became alcoholics or committed suicide. Tommy and Skippy remained good friends for life, and Tommy made it a point to visit him whenever he went to California.

Since everything happened alphabetically at school, George Kelleher and Tommy Leonard were usually in line together, and became fast friends. George was a very talented athlete and recalls a JV football game against Agawam at which Tommy was upset because he had forgotten his shoulder pads. Their coach, Coach Jenkins, was a former AIC gridder and a strict and successful coach.

"Oh, Jeez, George! I don't have my shoulder pads. Coach is going to kill me!" Tommy exclaimed. He knew that if the coach found out, he would read him the riot act about not being prepared or responsible. His ever-simmering mind led him into the men's room, where he collected all the toilet paper he could find. Then he went outside and gathered a bunch of tree branches, which he stuffed into his football jersey so he had the appearance of wearing shoulder pads.

Generally, Tommy was a bench warmer, but the crowd would often call, "We want Rainbow! We want Rainbow!" Coach knew that he couldn't be sure Tommy would run in the right direction if he got the ball, but at this game he shouted, "Leonard, get in there!" Tommy trotted onto the field with his makeshift toilet-paper shoulder pads. As soon as he was tackled, it looked as if his shoulder had been dislocated. Coach ran onto the field and gazed in disbelief at the collapsed branches and toilet paper. George doesn't remember Coach putting Tommy in another game after that one.

Tommy had a crush on Mary Jane Eagan, whose father was a Westfield firefighter. Mr. Eagan took a liking to Leonard and was aware of his situation at the poor farm.

He also knew Annie Murray, an elderly widow who lived on the Guilshan Homestead on Old Holyoke Road in Westfield. The Guilshan Homestead belonged to one of the earlier settlers of Westfield, who had four sons. One son, Dr. Henry Guilshan, and his wife, Nellie, lived in New York state but inherited the house on Old Holyoke Road. Nellie and Henry's only son had died of pneumonia, so once they passed on, the family divided up the considerable estate, and the Guilshan Homestead was given to Nellie's sister, Annie, and her husband, Monty Murray.

Monty Murray was heir to a large apparel business that his father had owned. He and Annie lived in New York City and had tremendous wealth. Annie's great niece, Carol Bannon Flynn, remembers Annie as very classy, refined, cultured, and soft-spoken. Annie and Monty lost most of their wealth in the 1929 stock market crash and were grateful to receive the house on the Homestead.

Annie had been widowed for a few years when Eddie Eagan approached her about taking Tommy in. Her house was the only house on Old Holyoke Road, which at the time was a dirt road. She was alone and aging, and liked the idea of having companionship and help around the house. She was also a very giving soul and wanted to provide a better life to young Tommy.

Bill Brown, Tommy's guardian, approved the paperwork, and suddenly Tommy found himself moved from a hellish existence to a heavenly one. Mrs. Murray treated Tommy with kindness, concern, and respect. The house was surrounded with woods and had a stream running through the backyard. Tommy had his own bedroom and harbored a natural affinity toward the birds and wildlife all around.

Although elderly, Mrs. Murray was indeed cultured and refined. She bought Tommy nice clothes and took him on trips to New York City. They would stay in hotels in Times Square and see shows such as *Where's Charlie?* with Ray Bolger on Broadway, and Radio City Music Hall's Christmas show. She took him to Midnight Mass at St. Patrick's Cathedral. He was being exposed to a world and culture he never expected to see, and he loved it.

One of Tommy's friends, Ann "Pinky" McGowan, met Tommy in the first grade, when they attended the Franklin Street School across the street from the Shurtleff Mission. After he transferred to St. Mary's, she didn't see him until he came to Westfield High School. She recalls how on Friday nights in high school, everyone would dial 2070 to see who was out at Kane's Dairy Bar, at the corner of Elm and Franklin streets. A gang of friends usually would gather there for ice cream, coffee, or fries. Eventually, a large group, who dubbed themselves the "Mugwumps," would go to Pinky's house, and they would harmonize such songs as In the Evening by the Moonlight, Shine on Harvest Moon, For Me and My Gal, Tennessee Waltz, Show Me the Way to Go Home, Moonlight Bay, and When You Were Sweet Sixteen into the wee hours of the morning. It is a memory that "Pinky", her future husband "Champ," Tommy, and all of the other singers cherish. Good, clean fun—singing and laughing into the night—that didn't cost a dime, but offered some of the best memories they have of their high school years.

Music and dancing were a very large part of Tommy's life. He introduced several of his friends to jazz, and his friends recall that he would go to the Newport Jazz Festival every year like a crusade. Right in Westfield, at Hampton Ponds, were dance halls called the Showboat and Couture's Garden, which held weekly dances. They'd go swimming at the beach on the lake and then go to the nightclub in the evening. The guys found it easy to be served alcohol and they would dance and drink the night away. Most of Tommy's friends recalled that at the end of an evening, they'd be dragging Tommy off the dance floor to call it a night. More than once, they woke up on a beach full of sunbathers the morning after a night of dancing and drinking at the Show-boat.

Many friends recall that Tommy thought nothing of dancing alone, and he had natural rhythm and great dance moves. One wall could be lined with girls and the other lined with guys, but Tommy would get out on the floor and enjoy himself. He dreamed of growing up to be another Gene Kelly. His friends described his dancing as comparable to the dancing seen in such movies as Dirty Dancing and Saturday Night Fever. Often, people would watch Tommy as part of the entertainment at the dances, although in the early 1950s Tommy was way ahead of the times, and not everyone was receptive to his style of dancing. Peter Butler recalled a couple of incidents when they had to pull Tommy off the floor to defuse a situation where someone had taken offense to his dancing style.

One year Westfield High School had a talent show, and Tom's friends "Moe" Placzek and "Blizzard" Barry helped him choreograph a dance routine. Entering the stage in a zoot suit and low-brimmed hat, Tommy electrified the audience with his dancing. During the routine, he pulled off his jacket and flung his hat into the crowd. The students erupted in applause and considered Tommy the winner of the contest. But the teachers were uncomfortable, and they overlooked him as a winner.

Tommy and his friends often went to the Valley Arena in Holyoke for concerts. The stage also was used for boxing matches and had a low balcony for viewing the fights. On January 6, 1952, the night the Professional Building in Westfield burned down, Tommy, Don Foley, and Eddie Bonnini went to see Lionel Hampton at the Valley Arena. Tommy was dancing up on the balcony and, in his enthusiasm, leapt down onto the stage, knocking over some of the drums and equipment. The joke of the evening among his friends was that no one could blame the Professional Building fire on Tommy Leonard because he was entangled in Lionel Hampton's musical equipment that night!

A slender boy with thick, black, wavy hair and eyebrows and twinkling Irish eyes, Tommy viewed being served a beer at age fifteen or sixteen as a challenge he was up to. One very cold winter evening, he was out with two of his closest friends, Bruno "Hoot" Fioroni, a very talented baseball player, and Don "Foley," admired by many for his skills on the basketball court. As they passed The Nook, a tavern on Franklin Street near Elm, Bruno challenged, "Tommy, I bet you can't get served in there." Raising his coat collar, Tommy went in, sauntered up to the bar, lowered his voice, and said, "I'll have a beer."

He enjoyed sipping that beer slowly in the warmth of the tavern while looking out at his friends, standing in the frigid cold.

Bruno's family was from Italy and they lived on East Mountain Road. There was a wine cellar or "cantina" in the basement with a dirt floor, where they fermented their own wine. Bruno, Tommy, and their friends would "occasionally" confiscate a bottle for the evening's entertainment and go find a parking lot to get soused in.

Peter Butler recalls the night he and Tommy got hold of a bottle of Haig and Haig whiskey. Peter drove a '34 Chevy with a rumble seat in which they sat talking and nipping away at the whiskey. By the end of the bottle, Peter was in no condition to drive. As he remembers it, he asked Tommy, who had little or no driving experience, to drive the car. Tommy drove the Chevy almost 15 miles to Peter's house. Their muddled minds had not registered that this was the worst place for them to drive to, and Peter's parents gave them hell for their behavior.

Tommy discovered his real athletic love and talent on the track. He ran the 100-yard dash and finished next to last in his first track meet. Then he jumped into the mile without his coach's permission and finished second, so he became a miler for Westfield. While his friends were practicing baseball, Tommy would just continue running around the track after his practice, waiting for them to finish and hang out. All of his friends recall Tommy running everywhere he went, not just at the track.

Tom heard of a 10-mile road race starting in Pynchon Park in Springfield during track season. It followed an out-and-back course to Forest Park, and he finished twenty-third out of forty runners. His coach gave him hell, but it was his first taste of long-distance racing and he definitely enjoyed it.

Tommy admits he wasn't always diligent about going to practice. Directly across the street from the high school was a lovely spot called Grandmother's Garden. In 1929 Albert E. Steiger donated land for a public park to Westfield with the hope that part of it be set aside for an old-fashioned colonial garden in memory of his mother, Mary Steiger. She was affectionately known by everyone in town as Grandmother Steiger. Thus Grandmother's Garden came into existence in 1934. Rather than show up at the track after school, Tommy often preferred taking the girls through the garden to show them the flowers and perhaps engage in some hanky-panky.

Tommy's carousing affected not only his running but also his grades. He never really took his studies seriously after the eighth grade and was always looking to have a good time with his friends. During his junior year, he was wrongly accused of setting off a firecracker and was suspended for a period. He ended up repeating his junior year.

Mrs. Murray was the first parent figure he ever had whom he was willing to open up to and share his feelings with. She could see that he was quite intelligent, and she wanted to give him more of a chance in life. She would often find his behavior maddening and threaten, "Tommy, I can't take this anymore. I am going to send you back to that poor farm." But she was genuinely fond of Tommy and couldn't remain irritated with him for any length of time.

She had many influential friends in New York City and once arranged a dinner at one of their homes so Tommy could meet them. They were going to use their influence to help him get accepted to Cornell or Columbia University. She and Tommy took the train to New York City, and Tommy went off to look at the city sights. He never returned to the dinner, and Mrs. Murray was greatly disappointed in him. Years later, Tommy shared with her great niece, Carol Bannon Flynn, that no one had ever been that good to him and he simply could not believe that it would ever happen, so he didn't see any reason to show up for the dinner.

Each Thanksgiving, Westfield High and Cathedral High of Springfield play a traditional football game. Once Tommy moved in with Mrs. Murray, they would have their Thanksgiving dinner at the home of Carol Bannon (Flynn)'s mother. Carol's mother was related to Annie Murray, as her Uncle Henry was married to Annie's sister, Nellie.

Carol was about thirteen when Tommy moved into Mrs. Murray's house and Tommy was about fifteen years old. Carol remembers having a crush on this handsome Irish lad with thick, black, curly hair and intense, twinkling, hazel eyes, who would come to Thanksgiving dinner. Carol's uncle, Charlie Morris, was married to her mother's sister, Alice. Uncle Charlie would pick up Tommy for the game to be played at Pynchon Park in Springfield at 10 AM, and they'd go back for Annie after the game and then drive to Springfield for dinner.

Charlie and Alice had three sons: Billy, the eldest, and the twins, Jimmy and Johnny, who were about a year older than Tommy. Carol had an older brother, Paul, and an older sister, Jane, who was a bit older than Tommy, as well as a younger brother, Doug. So there would be six boys, two girls, and the dog, "Chubbie," in addition to the adults. This was a real "family" gathering for Tommy, and Carol remembers him as somewhat quiet, perhaps overwhelmed by all the people sharing the dinner, but very happy and nice to have around. Tommy, of course, cheered for Westfield in the game and the Bannon family cheered for Cathedral, where the children were students, which made for a friendly rivalry. Later in the evening they would share sandwiches, dessert, coffee, tea, and Jell-O. Then Uncle Charlie would drive Tommy and Mrs. Murray back to the "country" in Westfield.

On the second Thanksgiving Day that Tommy lived with Mrs. Murray, when he was a junior in high school, he went to the Westfield-Cathedral game with Uncle Charlie and the boys. When they returned to Annie's house to pick her up for dinner, they found her on the floor, having a massive heart attack. They called for the police and an ambulance. Tommy was shocked and heartbroken. He could feel all the hope, happiness, and belief in a better future that had been his blessing since moving in with Mrs. Murray drain out of him as he watched the ambulance drive away.

4

A Family at Last

Training

"It's the *good life*."
—Another trademark Tommy Leonard expression

Mrs. Murray had introduced Tommy to her neighbors, the Tierneys, who lived on East Mountain Road. Francis X. and Eleanor (Cullinan) Tierney both grew up in Holyoke. Eleanor was the oldest of five girls (her three brothers had all died young). They lived in the "flats" of Holyoke. Her father was a bartender and her mother, a native of Ireland, had owned a beauty salon before she married.

Frank grew up on Walnut Street in Holyoke and was the fourth of five boys. His ancestor, Michael Tierney, came from Ireland and established a farm on East Mountain Road in Westfield in the 1850s. Frank's father was a postman and although money was tight, he greatly valued education, and all five boys attended college. Frank graduated from Holy Cross in 1928 at the age of twenty, having entered at age sixteen.

Frank got a job in insurance in New York City and started law school, but was never able to finish because there was not enough money. He later returned to Springfield and eventually became the head of General Accident Insurance. Frank and Eleanor married in 1939.

Two of Frank's uncles owned and operated the farm on East Mountain Road. Each summer, the five Tierney boys would live on and work the farm with their uncles and "Aunt Kate." Frank loved the farm and continued to help out on weekends even after finishing college. When the uncles died, the fifty-acre farm was left to Frank, and he built a new home on the land and moved his family into it in 1950.

Around this same time, Frank left General Accident and bought the Henry H. Noel Insurance Company in Holyoke. During the next decade, he bought several more agencies in Holyoke, Westfield, and Chicopee, managing them under their original names. In the late 1970s, he combined them into the Tierney Insurance Group.

Frank and Eleanor Tierney had two adopted children, Michael and Jane, as well as a daughter, Susan, who was a baby when they moved to the new house. Mrs. Murray had been friendly with the Tierney uncles and gotten to know Frank and Eleanor. She asked if Tommy could occasionally come over to the house for family companionship, as they were fairly isolated at her house. Tommy would sometimes baby-sit for the Tierney children, which was always an adventure. Francis X. recalled watching Tommy take his children on "magic carpet rides" or "safaris" for fun. Tommy remembers having picnics at Mrs. Murray's house for the children and putting the Coke bottles in the stream that flowed through the yard to keep them cold while he fixed hot dogs and marshmallows.

Frank Tierney was picking up the newspaper in a local shop when he learned that Mrs. Murray had taken ill on Thanksgiving Day. Tommy was distraught and walked over to the Tierneys' house after the ambulance left with Mrs. Murray. Putting his arm around Tommy's shoulder, Frank said, "Consider yourself part of the family."

Tommy moved into the Tierney home and began life with this kind and generous couple and their children. Although he never really took his studies very seriously again, he was being offered structure and discipline as well as love and guidance by the Tierneys. Tommy began to feel that he had finally found a real home and family. Looking back, Tommy says, "Frank and Eleanor Tierney were saints! Eleanor would tell her sisters how she would get so mad at me and shake me. Then I'd start laughing and she couldn't stay mad at me. I sure gave her reason to get mad sometimes. I was always out carousing and partying with my friends and coming home too late and things like that."

Like Eleanor, Frank found it difficult to stay mad at Tommy. Frank recalled, "He was always getting into trouble without meaning to. He'd come in late and be very apologetic saying, 'What can I do? I'll do anything. I'm sorry. I'll never do that again.' And then he had you laughing so you just couldn't stay mad at him."

In November of 1951, Tommy and Grace's mother passed away. They had not seen their mother during the years they were bouncing through the foster care system. Frank saw to it that she had a proper dress for her funeral and was buried in St. Michael's Cemetery with her husband rather than in a pauper's cemetery. Tommy told Frank that he had a sister who was working at Grant's Department Store, so Frank took it upon himself to give Grace the heartbreaking news that her mother had passed away.

Tommy wanted to go out every night to meet with his friends. Tommy and his friends continued going to the Showboat on weekends and the Quonset Hut in Amherst long after high school. Good music, dancing, and drinking remained their favorite activities.

During the summers, they would often travel to Misquamicut, Rhode Island. Peter Butler would drive a large group in his '34 Chevy with the rumble seat. They would hang out on the beaches looking for bathing beauties to attract and party with. Sometimes at night, they would pull adolescent pranks such as floating the lifeguard chair out into the water.

At the Tierneys', Tommy now lived just down the road from Bruno "Hoot" Fiorini. Bruno was one year older than Tommy, and the two of them had become the best of friends and were inseparable.

Tommy's Senior Prom was held at the Armory the night before the Western Massachusetts Track and Field Championships. Tommy was out on the dance floor with his date from Amherst when his friends Bruno (who had graduated the previous year), Foley, and "Doc" Koziol showed up and signaled for Tommy to come to the ramp in the back of the Armory. Excusing himself, Tommy left his date on the dance floor and discovered that his pals had bought some beer at the package store. With a glance back to the dance floor, Tommy left the Prom, probably with the intention of having a few beers and returning to his date. Being Tommy, though, he never did return to the Prom.

The next morning, he showed up in his tuxedo to run the mile for Westfield High School in the Western Massachusetts Track and Field championships. Just before the race, a girl whom Tommy had a crush on, Patty Keough, approached him and said coyly, "Tommy, I'll give you a big kiss if you win this race," so he blasted through the first quarter in 60 seconds, with his coach screaming, "Slow down! Slow down!" He recalls finishing fifth or sixth and breaking five minutes. In the State Championships Tommy would run against a miler from Arlington High School, who would become a very good friend later in life. His name was Bill Squires. Reflecting on these days, he claims, "I probably could have been a better runner if I paid more attention to running in high school and less attention to the girls."

Tommy had several girlfriends in high school. One was a very pretty fresh-man named Nancy Dickinson. She lived on a farm in Granville and was one of five lovely daughters. Tommy would often hitchhike up to her home on Fri-day nights and sleep on the sofa, and her father would drive him back to Westfield on Saturday. One evening, Tommy was jolted with surprise when Mr. Dickinson found Tommy and his daughter in a "compromising position" on the sofa. Seeing the look on Mr. Dickinson's face, Tommy flew to the door and ran right through the screen door, never opening it. He ran, terrified, in the bitter cold, all the way back to Westfield, about 12 miles. Upon reaching Westfield, he called his friend, George Kelleher, in the early morning from a phone booth, yelling "He's gonna kill me, George! You gotta see him! He's so mad!" George picked up Tommy and brought him to his house. Upon seeing Tommy, purple and frightened, Mrs. Kelleher exclaimed, "Oh my God, Tommy!" and helped him clean up all the little bloody scratches he had acquired from running through the screen door. To this day, George wonders where Tommy got a dime to call him from the phone booth early that morn-ing.

Years later, while retelling this story to Bud Collins for a biographical pro-file in the Boston Globe, Tommy was quoted as saying, "Normally I don't count the miles I run any more than I do the Molsons I drink. That's when even the runners I love can get boring. But that 12-miler is imprinted in my mind."

Tommy recalls that he was a senior in high school while dating Nancy, and at the same time he was seeing Carol Smith, who was a freshman at Westfield State. "Come to think of it, later I was dating Helen O'Connor, a freshman at Holyoke Community College, while I was dating Geraldine Whalley, a senior at Holyoke High. Guess I had a hard time making choices."

Although Tommy does not drive today, he did drive for a time in high school and when he first came home from the Marines. A number of different friends recounted various incidents when Tommy would be on a date and get a flat tire. More than once, he changed the flat and forgot to tighten the lug nuts on the wheel, and the tire rolled off the car down the road. At one time, he drove his car into a stream on the Tierney property, and it became perma-nently stuck until Frank had the old car towed away.

Graduation Day 1952 arrived, and Tommy was full of excitement. He was jumping around exclaiming, "I made it! I made it! I really did it! I'm getting my diploma!" Everyone cheered for Tommy as he returned to his seat with his envelope. Sitting down next to George, Tommy opened the envelope to find a note inside and no diploma.

It seems Tommy had gotten up on the art teacher's swivel chair when the teacher, Mr. Jim McDowell, had left the room. He started singing to all the girls a popular song at the time, I Give You All My Love. During his enthusiastic performance, the chair toppled over backward and broke into many pieces. He was promised his high school diploma when he paid for the broken chair. Frank Tierney received a call from the principal about five years later and made arrangements to get the diploma.

By the end of the summer of 1952, Frank and Eleanor were the legal guardians of both Tommy and Grace Leonard. Grace came to live with the Tierneys for the last two years of high school. Like Tommy, she had bounced in and out of seven or eight foster homes since leaving Shurtleff Mission. She, too, had an overwhelming sense of being a "child of the state" while growing up. The Tierneys were the first family to treat her not like that but as an individual. By the time she came to live with the Tierneys, Tommy had just entered the Marines.

Upon Grace's graduation from high school, Frank was instrumental in getting her a job at the telephone company, which put her on a career path that she would truly love. His influence helped her to transfer to Washington, DC, where she enjoyed independence for the first time in her life. She continued with the phone company until 1972 and then took a job with the union in Baltimore that provided her with the opportunity to do all the things she really wanted to do. She'd had visions of someday doing some kind of social work, and this job allowed her to help people through the arbitration and grievance procedure, negotiating contracts, and lobbying for the working man on Capitol Hill. It was a career she found very fulfilling, and she credits the Tierneys for helping to put her on a path where she at last found happiness.

Possessing a very giving nature like her brother's, Grace spends each Thanksgiving in Baltimore working in a soup kitchen, enjoying the opportunity to put smiles on the faces of others.

Tommy ponders his past. "Some people never get the love and support they need to help them through a rough time. I fear what would have happened to me if I had not landed in the Tierneys' home. I just think the Good Lord up above was looking out for me when I found Mrs. Murray and then the Tierneys. Before that, I had no direction. I was living day-to-day and failing in school. I really hated that old man's home. The Tierneys were my salvation. Without them, I probably would have been serving time somewhere."

Since the early 1950s, Grace and Tommy have considered the Tierneys to be their family. They continue to participate in the annual family holiday traditions and get-togethers with their adopted siblings, Susan and Michael, and their own families.

Eleanor Tierney passed away on July 25, 1993, and Francis X. Tierney passed away on January 5, 2001.

5

The Marines

The Challenge

"Keep the faith."

—Francis X Tierney, Tommy's foster father

At the time Tommy and his friends were graduating from high school in 1951–53, the Korean War was being fought and the memory of World War II was fresh in everyone's mind. For most of the graduating males, college was not even a consideration. Nearly everyone entered the service.

The summer after graduation, Tommy worked in the laundry room of the Westfield State Sanatorium folding sheets.

Tommy recalls, "I was very patriotic and always looking at John Wayne movies. When I was in seventh or eighth grade, I was talking to a TWA pilot who told me he had been all over the world and there was no country like the USA, and I should never forget that. I love my country and I graduated in an era when everyone was gung-ho. A couple of my buddies read about Guadalcanal and Iwo Jima. I wanted to be part of all that.

"I had always loved the Marine Corps Hymn and I wanted to be in the best outfit. I wanted to play my part and donate my three years." In high school, Bruno Fioroni was an extremely talented baseball pitcher and was approached by talent scouts from the Yankees, the Cleveland Indians, and other teams. He could have had a scholarship to Holy Cross or signed a professional con-

31

tract. Bruno's brother, Angelo, had been a Marine, and Bruno and Tommy as well as Don Foley all chose to join the Marines.

Bruno entered the service in January 1952.They tried hard to convince Jiggs Morrissey to quit Mt. Harmon Academy, where he was doing a year of postgraduate study, and join the Marines with them. Eventually, Jiggs did quit school and joined the Air Force.

Moe Placzek, one of eight boys, served in the Army, as did five of his brothers. Dante Malta, who was about three years older than Tommy, served in the Army and went to Korea. Dick "Blizzard" Barry, "Champ" Morris, Skippy White, and a large group of Westfield lads all joined the Navy. Champ recalls how ten of them all rode the train together to basic training, singing all the way. As they emerged with their newly shaven heads on the first day, the boys from Westfield already at the training camp were waiting and laughing like crazy as they welcomed them into the Navy.

On September 10, 1952, Tommy joined the Marines. Frank Tierney had had hopes of Tommy attending St. Michael's College, but when he heard Tommy wanted to enter the service, he felt it was the best decision. Frank Tierney drove Tommy to the train station that day. Shaking his hand, Frank looked at Tommy and his parting words were "Keep the faith."

Tommy reflected on basic training. "Boot camp at Parris Island—it was a big shock. They are always trying to break you so you won't break under combat. They try to humiliate you. After a few weeks, I adjusted. I enjoyed it; I was getting fit and I felt good.

"My drill instructors had just spent time in Korea and they were on the way back. Sergeant Brewer used to play the harmonica, and I would sometimes play for him and he'd get me off a lot of lousy details you have to perform. We'd pull fire walks (two hours on, four hours off), getting up in the middle of the night, walking around and patrolling the area. We'd do midnight to 2 AM, then sleep until 5 AM and get up again in the pitch black.

"I was homesick and I had three or four girlfriends in Westfield and I used to read their letters.... That would keep me going. I did go to Mass and Communion every Sunday. I also had this Mutt and Jeff cartoon on my fridge that said, 'If you have Faith, you can have Hope,' and it brought me through." Tommy starts to giggle, "I swear that pulled me through!"

Tommy was very proud of his platoon. "We had a great platoon. We became post-honor—the highest award you can get. A combination of written exam, rifle performance, and physical and mental tests they put you through. The final day you march on the parade field while they play the Marine Corps

Hymn. You swell up with pride. You are Private First Class. You can't wait to get home. I have a graduation picture somewhere that one friend, Sully, signed 'To one guy the Marine Corps couldn't break.'

"I got home for Thanksgiving in tremendous shape. I reported to Portsmouth, New Hampshire on a very dark gloomy day, December 7, 1952. I saw this big building, the Portsmouth Naval Retraining Command. They called it the Castle. It was a prison for servicemen (Marines, Navy and Coast Guard) who went AWOL, etc. You had an introductory two-week course with 1300 inmates. It was depressing but I liked when you had time off, 'Liberty,' and I'd go to downtown Portsmouth and the University of New Hampshire. It was great in the summer—the beaches!"

"They had a First Naval District cross-country race in South Boston. I came in second and Commander Colson asked, "Son, how did you get down here? How'd you hear about this? Congratulations on finishing second." I told him I came down on my own and he contacted my Commanding Officer, Colonel Ricksie. He sent me a nice letter and told me from now on I could have all the time off I needed to train, and an officer would escort me to any future races. I had the "red carpet" treatment. Next time I went to run in Boston, they drove me down. Captain Martin and I ate in one of the finest restaurants. I got three or four days off, 'Special Liberty.' So I had it pretty well off in Portsmouth. I ran a lot. I entered my first Boston Marathon at age 19, in 1953. There were 198 entrants that year and I ran about 4.5 hours.

"The duty was depressing, though. Watching young kids, maybe 75 percent of them shouldn't have been in the service in the first place. A judge who gave them the option of military service or prison confronted many. Many could not adjust to the regimentation and enforcement of rules and regulations. They had no motivation. I had a couple of prisoners who had gone through boot camp with me. That was tough, as I really liked one of them. They'd end up with dishonorable discharges or general discharges, which would restrict their benefits. At the time, a dishonorable discharge meant you could never vote again. I think they've lifted the bar on that one. A lot has changed. I spent three years there.

"The jail had three tiers of cell blocks and an annex with dormitories of seven or eight floors. There was an area called 'pre-release' for inmates who were preparing to go back to active duty. There were some guards on the third floor who were sadistic. I wasn't like that. I'd just say, 'Hey guys, I'll meet you halfway if you meet me halfway. If you try to screw me, I'll put you on report. It's as simple as that.'

"Murderers were in the cell blocks. Lesser criminals—they lived in the annex. I spent a lot of time in the guard towers, 'The Deadline.' You would do four hours on and eight hours off. I worked in the cellblocks doing prisoner counts, marching them to chow, watching over those in solitary, 'the hole.' They had an hour of daylight to read a Bible or missal and have some exercise. We'd throw a blanket at them. It was really depressing watching those kids.

"There was a tailor shop at Portsmouth where they sewed ugly-looking gray suits for inmates going home. They'd give you a small amount of money for transportation to get back to your home and maybe a little bit of spending money. It was sad to see that happen. You had access to their records; some seemed incorrigible. Maybe some of them got the raw end of the deal or maybe they brought it on themselves.

"With about a year and a half to go, they sent me to another Retraining Camp out in New Castle by the Sea. That was a bit more lenient. These guys were going back to active duty. That was nice…it wasn't as tough as Portsmouth. It looked like a college campus; that's when I really got into running. I could go off base, even if I was on duty. I'd sometimes go and lay on the beach when I was supposed to be running! In my days off, there was a beautiful resort called Wentworth by the Sea in New Castle. I'd work as a bus boy and make $25 a day. That was a lot of money back then. We could eat lobster, clams, and corn on the cob. It was nice up there. The Marriott has renovated it into a beautiful resort and spa.

"I had to go into Portsmouth to receive my discharge. There was a Marine Corps officer named Lieutenant John Archbold, a graduate of St. John's University, who was also a runner. He would always encourage my running. He helped to get my discharge quickly. In the Corps, you don't fraternize with the enlisted men. Once in a blue moon, he'd go out with the boys and just be one of the guys. We'd go to a place called "Lads." He was a very kind human, a true Marine.

"In 1968, I was working in a place called the Beachcomber on Cape Cod and was reading a column in the paper about now-Major John Archbold, who had just volunteered for his third tour of duty in Vietnam as a helicopter pilot and was recently married. The paper told how he was shot down and paid the eternal price. I was devastated. When the Vietnam Moving Wall came to Falmouth a few years ago, I punched out a ticket with his information. I have it on my refrigerator door. What a nice, nice man. God must have wanted him."

Tommy was discharged from the Marines on September 9, 1955, having served three years, and returned home to Westfield. He and his pals all recognized that the GI Bill was a godsend and provided them an opportunity to get a college education and pursue careers.

He has remained a loyal and true devotee of the United States Marine Corps. The Marine Corps flag, with its eagle, anchor, and globe symbols, flies daily by the front door of his bungalow in Falmouth, Massachusetts. He is proud of the Marine Corps' core values of honor, courage, and commitment. He has followed the Marine Corps Band to many concerts over the years. Anyone who has called his answering machine has probably heard some version of "Semper Fi" on his many different messages. He attends an annual Marine Corps Birthday Luncheon on November 10 in Boston, a celebration that occurs in many cities around the nation.

One of Tommy's greatest honors was receiving the William F. Degan Semper Fidelis Award at the birthday celebration luncheon in 1997. The award is given annually to a Marine in memory of William F. Degan, who was a U.S. Marshal and retired Marine colonel killed by a sniper at Ruby Ridge, Idaho, during the arrest of Randy Weaver for making and selling illegal weapons in 1992. It is a tremendous honor to receive this prestigious award. It is given to former Marines for acts of heroism or substantial acts of community service.

Tommy was not aware that he was going to receive the award, and his friend, Eddie Burke, also a Marine (1963–67) and a Viet Nam war veteran, had the unenviable job of making sure T.L. remained in the room long enough to hear the award announced. Eddie had previous experience introducing Tommy on numerous other occasions, only to discover he had disappeared while Eddie was making the introduction, so he knew the challenge he was facing. Tommy was being recognized for his many acts of charitable fund raising and community service over the years. Overcome with emotion and thrilled with the award, Tommy was actually at a loss for words as he accepted the award and tried to thank the crowd. He equated it to "my winning the Boston Marathon. It was my Academy Award."

In June 2004, Tommy was enjoying the festivities surrounding the annual Litchfield Road Race with Billy Harbilas, director of the Holyoke Elks Talking Turkey Road Race, and Billy's fiancée, Sally Rohan, as well as Steve Jones, former winner of the New York, Chicago, and London marathons and a world record holder in the marathon at one time. They were out to dinner with their Litchfield hosts, and Tommy was getting tired and announced to his table that he was going home for some rest.

As he was leaving, a bagpiper entered the restaurant. As he passed the bagpiper, Tommy leaned over and whispered to him. The piper nodded, his instrument hummed, and then the crowd began to hear the familiar tune—"From the halls of Montezuma to the shores of Tripoli"—the Marine Corps Hymn. As the piper finished, Tommy gestured for him to wait a moment, reached into his pocket, pulled out a harmonica, and proceeded to play the hymn and march in place. As he finished, the room was silent as the crowd sat stunned, and then everyone erupted in applause. Waving goodbye, Tommy exclaimed, "This Marine is toast. Good night, everybody!"

6

The Identity Search

Going the Distance

"If I knew where I was going, I'd be there by now."
—Don Foley's suggested title for Tommy's life story

Upon returning to Westfield after his discharge from the Marines, Tommy entered Holyoke Community College under the GI Bill in the fall of 1955. "I was really wild and should have waited at least a semester. Instead, I cut classes, chased women, and was a real hellion. I spent my money, wasted my time, and by December, I dropped out of school. I'd love to go to school today. I sure as hell had the opportunities. I don't blame anyone but myself."

So Tommy Leonard now began a long period of job hopping and carousing. Many of his high school friends were also getting out of the various branches of the service, so they all picked up where they had left off in the bars and dances at the Showboat, Couture's Garden, Amherst's Quonset Hut, the Valley Arena, Rahar's, and elsewhere.

Dante "Moldy" Molta is three years older than Tommy and had played football for Springfield Trade High. His mother's family came from the same village in northern Italy as Bruno Fioroni's family, so he got to know the Westfield athletes through his friendship with Bruno. Dante's mother referred to Tommy in her dialect as "Selvitaco Corsa," or the "Wild Runner," as she sensed Tommy's somewhat wild and free nature.

When he came home from service in Korea in the Army, Dante worked for a while as a bouncer at his brother's father-in-law's place, the Hofbraus House in West Springfield. Tommy went to hear a banjo band that had come in from Amherst one evening. Dante's twin sisters, Jenny and Dorothy, walked in with their friend Madeline Cremonti just as Tommy was pouring a pitcher of beer over Dante's head while standing on the table. Asking her friends, "Who are those fools up on the table?" Madeline never dreamed she would one day become the bride of the fool receiving the foamy shampoo. Tommy has had many unique ways of bringing people together over the years.

After Bruno got out of the Marines in 1955, he was working long hours and traveling to Amherst to visit and party with Dante at the University of Massachusetts. He would usually stay too long and leave too late. Dante and Tommy both worried about him and frequently would say, "Bruno, one day you are not going to make it home if you don't get enough sleep." But Bruno would drive with his head out the window to stay awake. One day he was a half-mile away from home when he hit a telephone pole and severed his spinal cord. The Tierneys called Tommy while he was in the Marines, and he came home devastated to see his formerly strong and athletic friend now paralyzed from the chest down.

Bruno spent over a year in rehab at the West Roxbury Veterans Hospital. Upon coming home from the hospital, he had a car outfitted with hand controls so he could drive in his wheelchair. As his friends recall, it was a rough spell for him when he first came home. He resumed going out to party and consumed up to a quart of whiskey a day for a period.

One autumn day, Tommy, Dante, and Bruno decided to go to the top of Mt. Greylock in Berkshire County to enjoy the view and have a few brews. When they left to drive home, they neglected to put the wheelchair in the back of the car. Dante dropped Tommy home before driving down the road to Bruno's house and discovering the wheelchair was missing. Dante wanted to carry Bruno into the house, but he would not hear of it. He was a proud Marine and was determined to play the cards he'd been dealt. Dante watched helplessly as Bruno pulled himself along with his elbows across the lawn and into his house. Bruno could see Mrs. Fioroni watching tearfully behind the curtain in the house.

Eventually, Bruno married the nurse who had taken care of him, Kate Curran. They had a house built and settled into a happy existence together until years later, when cancer took his life.

After the service, Tommy and his friends dated many of the girls at Westfield State College. At the time, there was a curfew for the students at the college. Westfield State President Scanlon acquired the nickname of "Sneakers," as he would sneak around looking for kids who were violating the curfew to smooch in their cars. He'd reprimand the girls and send them off to their dorms. One evening, Tommy was discovered generously displaying his charm in what he calls "a compromising position" inside the dormitory, which was a major violation of the rules. Westfield State banned Tommy from the campus permanently. Ironically, thirty years later, Tommy crossed the stage at Westfield State College to receive an Honorary Doctorate of Humane Letters for his contributions to the community and his role in promoting physical fitness and road racing. He also received the letter of congratulations from the Massachusetts State Senate shown here.

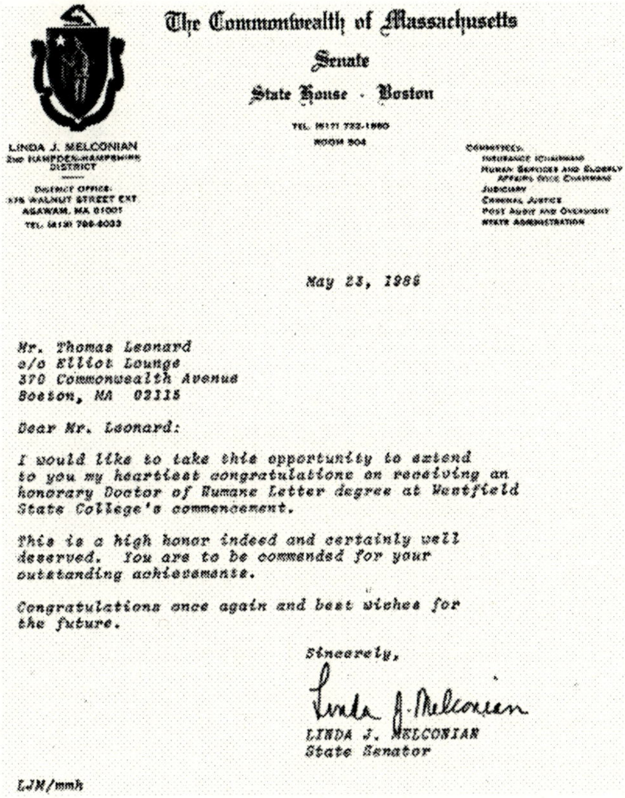

The Commonwealth of Massachusetts

Senate

State House · Boston

TEL. (617) 722-1440
ROOM 504

LINDA J. MELCONIAN
2nd HAMPDEN-HAMPSHIRE
DISTRICT

District Office:
375 WALNUT STREET EXT.
AGAWAM, MA 01001
TEL. (413) 786-6033

COMMITTEES:
INSURANCE (CHAIRMAN)
HUMAN SERVICES AND ELDERLY
AFFAIRS (VICE CHAIRMAN)
JUDICIARY
CRIMINAL JUSTICE
POST AUDIT AND OVERSIGHT
STATE ADMINISTRATION

May 23, 1988

Mr. Thomas Leonard
c/o Elliot Lounge
370 Commonwealth Avenue
Boston, MA 02115

Dear Mr. Leonard:

I would like to take this opportunity to extend to you my heartiest congratulations on receiving an honorary Doctor of Humane Letter degree at Westfield State College's commencement.

This is a high honor indeed and certainly well deserved. You are to be commended for your outstanding achievements.

Congratulations once again and best wishes for the future.

Sincerely,

Linda J. Melconian

LINDA J. MELCONIAN
State Senator

LJM/mmh

Frank's patience with Tommy's carousing when he came home from the Marines wore thin, and he suggested that Tommy go get himself a job. Having a flair for the dramatic, Tommy responded, "I know when I am not wanted around here. I'll take care of myself." And he spent the next couple of weeks sleeping in the car he had driven into the brook on the Tierney property after a few pops one night.

Tommy took a job driving a plumbing supply truck for Warner Supply Company. He invited a girlfriend to ride along while he made his deliveries one afternoon. Temptation was great, and Tommy found himself in another "compromising position." This time, however, his position shifted the gears on the column, sending the truck into the adjacent cow field, spewing bathtubs and copper tubing into the cow muck and horse manure.

For a period of time, seeking independence, Tommy lived in the supply truck he was driving. In the early morning he would go into the back door of the nearby Coffee Den to wash up and brush his teeth. One day, Tommy was backing up the truck to a loading platform with his co-worker, Jack Whalen. He accidentally hit the accelerator and nearly crushed Jack to death. This accident shook Tommy to the core, and shortly afterward he made a decision that would affect his whole life. Recognizing that he really did not have the temperament for driving, and not being sure if his drinking habits had affected his judgment that day, Tommy admitted to himself it was time to make a choice. He could drive or he could drink. He hasn't driven a car since.

Despite a lifetime of happy memories associated with drink and friends, both old and new, the choice to drink came with a price a few times in Tommy's life. Shortly after coming home from the Marines, Tommy was out in the bars of northern Springfield with friends Peter Butler, Tommy Carey, and Bobby King. After consuming a lot of beer, they walked down the street drunkenly hooting, singing, and ringing doorbells. A police paddy wagon appeared in response to a caller's complaint. Peter, Tommy Carey, and Bobby were put in the wagon, but Tommy Leonard figured he had the speed and fitness to outlast the police, so he took off running down the sidewalk. When the police caught up with him, they brutally beat his head with their clubs and threw them all in a jail cell for the night. No medical attention was given in the prison. His friends took him to the hospital the next day, and the doctor was astounded that he wasn't more severely injured as he closed Tommy's wounds with nearly thirty stitches.

For about a year after coming home, Tommy dated Geraldine Whalley, a high school senior in Holyoke. But the pull of the party always had a hold on him, and he would frequently go to frat parties in Amherst or Northampton when he'd promised Gerry he would take her out. When she had had enough of his lack of dependability, they broke up. "Wow," Tommy recalls. "That was another downslide in my life. I almost went over the deep end. But I brought it all down on myself."

Shortly after the breakup, Tommy went to an AIC–U Mass football game with Don Foley and Bruno in his wheelchair. "The breakup was on my mind. I was drinking 'Grappa,' Italian wine. The U Mass band had just started to perform at halftime. Bruno got me going and encouraged me to go out on the field. So I ran out between the lines of the marching band and the majorettes with their batons. The security police started to chase me but I would elude them, changing directions and running off. The band kept on marching and playing while I ran around and through the routine. The poor girls were dropping their batons, and more and more security came out to chase me. It began to look like a Keystone Cops episode, and the crowd began to cheer and really enjoy the chase. They booed when the cops finally took me off the field.

"That's not a memory I am too fond of. I don't think the Tierneys ever heard of that; I didn't want them to hear about it. It was embarrassing...I was a jackass. Everyone got a big laugh out of it, but I'm not proud of it. I was going through a rough time."

Kenny Balducci had just gotten out of the Army and was playing football for AIC on the day of the "Keystone Cops" incident. It was his introduction to a guy who would become a close friend for life.

During high school, an aunt raised Don Foley. His mother lived in Brooklyn, and Don and Tommy would sometimes hitchhike to visit her. When Tommy lost his job at Warner Supply, he decided to go visit Mrs. Foley for a weekend. A year and a half later, Tommy was still calling Mrs. Foley's apartment home and working for New York Life Insurance in Manhattan. It didn't take him long to make new friends and continue his lifestyle of drinking and dancing, on tabletops as well as dance floors, at Kaufman's, Kennedy's, Runyan's, and many other night spots.

One fateful night Tommy decided to travel out to a pub called the Irish Circle, across from Maguire's on Rockaway Beach. He was flinging money on the bar while buying drinks for people as the night progressed. When he went into the men's room, three thugs jumped him and beat him so severely that he spent a week in New York Hospital. That beating cost him most of the hearing in his left ear.

A herald of optimism, Tommy has never lost faith in the goodness of mankind. He has continued to seek the joy in life in all of his endeavors. After recovering from his hospital stay, he returned to work and play in his own rare form. Ever proud of his Irish heritage, Tommy considers St. Patrick's Day to be one of the year's primary holidays. He once painted his entire body green to help him fully celebrate the festivities and mood of the day.

Before entering the Marines, Don Foley had been asked to leave Westfield High. At age twenty-one, he returned to Westfield to complete his high school degree. He organized weekly Wednesday dances at the Whippernon Country Club for the local guys and the girls at Westfield State. Tommy had been elevated to the status of Senator Rainbow Rainmaker of Raintree County by his friends. One Wednesday evening, the "Senator" arrived at the Whippernon from his job at New York Life, sporting a brand new seersucker suit he had purchased that Monday. The limbo was popular at the time—an eccentric dance to a Caribbean rhythm in which the dancer bends over backward and passes under a stick held by a person on each end without knocking or touching the stick. As the evening wore on, Tommy felt that his long suit pants were interfering with the true spirit of limbo dancing, so he simply cut them into short pants to better capture the mood and movements of the limbo.

In the early 1960s, Tommy began to spend his summers on Cape Cod. His first jobs were at the Falmouth Playhouse and Clausen's Inn as a waiter. One evening, after working at the Falmouth Playhouse, Tommy went to the Hunt Club with some waitresses, who bought him a few too many "Planter's Punches" for his birthday. Walking by the Playhouse later that night, Tommy noticed the actor William Bendix checking into the actor's cottage. He staggered toward Mr. Bendix, saying, "Welcome to Falmouth" with his fist full of about $100 in singles he had earned in tips and was trying to offer to the actor. A summer breeze then blew all of the money into the pond. Mr. Bendix was not amused by this drunken welcome and complained to management. That was the end of his job at the Falmouth Playhouse. The very next day, Gerry Lopez, the manager of the restaurant at Clausen's Inn, gave Tommy a job as a waiter and busboy.

By the mid-1960s, Tommy was tending bar at the Beachcomber in north Falmouth, where he stayed for four or five summers. The Beachcomber had a large performance hall and would draw top bands. One summer, Tommy called George Kelleher: "Georgie, I've got a summer job for you as a bouncer. And a place to stay! Come on down!" Upon his arrival, Tommy led George upstairs by the owner's quarters and then across two narrow planks high above the performance hall to a loft at the other end, where two mattresses lay on the floor. This was Tommy's living quarters for a couple of summers. George, a husky football player, took the job but opted to find less perilous housing after a couple of days of plank walking.

Neighbors of the Beachcomber, the O'Rourkes owned a Saint Bernard dog named Mickey Finn. Mickey became a kind of house pet for the Beachcomber and followed Tommy everywhere. On a very hot and humid Cape Cod day, the Beachcomber softball team was having a clambake. A hole was dug in the ground for the clams, and everyone was feeling the heaviness in the air. Tommy felt sorry for Mickey Finn, so he put him in the walk-in cooler to give him relief from the heat. Unfortunately, Tommy then went to the clam bake and beach party, forgetting all about the poor dog. Opening up for work the next day, Tommy heard a muffled "WOOF" come from the cooler and realized his folly. Tommy opened the door and the huge, frosty dog with frozen whiskers dove at him with a cross-body block, spinning Tommy in the air like a pinwheel. The dog then crawled under the porch of the Beachcomber, where he stayed for a couple of days. Eventually, they called the police to get some help coaxing the dog out from under the porch. Tommy has tried to be extremely careful with pets ever since.

Tommy does have a love of animals, and they often take to him immediately. Years after the Mickey Finn incident, John Connolly of the Boston Herald would recall watching Tommy sitting with his brother-in-law Reid Oslin's big black Labrador. The dog idolized Tommy and would sit at his feet. As Tommy drank his Budweiser, he'd set the can on the dog's nose, and the dog would patiently sit holding the can and watching Tommy.

As summer came to a close and the Cape experienced its annual mass exodus of tourists and second home–owners, Tommy would return to Westfield to find work. For a brief while, Tommy moved to Hartford and lived with his high school buddy Fred "Moe" Plazcek. He tried a job at Pratt-Whitney where Moe worked, running IBM machines such as collators and sorters. It was a short-lived experience.

Tommy decided to give California a chance in the early 1960s and took a job at UCLA running electrical accounting machines. He was quickly afflicted with what he terms "beach blanket syndrome." After missing six Mondays of work in a row, his bosses suggested they terminate the relationship and that he not use them as a reference.

Tommy headed to Santa Monica, where he knew John O'Connor lived. John had graduated from St. Mary's High with Grace and had never actually met Tommy. When he finished his stint in the Army, he moved to California and was working as a bartender at Chez Jay. Being a Westfielder, he welcomed Tommy with open arms and invited him to stay at his place.

Tommy spent lots of time at Chez Jay, which is situated on a bluff above Santa Monica beach. Known as a celebrity dive through its forty-five-year old history, the decor is described on AOL's city guide for LA as "classic seafood shack: red and white checked tablecloths, cement floor littered with peanut shells and rough-finished wood walls plastered with memorabilia. Photos and newspaper clippings commemorate the night Marlon Brando made off with one of the waitresses, the day a Chez Jay peanut went to the moon and the time when Jay bought the hot air balloon from the film 'The Great Race' and flew it all over Southern California."

When owner Jay Fiondella opened Chez Jay in 1959, he was appearing in films. The celebrities of the day, seeking anonymity from their star status, flocked to Jay's. To this day, the policy of no cameras or autographs is enforced, so movie stars continue to enjoy a rare degree of privacy while there. Tommy is in his element when he feels that the circle of humanity has blended into a "Noah's Ark of Life"—people of all social and economic strata enjoying life together—which he felt happened regularly at Jay's. He quickly became a legend during his brief stay in California.

John O'Connor, or "Okey," recalls that Tommy would borrow clothes for a job interview and then disappear for a week. "Tommy would befriend someone on the beach or at a party and end up staying with them for three or four days. People would adopt him. He lives for today. I was working full-time and it seemed like he was playing full-time. But he did miss Boston; he's a die-hard Boston fan."

Tommy did find himself a job as a waiter at La Mer in Malibu and enjoyed interacting with people. He began to feel that he was finding his niche in the world of bars and restaurants.

The owner of La Mer was an eccentric elderly lady from Tennessee who wanted her staff to live on the premises. Tommy found himself sleeping in what was basically a boiler room into which she had put a bed. This was not one of his favorite haciendas, but this fact seemed irrelevant to him while he enjoyed the beaches and bars of California. He held on to that job until he tripped while delivering a Baked Alaska to a table and nearly burnt his eyebrows off when his face landed in the flaming dessert.

The pull of Boston and Cape Cod on his heartstrings eventually landed him back on the East Coast working at the Banjo Room as a waiter in north

Falmouth in the summer of 1963. The owners, Paul O'Donnell and John Ashton, opened another Banjo Room in Lechmere Square in Cambridge, and Tommy took a job bartending there in the fall.

The Banjo Room also had the casual "checkered tablecloth/peanuts and sawdust on the floor" atmosphere that was so popular at the time. Frequently featured was the Gaslight Gang, a banjo band composed of three banjos, a piano, washboard, ukulele, and drums. Tommy would often jump in to play the washboard and sing with the band.

Throughout all of his job hopping of the 1950s and 1960s, Tommy's love of running never ceased. He continued to enter marathons and long-distance races. In 1965 he arranged for the Gaslight Gang to set up on a flatbed truck at the end of the Boston Marathon. Seeing the band as he was completing the 26.2 miles from Hopkington to Boston, he finished like a racehorse and kept running up onto the truck with the band, where he belted out an exuberant rendition of Won't You Come Home, Bill Bailey?

Tommy met two of his closest friends at the Banjo Room in the 1960s: Jackie Pierce, now a retired Detective with the Boston Police Department, and Eddie Doyle, renowned bartender of Bull & Finch/Cheers fame. Jackie was living in Charlestown at the time and was a frequent patron of the Banjo Room on Saturday nights with a group of pals, many with their own nicknames—"YP," "Muff," "Ratso," Marty, and others." Many of the patrons of the Banjo Room came from Southie, Dorchester, Charlestown, and Cambridge. Altercations of some type were not infrequent. Jackie noticed that in addition to being a charismatic bartender with a flair for bringing people together, Tommy was keenly observant and could pinpoint the peacemaker in a crowd. He often took advantage of this ability to defuse some potentially hot situations.

In the late 1960s, Eddie Doyle was a student at the Museum School of Fine Art in Boston and was bartending at the Harvard Club a few nights a week. He took a job as a waiter at the Banjo Room during a time when it was transitioning from a banjo/peanuts/sawdust type of place to more of a rock band milieu. Eddie remembers such bands playing there as the Crumpets (a black band from England) and Monty and the Barbarians (a band whose drummer had a hook for a hand).

On Eddie's first night as a waiter, a Golden Glove boxer named Frank Calabro was working as the bouncer. The staff would pay for their drink orders up front at the service bar and then collect from the patrons. Eddie's first table was a group of five wise guys who denied they ordered the beer he delivered to them, but grabbed the pitcher and began pouring it, thanking Ed for his generosity. Seeing this, Frank approached the table and suggested they pay for their beer. One of the buys pulled out a handful of his father's business cards, subtly suggesting that they shouldn't be bothered or expected to pay. Dropping the cards on the floor, Frank told them to pay and get lost. Before Eddie realized what was happening, Frank was in the middle of a fistfight with the gang outside the building, sending them on their way.

The last night that Eddie worked at the Banjo Room, the bouncer had the night off. A large group of hefty drunken guys sauntered in from a wedding reception they had attended. Before the night was over, Eddie found himself in the center of a monumental brawl. Tommy pulled him away from the melee, letting him know the cops were on the way. Eddie decided this was not the atmosphere for him. He would not see Tommy again for several years. Eventually, the Banjo Room succumbed to a fire.

Throughout most of the mid- to late 1960s, Tommy continued to work at the Beachcomber on Cape Cod during the summers. Many of his loyal friends at the Banjo Room would head to the Cape late on Friday night, avoiding the traffic, and arrive at the Beachcomber in time for last call. Jackie Pierce remembers that the place was always packed, as Tommy's humor, storytelling, and charisma were already becoming a magnetic force.

Jackie vividly remembers one June weekend in 1968 when he went to the Beachcomber and Tommy was nowhere to be found for several days. Eventually, Tommy called from New York City, where he had traveled to honor Robert F. Kennedy, whose funeral was being held at St. Patrick's Cathedral. Although he was known for his penchant for parties and good times, he has always had a profound sense of what really matters and a willingness and need to pay his respects when he feels it is called for.

In 1968 Tommy introduced Jackie to Jacqueline Finnerty, whose pitching abilities led the Beachcomber softball team to the summer championship. On June 27, 1970, Jackie wed Jacqueline in a huge ceremony with 300 guests at Florian Hall, a firefighter's post in Dorchester. Tommy served as an usher in the wedding. In true Leonard fashion, he was the last to arrive and had only the clothes on his back. Jackie brought Tommy to his parents' house to shower and then gave him his tuxedo to wear, and says, "I think I provided him with clean socks and underwear, as well!"

Another job that Tommy took in the 1960s was bartender at the Crossroads Irish Pub on Beacon Street in Boston. Sharpless Jones remembers the day he met Tommy Leonard at Crossroads. It was Christmas Eve of Sharpless's eighteenth year. He and his friend, the late Fran Coffey, had decided to quaff a couple of beers before heading out to do their (timely) Christmas shopping. Tommy kept both the pitchers and the stories flowing for hours, and they very nearly missed Christmas with their families, but they did have a Christmas Eve they would never forget. This was the beginning of another lifelong friendship. Fran and Sharpless also began to share the joys of summer with Tommy in Falmouth.

It was while he was employed as a bartender at the Crossroads Irish Pub that Tommy Leonard got to know one of his patrons, Mark Aiken, in 1972. This relationship would be the catalyst to the most significant job of Tommy's life.

7

The Eliot Lounge, Part One

Reaching Goals

"I tried to bring the world together."

—Tommy Leonard

On the corner of Massachusetts Avenue and Commonwealth Avenue in Boston Massachusetts, next to the Harvard Club, is the Eliot Hotel. Behind the hotel for fifty years sat the Eliot Lounge with its own entrance on Massachusetts Avenue and a direct entrance inside to the hotel. Established in 1946 when hard drinks were 29 cents, the Eliot was a tri-level lounge that began as a Back Bay bistro. There was a balcony for dining couples and a lower level for more raucous socializing. At one time, an organ was suspended above the bar on the street level.

The business waxed and waned over the years, and by the early 1970s it had become a dark and somewhat dismal watering hole with a lone Indian jukebox. It's decor would later be described in the Boston Globe as "Early Grandfather's Attic"—"decaying deer head, an old (stalled) clock, an Irish flag, hanging plants, framed pictures." Veteran patrons of the era recalled, "The place was so dead, they'd be playing chess on Saturday nights. It was in the ashes."

The lounge and its huge basement offered Mark and Don Aiken the perfect solution to their long search for a location for their new business venture, Medieval Manor, Inc.

Don and Mark had both previously worked for Your Father's Mustache, a national chain of nostalgia-themed saloons with audience participation, sing-along banjo bands, and crazy antics from the wait staff and bartenders. In 1971 Don was a student at Yale with an interest in theater. He went to British Columbia in Vancouver, Canada, to assist with the opening of the Medieval Inn—a restaurant/inn based on the medieval period, with traditional multi-course English feasts accompanied by wenches, minstrels, jesters, and such. Mark and Don felt that if they combined the Medieval Inn concept with the audience participation of Your Father's Mustache, they'd have a great business concept. Mark was most interested in running a local corner bar, and Don was interested in the theatrical end of the Manor.

They purchased the business in February 1972. They took over the lounge and outfitted the basement for the Medieval Manor Theatre Restaurant, where the Lord of the Manor's every whim was responded to with song, story, and slapstick. Mark asked Tommy to stop over and meet his brother, Don. He told Don what a great guy and friendly bartender Tommy was. They offered Tommy a job, but he had a commitment to bartend at the Brothers Four in Falmouth on Cape Cod for the summer. He agreed to return in September and began his tenure as the "daylight bartender," which would last for almost a quarter-century.

In their wildest dreams, the Aikens could not have imagined the transformation that would occur within a few short years of their acquiring the little corner bar. Tommy's passion, enthusiasm, and common touch would shape the metamorphosis. His title as "daylight bartender" would be as symbolic as it was factual, as his personality would soon coruscate into the hearts of many. Even the Indian jukebox would receive postcards from around the globe with good-natured fondness from the senders.

In the summer of 1972, while Tommy was bartending at the Brothers Four, Frank Shorter won the Olympic gold medal in the marathon. Shorter's victory happened just as the country was waking up to fitness and exercise. The running boom would grow and develop over the next few years and would lead the way to the development of many annual marathons, road races, and triathlons around the globe.

When Tommy began his job at the Eliot in September 1972, he was pumped up and enthused about running. His sport was finally coming of age.

He suggested to the Aikens that they offer a free beer to any runner in the 1973 Boston Marathon who came in with their number. The Aikens gave their full support. Tommy acquired the mailing list of all the registered entrants and sent them a postcard invitation to the Eliot Lounge. This would be his first marketing attempt, and preceded many incredibly successful events in the next few years.

Tommy once described the Boston Marathon to Alan Bruce of the Associated Press as "the longest stage in the world. I like show biz. All the love comes out in people that day. The Marathon is like Christmas Eve, St. Patrick's Day, the Mardi Gras, and Thanksgiving all rolled into one. All the happiness comes out in people."

In one of Tommy's earliest experiences as a bartender at the Eliot, he was approached by a guy with a gun who wanted the cash in the register. Tommy took a look and said, "Hey, I'm a runner. I know a starter's pistol when I see one." The fellow responded by blowing out a large hole in the wall behind the bar, which remained for many years. Don Aiken installed a Guinness mirror over that hole, an ale the Eliot did not serve.

In 1974 Tommy was living near Cleveland Circle and would occasionally work out on the track at Boston College, where the Greater Boston Track Club did their workouts. His intense interest in running led to a natural friendliness with the members of the GBTC.

The club was formed in 1973 when a group of talented postgraduate athletes were looking for a place to run and an organization to help them continue to develop their talents. BC's track coach at the time, Jack McDonald, a talented track runner, nurtured the club in its infancy on the BC track. Bill Squires, a former All-American from Notre Dame and then the coach at Boston State, agreed to coach the GBTC without pay. Although the club was a track club, road running in New England was strong and the top distance runners gravitated to the GBTC.

The club would soon spawn such talented running giants as Bill Rodgers (four-time winner of the Boston Marathon, four-time winner of the New York City Marathon, winner of Fukuoka), Greg Meyer (Boston Marathon champ and national AAU Cross-Country champ), Alberto Salazar (three-time New York City Marathon winner and 1982 world record holder at Boston), Vinnie Fleming, Dick Mahoney, Bobby Hodge, Bob Sevene, and Jack Fultz, among others. By 1977 the GBTC would take four of the top ten places at the Boston Marathon.

When the club first formed, they made a commitment to meet on Tuesdays at Boston College at 6 PM and later moved their workouts to Tufts in the winter. Tommy invited the members of the GBTC to stop into the Eliot after their workouts. Tommy's intense interest in and knowledge of running combined with his friendly and enthusiastic personality made the club feel very welcome. It didn't take long before the Eliot became the unofficial clubhouse of the GBTC and "Coach's Corner" developed, where Coach Squires happily offered training advice to anyone who asked. Tommy made sure pitchers of beer flowed freely to the club, whose talents he admired tremendously.

These athletes would regularly run 8, 15, or 20 miles in about a 5:30 pace. This was the era before shoe deals, appearance money, or corporate sponsorship. JJ Larner, BC graduate and part-time bartender at the Eliot, wrote in a history of the lounge, "It was truly about running, testing yourself, seeing what you could do, enjoying it and then having a few beers at the Eliot afterwards."

For several members of the club, the Eliot became a favorite mid-way stop during daytime workouts. Toni Reavis, current sports reporter for ESPN and Fox Sports Net, was a co-host of Runner's Digest, the first radio show devoted to running in the 1970s. He would regularly meet Bobby Hodge and Vinnie Fleming at the New Balance factory in Brighton for an 8-mile run along the Charles River. As he recalls, "This was during the hot, sweaty summer months, and we ran shirtless and free, all skin and bone, sweating like glistening malnourished pigs in the trough of New England humidity." In the middle of the run, they'd stop to see Tommy at the Eliot. "Upon seeing us enter the darkened tavern, he'd break into one of his warm summer smiles, remark floridly about the 'powder puff clouds and cerulean blue skies' as he welcomed us with open arms and gave us each a Sea Breeze...which would refresh us mightily before we embarked on our final 3–4 miles west back to Brighton.

"It was just Tommy being himself, welcoming runners just as his day was beginning behind the bar....We'd spend those few minutes with sweat dripping from our bony frames as the warmth of Tommy's welcome ushered us through the mid-point of our run. The very nothing-special-about-it element lent it, in reflection, the quality of true bonhomie which came to define Tommy to all who were and are lucky enough to brush through his briar patch of good cheer."

During the summer of 1973, while working back at the Brothers Four in Falmouth, Tommy started a little 7.1-mile road race that would grow and grow into one of America's premier road races, the Falmouth Road Race. It will be discussed in detail later in this book. In the summer of 1974, he enticed

several members of the GBTC to run in the Falmouth Road Race with prom-
ises of "girls in bikinis handing out water along the beach route." Billy Rodgers at the time was a virtual unknown, a quiet conscientious objector who had
graduated from Wesleyan University and Boston College. His surprise victory
over America's premier middle-distance runner, Marty Liquori, a graduate of
Villanova, brought him to the forefront of New England road running.

Eight months later, on Patriot's Day, Rodgers ran to a stunning win in the
Boston Marathon with an American and course record of 2:09:55. After the
race, with national TV cameras in his face, Billy was asked what he was going
to do and he replied, "I'm going to the Eliot Lounge to have a Blue Whale."
This created an immediate media frenzy to discover what this Eliot Lounge
was all about. Tommy would often say, "That statement put us on the map,
the switchboard was jammed, it pioneered us. I owe a lot to Rodgers."

The day of Billy's first Boston victory, Tommy also ran in the marathon.
He described the race to John Schulian of the Chicago Sun–Times, saying,
"Billy's fighting to prove how good he is and I'm way back in the pack. I'm
ready to drop out and just then I hear the crowd roar—Billy's just pulled into
the lead. I'm telling you, he gave off mystical vibrations. I got so high I ran my
best marathon ever. Three hours and seventeen minutes."

That evening Billy celebrated with his girlfriend Ellen, Coach Squires,
brother Charlie, and former college roommate and 1968 winner of the Boston
Marathon Amby Burfoot into the wee hours of the morning at the Eliot.
Tommy had rented a room at the Eliot Hotel. He climbed into a hot tub with
a couple boxes of fried rice and a few beers to replenish and refuel. "The next
thing I knew, I woke up freezing with a ring of fried rice around the tub and a
flotilla of beer bottles. I wouldn't want to say I drank too much," he laughingly
recalls. He never did make it to Billy's victory party.

The infamous Blue Whale, which Billy described as looking like a large
glass of Windex, was actually the brainchild of Eliot bartenders Ed Jones and
the late Fran Coffey. Ed explained its history in an article written by Paul
Kenney for the Patriot Ledger: "The Eliot's charm was the sense of comfort it
gave to each of its patrons, particularly the women, which led to the creation
of the Blue Whale.

"The Eliot was one of the last places a girl could come in and stand alone
without being bothered....We kept an eye on things. At that time, the drink
of the day was 'Skip and Go Naked.' We'd have these dizzy broads come in
and ask us to cook something up. Well, I was in the depths of the cellar one
day and pulled up a bottle of blue Curacao and along with a mixture of vodka,

gin, rum, and a couple of cherries, the Blue Whale was born. I think the whale came from the big girl who ordered the first one," said Jones, laughing.

1975 was the year Doug Brown was offered a weekend bartending job at the Eliot. At the time, he was Beverage Manager at the Harvard Club, putting in 80-hour work weeks. He discovered he could earn more money in two days at the Eliot than he did in 80 hours at the Club. Doug says, "I was always trying to figure out what I didn't want to be when I grew up. Once I found the Eliot, all bets were off."

Doug first met Tommy when he stopped into the Eliot after work. In a short span of time, Tommy discovered that Doug was from a small town near White Plains, New York. As was the case with virtually anyone who came into the Eliot, Tommy knew either a fact or a person related to their locale. "Oh, White Plains, that's Craig Masback territory. He's the greatest miler in America!" The next time Doug went into the Eliot, Tommy greeted him with "Hey, White Plains! How ya doing?" Doug would thoroughly enjoy caddying for Tommy and watching his people skills for the next nineteen years.

Six months after Boston Billy's "Blue Whale" remark, "Spaceman" Bill Lee, pitcher for the Boston Red Sox, was preparing to pitch game 7 of the 1975 World Series against the Cincinnati Reds. Sparky Anderson, manager of the Reds, had nominated Lee's game 7 adversary, Don Gullett, for inauguration to the Baseball Hall of Fame in Cooperstown, New York. During a press conference on national TV, Spaceman said, "Gullett may be going to the Hall of Fame, but I'm going to the Eliot Lounge." The watershed comments of Rodgers and Lee catapulted the Eliot into the world of famous sporting saloons.

Bill Lee was already a frequent customer of the Eliot, as were several of his Sox teammates. A portrait of the Buffalo Head Gang—Bill Lee, Jim Willoughby, Fergie Jenkins, Rick Wise, and Bernie Carbo (all members of the Red Sox pitching staff)—hung in a place of honor near the bar. They considered the Eliot their unofficial headquarters as well.

Bill Lee recalled, "During a rain delay, Tommy always had a beer waiting for me, as he knew I had a way of getting out of the bullpen, going underneath, and taking the back alley across the bridge. He could hear me clipping and clopping along in my spikes. I'd usually take my Red Sox jersey off so I wouldn't be conspicuous and we'd watch the TV. He'd let me know when they started pulling up the tarp, and I'd run back to the game.

"I loved that bar…seeing Prefontaine's picture there. You could kind of hide out there. It was more working class, not the jet-set crowd of Daisy's or Lucifer's. I think I went there mostly because of Tommy."

Doug Brown recalled his first experience with a "Bill Lee rain delay appearance" during his second week on the job. While he was cutting fruit for the bar, Bill Lee walked in dressed in full uniform, cleats, and cap. It wasn't long before Bill Lee was deep in conversation with Coach Squires, who was interested in anything related to sports, about the technicalities of throwing a curve ball. Looking up at the TV to see the game restarting, Lee exclaimed, "Oh crap, I need to go before Zimmer knows I'm gone!" It was Doug's first exposure to the unusual and memorable events that would occur over the next nineteen years.

JJ Larner, the part-time bartender and active Dana-Farber Marathon challenger, once described Tommy as the "quintessential Irish bartender, the delightfully daffy, the wonderfully wacky, the one and only, the master of disaster, often imitated—never duplicated Tommy Leonard!" With such a barkeep to entertain them, it is no wonder the GBTC and the Red Sox Buffalo Head Gang adopted the Eliot as their headquarters. Off-duty Patriots, Celtics, and Bruins also found their way to the Eliot, as did members of teams from the many colleges and universities of Boston. Sportswriters from the Globe, the Herald and the Boston Phoenix regularly edited their articles from their barstools. Runners of every talent, from world-record holders to the back-of-the-pack plodders, all were finding their way to the Eliot. Politicians, truck drivers, police, delivery men, business women—everyone felt comfortable at the Eliot Lounge and knew their paths had crossed with someone unique when they met the fellow behind the stick who wore the map of Ireland on his smiling face.

Although Tommy was having an extremely positive influence as the "daylight bartender," there were some unsavory and disreputable characters coming around at night. Mark Aiken was developing a serious problem with drugs and alcohol. Don tried to intervene on his brother's behalf but lost his family's support in the process. He chose to go to the West Coast and divorced his first wife due to all the stress. Don returned to Boston to reconcile with his mother and grandmother on Mother's Day, May 9, 1976. Unfortunately, Mark succumbed to his problems and passed away one week later at age twenty-nine. Mark had always been very supportive of Tommy's efforts and events, donating oranges and money to the Falmouth Road Race and other causes. Tommy would later arrange for a memorial plaque, signed by the members of the

GBTC and other Eliot patrons, to be given to Mark and Don's mother at the Falmouth Road Race.

Don picked up the pieces and took over operation of the Eliot Lounge and the Medieval Manor. He remained fully supportive of every one of Tommy's new ideas.

Twice a year, Don threw the "Spring Fling" and the "Fall Call," which were customer appreciation days featuring shrimp, steamship roasts, and other delectable delights. It gave him the opportunity to bring his customers together and say thank you. Doug and Tommy both remember Don as a very generous soul. Don often wonders how many Boston cab drivers ended up with the $100 bills he used to stick in Tommy's back pocket at the end of the night.

Coach Squires recalls an evening when a friend of the Eliot's bartenders wanted to do a gig as a DJ. Lots of young kids were in that night, but it had the atmosphere of a junior high dance, with girls on one side and guys on the other. No one was dancing, and the DJ was ready to pack it in about 10 PM. Squires grabbed a couple of girls and started dancing. He spun one off to a fellow and picked up another, spinning her off to another guy. Soon the entire dance floor was hopping to the music of the '50s and '60s that the DJ was spinning. The place came alive, and the bartenders told Squires he could drink there forever.

By 1977, the Boston Marathon had 3,016 official entrants and Tommy had hung twenty-three foreign flags representing the nations that had sent runners to the marathon. Don agreed to Tommy's idea of offering a spaghetti dinner for $1 per person the day before the marathon to boost the runners' carbohydrate load for the race. The bar was stocked with over 300 cases of beer. Tommy convinced Budweiser to donate the plates, mats, and pasta that first year. People came in droves to feast at the Eliot. Tommy's dream was to create a place for people to rendezvous and enjoy being together, not only for the race but après-race as well. Before Tommy Leonard's days at the Eliot, the only distance runners who had ever dropped by were the Harvard varsity, who came to hear teammate Spider McLoone on the piano. By the end of 1977, Tommy had so endeared himself with his selfless qualities to the patrons of the lounge and the running community, they bought 400 tickets at $5 a piece to send Tommy to Fukuoka, Japan, to see the marathon on December 4, 1977, without his knowing about it.

After his shift one Wednesday evening, he was taken to the Exchange Restaurant, where he was promptly engulfed in a kimono and led to his waiting friends, who announced the news of his trip. After recovering from the shock, Tommy tried unsuccessfully to put the money raised toward a schoolboy track.

Bill Rodgers was one of the favorites for that year's Fukuoka Marathon and said, "The thing about Tommy Leonard is his spirit. He's got so much enthusiasm, which he doesn't restrain at all. He's also so very unselfish."

Tommy would travel with Billy, Joe Concannon of the Globe, and Tom Fleming, who in 1977 was ranked fourth in the world in the marathon. When he went to apply for his passport, Tommy said, "The realization of it all started to set in. I don't know how to thank anybody. I wish I could hire that Concorde and take everyone with me. The shock has worn off. I'm starting to dream about the saki, the Geisha girls…"

Billy Rodgers described the Fukuoka Marathon as the "Holy Grail, the Super Bowl of Marathoning" in his book Marathoning, which he wrote with Joe Concannon. He wrote that any runner conscious of his position on the world lists wanted to run Fukuoka. He considers it one of the top marathons in the world—Boston, London, New York, Fukuoka, Chicago, and perhaps Tokyo.

Fukuoka is on the island of Kyushu, the southernmost in the Japanese archipelago. The Japanese people take a tremendous interest in the marathon and are extremely knowledgeable. Billy and Tom found it great to run in Japan, as they were treated the way American baseball players are treated in the States. They often felt like royalty while in Japan.

The race is highly organized and well managed. The crowds are enthusiastic but more disciplined than American crowds. The race is televised live in Japan by a major network. The press truck stays behind the lead runners during the race.

Yoichi Furukawa, editor and sports writer for the Hochi newspaper of Tokyo, hosted the American entourage. Tommy desperately wanted to personally cheer Billy along in the race, so he registered with the Japan Athletic Federation as a journalist who would cover the race on the press bus. There were thirty or forty members of the press, both Japanese and international, on the bus carefully watching the race. The atmosphere on the bus was generally quiet, as everyone was concentrating on taking notes and not missing any strategies during the race. Tommy sat quietly for the first half of the race, but by 30 km he had flung the window open and started shouting, "Come on, Billy! This is your race, Billy! You can do it, Billy!" He continued shouting until Billy crossed the finish line as the winner. The members of the press corps were stunned, never having seen a "foreign journalist" open the window and shout hysterically as loud as possible for their favorite son. However, Tommy's enthusiasm and happiness were infectious, and he was widely accepted by all he met in Japan. Billy himself describes Tommy as "very, very un-Japanese. He's a force of nature, a hurricane!"

At the finishing ceremony, Billy began to feel a bit chill while sitting on the winner's platform, so Tommy offered him his jacket. Billy felt like a warm but incongruous king on a throne, answering questions and being photographed while wrapped in a Falmouth Track Club jacket.

That evening there was a lavish all-you-can-eat-and-drink banquet at the Nishitetsu Grand Hotel attended by the race officials, the American consul, Princess Nichitibi, the media, and all the runners and coaches. Never missing an opportunity to spread goodwill and happiness, Tommy climbed on the stage and started singing You Are My Sunshine, and all the Americans joined in. The runners from Australia then sang Waltzing Matilda, which led to the runners from all the different countries singing songs of their homelands. The next year the tradition was picked up, and Tommy Leonard's legacy now stretches as far away as Japan.

Yoichi has fond memories of walking the streets of Tokyo with Tommy, Billy Rodgers, and Joe Concannon after midnight, singing joyfully as loud as they could after a night of fine dining and plum wine. Tommy's smile and happiness of thirty years ago lingers in Yoichi's mind as the start of a lifetime friendship. Billy seems to recall that Tommy got lost in Tokyo, probably after walking off talking to people, and he thinks Joe somehow managed to find him.

Renee Loth once described Tommy, in an article she wrote for the New England Monthly, "Why I Drink Where I Drink," as "a great interview, exuding childlike glee verging on hysteria." Tommy's innocence, generosity, and enthusiasm draws people like magnets. Even the Japanese could not escape his charm.

On the way back to the States, the group stopped in Honolulu, where Tommy planned to run in the Honolulu Marathon. He entered the race, picked up his number, and got his room at the Sheraton Moana in Waikiki.

Being the "master of disaster" that he is, he overslept and missed the 4:30 AM bus to the starting line. At 5:45 AM, Billy woke to a loud knocking on his door. "Billy, wake up! Billy, wake up!" The race was set to start at 6:00 AM, four miles away, and Tommy was in search of a pin for his number. He began to run toward the starting line, and soon some 4,000 runners started coming at him. He said, "I wasn't going to run 30 miles. That's more than I did in training. I had sake'ed myself to death in Japan. But it was worth it."

The group watched the marathon and enjoyed some terrific rest and relaxation on the beach. Tommy had a friend in Honolulu who tried to teach them to surf, not with much success but with a great deal of enjoyment.

As the Boston Marathon or the Falmouth Road Race approached each year, Doug Brown recalled that the phone would really start ringing about a month before the event. If Tommy knew the caller or knew a friend of the caller, he would try to help in any way he could, often with travel plans or accommodations. Then the interviews would begin—calls would come in from Fresno, Sacramento, Phoenix, Houston, and Japan asking Tommy about the outlook for the races. He had such a reputation for his knowledge that the Boston Herald included him in their annual predictions column for the marathon along with the likes of Coach Squires, Amby Burfoot, Jack Hines of WCVB-TV, Randy Thomas, and Steve Harris of the Herald.

Tommy would be so distracted by his many phone calls that his regular customers would affectionately walk downstairs to the pay phone, ring the bar, and ask, "Hey, can you deliver a G&T to the third stool on the left?" (as described in the BAA 101st Boston Marathon Program article "Requiem for the Eliot").

Don Aiken would good-naturedly look at the phone bill and say, "Oh, this wasn't such a bad month. Only $350 for the phone."

Doug has often been quoted as saying, "I'll go on record saying that Tommy Leonard is a lousy bartender. But there's no one better at getting people together and finding common ground. If there was an Australian guy at one end of the bar and a Lithuanian on the other, Tommy would have them talking together in five minutes. I like to think of him as the Tom Sawyer of bartending. He always has his ideas, and his forte is gathering his troops for different causes."

None of the bartenders looked forward to having the shift after Tommy's. Doug called it the "fear of the unknown" as he tied on his apron. Once he stepped behind the bar, he'd look around and close his eyes, shaking his head. Tommy would now usually be on his stool on the other side of the bar, and he'd take a look around at all the tables full of glasses and ashtrays and exclaim, "Oh, Marine Corps Field Day!" He'd promptly get up, Bud in hand, and do his part to clean up and get the place in shape for the evening.

Tommy's money skills were aptly described by Charlie Pierce in his GQ article "The Last Sports Bar": "When Leonard was on duty, it was equally possible to receive 2 fives for a ten, one five for a ten, 3 fives for a ten or your own ten back."

By the late 1970's the staff at the Eliot were dressed in tuxedos and yellow Nike waffles on Patriot's Day, the day of the running of the Boston Marathon. The staff considered that day a "full-tilt boogie," as they never stopped and they never saw a runner go by.

NBC was filming live from the Eliot the night before the race; major athletic shoe companies such as Nike, Puma, New Balance, and Reebok began to host private parties on race day; and the lines to get into the bar on the night of the marathon stretched down the block in Studio 54 fashion. Former winners of the marathon and Olympic champions all cooled their heels waiting for entrance to this holy shrine of running, with its limited capacity. The doormen's most frequent complaint was that every person who approached the door would say, "I'm a friend of Tommy Leonard's" and "the problem was that everyone was." Robin Young of Evening Magazine began to film several episodes from the Eliot. Sunday Night NBC News did a special on carbohydrate loading at the Eliot.

Don Aiken would claim to George Kimball of the Herald, "You could not put a stripper on the sidewalk outside and bring in more people than Tommy does. The man is simply amazing." The week before the marathon or the Falmouth Road Race, Tommy would get caught up in what he termed "a tidal wave of exuberance," so Don gave him those weeks off with pay. He acknowledged, "He'd just go nuts anyway."

After Bill Rodgers' 1978 win in 2:10:13, Tommy would reflect on the 1,200 customers who passed through the Eliot on race day. He told John Powers of the Globe, "It killed me to have to keep people waiting outside, to tell them we didn't have enough space. I tried to tell them at the race that there were other places to go in the city…but they all wanted to come to the Eliot." When Bill Rodgers arrived at the Eliot that night, he found four of the top ten finishers waiting for him: New Zealand's Kevin Ryan, Jack Fultz, Randy Thomas, and Don Kardong.

By 1979, in the week before the Boston Marathon, Tommy would say, "I am going through three states of anxiety this week. Who to let into the Falmouth Road Race, who to let into the Eliot Lounge Monday night, and who to let into the spaghetti feed on Sunday." Admission to the Eliot on Monday was now by invite only. "I never wanted that to happen. But it's gotten too big." There were 8,000 runners who qualified to run Boston in 1979; every state in the nation was represented, as well as twenty-eight other nations, and over 500 women participated.

Tommy was now regularly referred to as the "Guru of New England road running," and he was trying to shy away from all the international publicity. As he told John Powers of the Globe, "I've had more ink in the past three years than the Middle East. I think I'd like to kind of fade off into the sunset."

Fading into the sunset, however, was not an option for Tommy Leonard. His mind is like popcorn, with multiple schemes, dreams, and ideas always popping around in his head. He lives by a mantra that he picked up from the late John F Kennedy—"We can always do better"—and never ceases to look for ways to make life better for others.

Most of Tommy's ideas begin as spontaneous acts of charity, such as the night the Stanford Band made an appearance as the "house group" at the Eliot. One Thursday afternoon in the fall of 1980, a group of writers from the Boston Phoenix, which was located directly across the street, were in discussing the upcoming Boston College–Stanford U football game that Saturday. One of the writers told Tommy about the Stanford Band, famous for its zany antics and funky dress. The band was being housed in the BC hockey rink for the weekend. Tommy has always felt that the athletes are given all the recognition, and the "supporting cast" is largely overlooked. He got on the phone to BC, and by 6 PM Thursday the Stanford Band was scheduled to appear at the Eliot on Friday.

Doug recalls the staff being a bit dubious, saying, "Tommy, you can barely fit them inside a football field. They're a marching band!" But Tommy was undeterred and excitedly told everyone on Friday, "They are coming tonight! They are coming tonight!" Doug recalls hearing a huge noise and thinking there must have been an accident on Mass Ave. The sound grew closer, and they began to recognize the tune of the Grateful Dead's Truckin as first the cheerleaders and then about twenty members of the band marched in. The cheerleaders climbed up on the bar and flipped off while the tuba players were hoisted onto the shelves from which the TVs had been moved to make room for them. The place went wild while the building shook, rattled, and rolled. "They blew the walls off the place," Tommy fondly remembers.

Tommy had arranged for free beer and pizza for the band members and talked a shoe company into donating new shoes for the cheerleaders. When the manager of the Eliot Hotel came raging into the lounge threatening to pull the lease, the band marched into the night, playing White Punks on

Dope. As Charlie Pierce noted in his GQ article, "It was not a night strictly about sports but it was about everything that is interesting about them."

After Pierce's GQ article was published in 1996, it would become the ace-in-the-hole for Tommy's cousin, Jimmy Tierney, when he was out socializing in pubs with Tommy. Jimmy would say to people, "You see that guy over there, Mr. Magoo?" pointing to Tommy. "There's a three-page spread about him in GQ." Tommy would be sitting stoop-shouldered in his baseball cap of choice, head tilted with his good ear toward whomever he was talking with, eyes intent on his or her face, and a slight beer belly resting on his belt. They would take a look over at Tommy, knowing that GQ generally profiles buff, brawny, and chiseled young men, and say, "Nah, there can't be." Jimmy would wager a couple of Sam Adams that he was right, and once the bet was on, he'd retreat to his car, where he kept a copy of the issue handy for just such occasions.

The Stanford Band experience fired up Tommy and he got to thinking about other bands he could invite to the Eliot. He invited the Clemson University Tigers Band one night. Eddie Doyle, whom Tommy had rediscovered bartending at the Bull & Finch on Beacon Street in 1974, created stencils which they used to paint tiger paws up and down the Mass Ave sidewalk, with permission from the city to use washable ink. Tommy went to Logan Airport with a state trooper friend, who drove him out on the tarmac in a police cruiser to greet the band, the cheerleaders, and the football team. That evening the bus drove up onto the sidewalk outside the Eliot, and half the band marched in playing Hold That Tiger while the other half played out on the sidewalk. It was another memorable evening of oom-pah songs and flipping cheerleaders. Tommy was presented with their orange flag with the tiger paw, which found a place of honor on the bar's ceiling.

Tommy then invited the Syracuse Citrus Society Band to the Eliot, and they returned three or four times because they found the experience so enjoyable. "The whole idea behind the bands coming to the Eliot," Tommy said, "was to offer some Beantown/Eliot Lounge hospitality." Tommy's brother-in-law, Reid Oslin, was the Sports Information Director at Boston College and was able to get Tommy in touch with the right musical directors so Tommy could extend the invitations. As the band buses got ready to leave at the end of an evening, Tommy would pass out donated sandwiches and drinks he'd acquired for the ride home.

Also in the late 1970s, Tommy began a tradition at the Eliot that would not leave a dry eye in the place. For many, it became the unofficial yet traditional opening ceremony of the world's oldest marathon, the "Grande Dame," the Boston Marathon. It was the flag-raising ceremony that occurred on the Thursday night before the race.

Around 10 PM that night, the house lights would dim, spotlights shone over the bar, and Tommy would snip fishing line that would unfurl flags, one by one, of the nations being represented in the race on Monday. As each flag unfurled, a representative song would play. These were not national anthems but songs to celebrate both the nation and the fellowship of running. Since Greece was the sight of the first Olympics, it would always be first. Tommy would play a medley of Chieftain hits for the "Olde Sod" and even give Boston, the host city, a place of honor with the playing of Charlie on the MTA. In 1984 the New Zealand flag fell to the floor. This was the same year New Zealander Allison Roe, the race favorite, had to drop out. In 1991 Tommy began the ceremony with Young at Heart to honor Johnny "the Elder" Kelley, age eighty-three, who ran his sixtieth Boston Marathon that year.

Those present often included Coach Bill Squires of the Greater Boston Track Club, finish-line announcer Toni Reavis, former marathon winners and runners of all kinds, sportswriters of the various Boston papers, and regular patrons and former staff of the Eliot. The evening had its pauses, with beer breaks and peeks at ESPN here and there.

As midnight approached, Tommy would ever so slowly unfurl the Stars and Stripes while playing Ray Charles's version of America the Beautiful. Just as everyone's heart was ready to explode with emotion, Louis Armstrong's deep, guttural voice would begin:

> I see trees of green, red roses too
> I see them bloom for me and for you
> And I think to myself, what a wonderful world…

(What a Wonderful World, George Weiss/Bob Thiele)

The celebration of the fellowship of running and the beauty of being a part of the great Boston Marathon was achieved in high and memorable style. For those present, it was a wonderful world indeed.

In April 1978, Boston Herald writer Tim Horgan wrote, "The BAA Marathon just might be the most singular and prestigious event in international sports in any non-Olympic year." Hal Higdon, author of A Century of Running Boston has written, "It is the biggest love-in in the country. Every runner wants to come here at least once before he dies. It's the one place where people line the streets to see you. You feel loved, wanted in Boston."

Tommy's dream of combining the competition of the marathon with après-race socializing and celebrating had indeed become a reality. He was creating a museum of marathon memorabilia as well as other sports recognitions and souvenirs that would continue to grow over the next several years. There was Jock Semple's famous 1967 sequence of photos where he tried to push Katherine Switzer off the course as an unwelcome female before women were allowed to enter; the Rodgers victories of 1975, 1978, 1979, and 1980; Steve Prefontaine; Allison Roe; Joanie Benoit; Rob de Castella; the Salazar-Beardsley duel; and many, many more. Prominently displayed over or behind the bar were various flags of the world, NBC and ABC banners from major marathons and the Olympics, Ray Bourke's autographed Bruins hockey stick, Wade Boggs's bat, a pair of Rodgers's running shoes, and a "Bill Lee for President" sweatshirt, among other equipment and apparel. There was even a framed Sports Illustrated photo of Tommy in the 1956 Boston Marathon, where he finished 87th out of 211 entrants. A gallery of Celtics action photo shots was featured in the balcony, and there was a calligraphy copy of Globe sportswriter Ray Fitzgerald's "Ode to Baseball." Tommy had Carl Lewis's 28'10¼" long jump taped out on the floor, and he later put Mike Powell's jump of 29'4" next to it. In 1989 he added Javier Sotomayor's world-record high jump to the wall.

Without realizing it, Tommy was also creating that elusive family of adults who would love and respect him that he had so often dreamed about as a child. After years of searching for the right fit, his life was becoming a daily joyous experience.

In 1979 Tommy had a day proclaimed in his honor for the first time. This one was in the city of New London, Connecticut.

Office of the Mayor
CITY OF NEW LONDON
CONNECTICUT

Proclamation

WHEREAS, Tommy Leonard has long been one of the United States foremost supporters of distance running; and

WHEREAS, among the athletes he has especially encouraged are Bill Rogers, Randy Thomas, Joan Benoit and Patti Lyons; and

WHEREAS, Tommy Leonard has shown a warm and open heart to all runners, even those not nearly as talented as the aforementioned; and

WHEREAS, Tommy's workplace, the Eliot Lounge, has always provided a friendly and secure environment for runners of Boston, and for those merely visiting Boston; and

WHEREAS, Tommy has played a principle role in organizing some of the Country's best road races such as the Falmouth Road Race, the Holyoke Road Race and the Freedom Trail Road Race; and

WHEREAS, Tommy Leonard is himself a runner of notable accomplishments, most significantly his more than 25 completions of the world renown Boston Marathon; and

WHEREAS, Tommy has taken his running goodwill from Boston to various and sundry points around the world and everywhere amazed his hosts with his energy, enthusiasm and love of people and running and life, bringing with him everywhere his ready ruddy smile and a bellowing belly of laughter.

NOW, THEREFORE, I, Carl Stoner, Mayor of the City of New London, do find it fitting and proper to proclaim this day, Friday, August 3, 1979, as

TOMMY LEONARD DAY

in the City of New London in connection with our Annual John J. Kelley Twelve-Mile Road Race, and take this opportunity to wish Mr. Leonard and the other many participants every success in tomorrow's Race.

IN WITNESS WHEREOF, I have hereunto set my hand and caused to be affixed the Seal of the City of New London, Connecticut, this third day of August, 1979.

As the marathon approached, Tommy would greet his customers with "Happy 7 (6, 5, 4, 3, 2) days to the marathon!" He kept a large annual countdown calendar behind the bar with the number of days to the next Boston Marathon posted, and he would tear off a page each day. Reebok would eventually give him an electronic countdown sign that blazed in the Eliot for several years.

Those who had any remote connection with running considered the Eliot their corner bar. Other road races began to mushroom, and all had courses that passed the intersection of Massachusetts and Commonwealth avenues: the Bonne Belle (now Tufts 10K), the Milk Run (which became the Fenway Five), the Corporate Challenge, the Police Chase (run by former Eliot doorman and Tommy's favorite Marine, Eddie Burke), and the late Freedom Trail Road Race.

Eddie Burke worked the door at the Eliot for most of the major parties and helped Tommy with the many events he created. While serving in Viet Nam, Eddie had gotten exposed to Agent Orange, and his three children have all had cancer. He lost his youngest at age three. He was particularly involved with fundraisers for the Jimmy Fund.

Eddie recalls that for the Bonne Belle 10K, the Boston Police allowed them to block off Mass Ave in front of the Eliot for the "Eliot Lounge Celebrity Water Stop." Members of the Red Sox and Celtics whose wives were running worked the water stop. Tommy, in his usual exuberance, was high-fiving the runners and having the time of his life. Although the race organizers had a post-race function in Boston Common, where the race finished, runners like Joan Benoit Samuelson and Patti Catalano quickly made their way to the Eliot as soon as they could for what they considered the "real" party.

Eddie recalled that one year, a few days after the Bonne Belle, Joe Concannon of the Globe was giving a talk at the Hynes Convention Center. He told the approximate 1,000 people present, "You know, the other day 8,000 women ran in the Bonne Belle. You know how excited Tommy Leonard can get. Of the 8,000 runners, I think 7,997 had Tommy's fingerprints on their derrieres."

In 1980 Jacqueline Gareau, a petite, dark-haired runner from Quebec, Canada, thought she was going to win the women's race in the Boston Marathon with her time of 2:34:28, until she heard her name announced as the second-place woman as she neared the finish line. Rosie Ruiz had jumped into the race with less than a mile to go and stole the crowning moment from Jackie Gareau. Although there was suspicion among race officials about the possible deception, they placed the laurel wreath on Rosie's head at the finish line ceremony.

Within a week, the Boston Athletic Association acknowledged that Rosie was a fraud. Race director Will Cloney asked her to return her medal, but she refused and disappeared into obscurity.

The BAA invited Jacqueline Gareau back to Boston for a brief ceremony in which she was presented with her well-deserved medal and laurel wreath. Tommy had helped to coax Jackie back to Boston for her honors. He quickly became engaged in another spontaneous act of charity. Roses were purchased, a bottle of Dom Perignon was put on ice, the troops were gathered (including the regulars who were writers from the Globe, Herald, and Phoenix and those who attended the BAA ceremony). Tommy took down all the flags except for Canada's. A couple of writers from Montreal sat down at the piano, and those present did their best to come up with the words to O Canada, which they sang respectfully, if not accurately, as Jacqueline came through the door. She smiled, she wept, and she politely listened as the group courageously decided to sing the national anthem a second time. She was honored. She knew she was among people who had a true appreciation for her achievement of breaking Joan Benoit Samuelson's course record of 2:35:15 the year before and the tragedy of having her moment of glory stolen from her. It was another moment of sports history that played itself out within the walls of the Eliot and contributed to its now legendary reputation for demonstrating respect for athletes, especially runners, and doing the right thing for humanity.

Throughout his first decade of working at the Eliot, Tommy continued to run in marathons. He has completed about twenty-five in his lifetime, with the last one in 1981. He says he never really kept a record of his marathons. "My idea of running is to take it easy and smell the roses along the way. I run with the speed of a tugboat," he says. "The best I ever ran was in Phoenix—I did 3:14." Others describe Tommy as looking like "he has a suitcase in each hand" as he runs along.

Tommy's journey on Patriot's Day along the Boston Marathon course would often include pit stops at the Happy Swallow in Framingham, Mary's Cafe (now closed) in Newton, and the Tam-O-Shanter on Beacon Street in Brookline. One year the staff of the "Tam" had a bottle of champagne waiting for Tommy.

"In Houston, I was on a sub-3:00 pace for 23 miles. When I reached the bar I was working at, I had nothing left in the tank. I just walked off the course and said to myself, 'That's it for running marathons'…and it was my last marathon."

Each Thanksgiving and Christmas, Tommy has always returned to Westfield for the family holiday dinners with the Tierneys. Don Aiken recalls one holiday when he and his wife gave Tommy a ride home on their way to visit Don's mother in Hamden, Connecticut. The Jaguar moving a bit too fast, a state trooper stopped them near Sturbridge on the Massachusetts Turnpike. "License and registration, please. Do you have a reason for traveling so fast today?" the officer asked. "Just trying to get a jump on the holiday traffic, Officer," said Don. Looking in the back seat, the officer exclaimed, "Tommy, what the hell are you doing back there?" He then asked Don, "And why didn't you tell me Tommy Leonard was riding in the back of your car?" Needless to say, the holidays were celebrated without being hampered by a speeding ticket.

On one of those visits home to Westfield Tommy was staying with his adopted brother, Michael Tierney, and his wife, Robin. After helping with yard chores in the morning, Tommy went down to a local pub around lunchtime. After several hours, Michael and Robin went down to collect Tommy and they realized he'd been drinking his lunch all afternoon, so they encouraged him to go next door for some Chinese food.

When Tommy's chicken fried rice arrived, the drink got the better of him and his face landed in the center of his place. Hearing an ambulance siren next door, Michael and Robin ran out of the pub in time to see Tommy being carried out on a stretcher while the owner of the restaurant ran alongside crying, "He have heart attack! He have heart attack! We have clean restaurant! He have heart attack!" At this point, Tommy was starting to rouse and became aware of the blue lights of the ambulance. He shot up like Tim Finnegan at his wake, exclaiming through his soy-soaked mustache, "I've got the strongest heart of any man in Westfield! Do you think I'm dead?" He scrambled off the stretcher as the startled ambulance drivers looked on in disbelief and amazement.

On another visit home for the St. Patrick's Day Parade, Tommy was staying with his cousin, Jimmy Tierney, in Holyoke. The snow was deep and the night was cold. Tommy walked home from the pub to discover that the house was locked and he didn't have a key. While he was trying all the doors and windows he could reach in an effort to get in the house, a neighbor noticed him and called the police. Having had a few pops, he flopped into a snow bank and settled in for a bit of a snooze. When the police arrived, they found

Tommy sleeping in the snow. The family affectionately refers to that night as Tommy's "angel in the snow" night.

In 1982 the landlord made it clear to Don Aiken that he didn't want the Medieval Manor to operate in the basement any longer. Don moved his business to 246 East Berkley Street in Boston's South End, where it continues successfully today.

Hank Hankinson was another well-loved daylight bartender at the Eliot Lounge. In addition to bartending at the Eliot and the Newbury Steakhouse, Hank taught jazz at the Berklee College of Music. Tommy would sometimes break out the banjo and play with Hank's band at the Eliot.

Don tried to pass on the ownership of the Eliot to Hank, Doug Brown, and Tommy but was not able to work out his offer with the owners of the building. After a protracted period, the business was sold to John Hanrahan, John Ryan, Jack Hines, and Mike King—all young, energetic, and sports-minded. Although Ryan and Hanrahan became involved primarily as an investment, Mike King's family had owned bars in Charlestown and he had some knowledge of the business. He was also married to Karen Smyers, a former swimmer at Princeton who went on to win the famed Ironman Triathlon in Hawaii (2.5mile ocean swim, 212-mile bike ride, followed by a 26.2-mile marathon run). A triathlete himself, Mike had an acute appreciation of the commitment, sacrifice, and effort required of athletes, so he was a natural for the Eliot Lounge.

Hank chose to go with Don to the Medieval Manor and Tommy remained at the Eliot. The new owners had enough business savvy to understand that Tommy was one of the Eliot's greatest assets. In an article in Runner's World written by Amby Burfoot, new owner John Ryan said, "For us, Tommy represents tradition, goodwill, and just about everything a place should have."

Although many people thought that Tommy owned the Eliot, he was simply what Amby coined "the Good Shepherd of running....He tends his flock daily, making the lonesome feel wanted, fetching back the lost." And Tommy would say, "There are no strangers here in the Eliot, just friends who haven't met yet."

In 1982 the Boston Marathon saw one of the most memorable duels in marathon history: the race between Alberto Salazar, NCAA cross-country champion from the University of Oregon and 1980 winner of the New York City Marathon, and Dick Beardsley, a dairy farmer from Minnesota. Both runners had been coached by Bill Squires—Salazar while a runner in high school and as the "rookie" with the GBTC, and Beardsley as a newly sponsored runner for New Balance.

In the early 1980s Coach Squires was a consultant for New Balance and offered to help Beardsley with his training. Squires would deliver his weekly workouts from the phone booth downstairs at the Eliot or mail them to Beardsley on the backs of napkins.

The race was a "me and my shadow" duel to the end, with Alberto breaking the tape in 2:08:52 and Beardsley following a couple seconds later at 2:08:54, after being clipped twice by a motorcycle cop.

Several years later, Tommy's co-worker at the Eliot, JJ Larner, recalled being at a function honoring Joan Benoit Samuelson for her gold medal in the first Olympic Marathon for women in 1984. At the function, someone asked Tommy, "What's your greatest marathon moment?" Tommy began extolling Salazar vs. Beardsley as only he can: "It was like Ali-Frazier in Nike's, mano a mano, back and forth they went," with Tommy absolutely apoplectic in the retelling. "Remember that race, Joanie?" he said, turning to the Olympic gold medalist. "Yeah," she said. "I think that was around the time I set the American, course and world record" (2:22:43). Leonard, Nike-in-mouth, said, "Oh yeah. That was pretty good, too."

In 1982 Mayor Kevin White of the city of Boston dedicated the bridge that crosses an underpass on Commonwealth Avenue next to the Eliot Hotel as the Tommy Leonard Bridge. During a light mist, the dedication ceremony was held and a wooden marker installed. Tommy's high school friends Champ Morris and Jiggs Morrissey of Westfield and the sons of Carol Bannon Flynn (old Mrs. Murray's niece) planted tulips along the bridge. Tommy's humble reaction was "Christ, I thought you had to be dead to have a bridge named after you." Mayor White proclaimed July 20, 1982, as Tommy Leonard Day, with the following proclamation:

♦WHEREAS: Tommy Leonard has graced our city with his residence and dedicated himself to establishing Boston as the running capital of the United States; and

♦WHEREAS: Tommy Leonard has personally inspired, helped subsidize, and arranged for the participation of hundreds of runners from all over America in the Boston Marathon; and

♦WHEREAS: Tommy Leonard has achieved international recognition in running circles for establishing one of the most popular, professionally organized, and beautiful road races in the world, the Falmouth and, as a member of the Greater Boston Track Club, being a founder of another great race, our own Freedom Trail Classic; and

♦WHEREAS: Tommy Leonard, manager of the Eliot Lounge, has made that establishment the world headquarters of marathoning every Patriot's Day while at the same time extending hospitality and friendship to all who patronize the Eliot during the year; and

♦WHEREAS: The family, friends, track aficionados, and legions of runners from all over our country wish to pay him honor and express their gratitude to him for his kindness, friendship, encouragement and skilled advice;

NOW, THEREFORE

I, Kevin H. White, Mayor of the City of Boston, do hereby proclaim Tuesday the twentieth day of July in the year of Our Lord, one thousand nine hundred and eighty-two as:

TOMMY LEONARD DAY

And urge all of our citizens to participate in this wonderful event.

Kevin H. White

That evening there was a kickoff testimonial gathering for the Tommy Leonard Scholarship fund at the Exchange Restaurant. Tommy's friends created the fund to defray college costs for deserving runners from Falmouth and Westfield high schools. Billy Rodgers served as the guest speaker, much to Tommy's delight.

After the bridge was dedicated, Tommy's friend Jack Kearney, former vice president of WBCN radio and regular Eliot patron, wrote the following ballad, reprinted here with permission of the author:

The Ballad of the Eliot Lounge

"The Eliot" is
"A haven of cheer"
Where good conversation
Follows a beer.

It really is
"The Noah's Ark of Folk"
Who laugh, talk, and joke
Of things to come,

Of things in the past,
And drink liquid wisdom
Right out of a glass.

"Hey, Silver Star John,
How about Omaha Beach?
Tell us how
You were 'pinned down
In the breach.'"

They absorb the nectar
From the fountain of youth.
But don't weed out nostalgia
To get at the truth.

"Why…that Olympic champion
From Freeport, Maine,
Could even win a marathon
Down 'Memory Lane'!"

They say a bar is a place to drink
But the Eliot Lounge
Can make you think.
"Didn't Billy run a great 'twenty-six'?"
"Hey Tom, play Sinatra.
And then maybe some Bix."

Stories of runners
And the real "Sugar Ray."
But nothing saccharin,
Like "Have a nice day."

"There was never anyone
Like old 'Number Nine.'"

"And couldn't Dalton Jones hit 'em
Right on a line?"

So...when you're in Boston
Make "The Eliot" your port of call
It's right next to the Tommy Leonard Bridge.
And that
Says it all.

Tommy's close friends who were regular patrons of the Eliot, such as Bernie Corbett (the voice of Harvard football and the voice of the Terriers of BU hockey), Coach Squires, Dr. Charles Tifft, Charlie Pierce, Jack Kearney, and others, teased Tommy about the bridge, saying, "Excuse me, I need to meet someone at the Tommy Leonard Bridge. Could you give me directions, please?" Tommy would humbly laugh, saying, "Yeah, I know, I probably only have a couple of years left. It's all downhill from here."

Joe Concannon, most noted for his annual coverage in the Boston Globe of the Boston Marathon, the Falmouth Road Race, major golf tournaments, the Head of the Charles Regatta, and the Beanpot hockey tournament, began the year 1983 with an award of his own to Tommy in the January 1 issue of the Globe. It was the "Don't Let Facts Get in the Way of a Good Quote" Award:

"To Tommy Leonard, the running guru who founded the Falmouth Road Race, who was asked, after saying he wanted to retire and 'run into a tangerine sunset,' when he last saw a tangerine sunset. "I remember it well," he replied, sipping on a Michelob in Falmouth last August. "I was sitting on the bluffs in Nauset, drinking a carafe of wine with a little chickadee, looking out over the water and thinking the next stop was Spain." It didn't matter to Leonard that Spain was to the east and the sun sets in the west."

In July 1983, the Boston Globe published a list of the fifty most overrated people, places, or events in Boston, compiled by Nathan Cobb. The Eliot was given a prominent spot at number 6 on the list.

Tommy viewed this as another opportunity to bring people together and celebrate our commonality. He sent an invitation to each of the "overrated" recipients that read, on the front, "You Were Overrated" and inside, "So Were We."

Will you join us, along with
The remaining forty-eight listed
To celebrate this honor, at the Eliot Lounge
On the first of September at 8:00 PM
Please come and enjoy
We all have something in Common!

(*One dollar charitable donation requested at the door)

Naturally, Tommy wouldn't just throw a dull and ordinary party. He acquired as many symbols or representatives from the list that he could. The 50 most overrated of 1983 were

Plymouth Rock—Tommy put a rock on the bar
Bleachers at Fenway—An old set of bleachers from Fenway were put on the stage
Dinner at Durgin Park
The Harvard Mystique
Patti Page was never there on Labor Day—Tommy played her singing Old Cape Cod in the background
The Eliot
Steve's Ice Cream—Tommy had a cup of Steve's (melting) ice cream on the bar
Brother Blue
North End festivals
"Gossage Winds Up...Here's the Pitch..."
Everyone running for mayor—A representative from Mayor Kevin White's office attended the party
Alan Richman
The Brinks Heist
Kennedy Charisma
The Eire Pub—A bartender from the pub attended
BC football—A game program was on the bar
Walden Pond—A bottle of water from the pond was brought in
Attending a Pops concert—A few members of the Pops attended
Orson Welles Cinema

Celtics Pride—The Eliot had numerous Celtics memorabilia on the walls
Institute of Politics at the Kennedy School of Government
The Premiere Deli—A menu was on the bar
Fenway Franks—A representative dog in bun was on the bar
Any appearance of Tall Ships
Parkman House
The Eye—Writer Noma Nathan made an appearance
The New Boston
Hasty Pudding Woman of the Year Parade
Freedom Trail—A map was on the bar
Guardian Angels—The requisite red beret was displayed
Robert J Lurtsema
No Name Restaurant—A menu was on the bar
Boston baked beans—A can of beans was present
Robin Cook
Guy Lombardo, First Night—A tape of Auld Lang Syne played
Any plan for a new sports arena
L Street Brownies—A member attended
Larry Glick
William Bulger's annual St. Pat's Day Roast
"Put it on! Put it on!"…the Golden Banana
Christmas Eve in Louisburg Square
Locke-Ober
Bob Lobel—He attended the party
Charles Laquidara
Breakfast in the Cafe at the Ritz-Carlton—A menu was on the bar
Veggies at the Haymarket
Jason's
Taking the train to New York
Bob Woolf
Regina Pizzeria

Nathan Cobb, the author of the list, made a good-natured appearance at the party. By the end of the evening, the guests had made up their own song about being "overrated," and a positive twist of pride descended on the honorees. Once again, Tommy had taken a divergent group of people and found the common core to bring them together in fellowship and joy.

The 1980s saw many an interesting and unexpected guest at the Eliot. One evening, Fuzzy Urban Zoeller, winner of the 1979 Masters golf tournament and ten PGA tours, came in for a drink. Sipping his scotch and blithely blowing smoke in the health-conscious faces of the staff and customers, his stories soon had everyone bowled over in laughter. Stepping behind the bar, this unscheduled guest bartender closed the place well into the wee hours of the morning. A large poster that arrived a week later, inscribed "To Tommy and my friends at the Eliot," held a place of honor in memory of a great night in the history of this unusual saloon.

There were a couple of recording studios on Newbury Street around the corner from the Eliot whose technicians were regulars at the bar. One of them mentioned to Tommy that Joe Cocker was recording the next day, and he'd like to bring him over to the Eliot. Although excited, Tommy managed to stay quiet about it. About 6 PM the next day, Cocker walked in, ordered a whiskey, and talked about the crazy "Mad Dogs and Englishmen" tour and life in general for several hours with the locals fortunate enough to be on their stools that night.

Jack Kearney, the radio exec, often came to the Eliot on Tuesdays, when he'd get together with Charlie Pierce and Michael Gee of the Phoenix, Bernie Corbett, Dr. Charles Tifft, and Coach Squires for some fun baseball and movie trivia contests. Jack was also a good friend of world-renowned jazz pianist Dave McKenna. At the time, Dave was playing at the Copley Plaza, and Jack convinced him to come play a few songs at the Eliot. As noted by Pierce in his GQ article, piano tuner Laurie Cote managed to get the piano out of the "key of 1937," word hit the streets that Dave was going to play, and the place filled to capacity with customers. The Eliot turned astoundingly quiet. Tommy never rang the register. Dave took requests and played for over two hours. The guests knew this was going to be one of the most memorable and unique concerts they would ever attend. "It was like listening to Vladimir Horowitz at Symphony Hall," said Ron Della Chiesa of WGBH radio.

Two-time Boston Marathon winner Geoff Smith recalled to Katy Matheson of the Middlesex News the night he came to the Eliot and Tommy began showing him around, introducing him to everyone without ever mentioning his name. After meeting lots of people, Tommy bought him a beer and then continued making introductions, still never mentioning Geoff's name.

Smith quaffed his beer and then pointed out to Tommy that he had not once mentioned his name. Looking at Smith, Tommy cried, "Jesus, Geoff, I thought you were Eamonn Coghlan!" (world-class miler from Ireland). "You mean you bought this beer for Eamonn Coghlan? Now you can buy one for Geoff Smith," Geoff replied.

Eamonn has also quaffed a few in the Eliot, and Tommy fondly recalls, "Like a good Irishman, he closed the place."

One of the most unexpected guest appearances at the Eliot occurred on August 15, 1983, Tommy's fiftieth birthday. This was by far one of the most memorable nights at this saloon, and no one is able to retell this story without succumbing to raucous fits of laughter.

Tommy, who prefers to create events and then slip off to the side to enjoy them being played out, tried to tell the staff not to do anything special for his fiftieth. The staff made it clear that many of his friends would be at the Eliot to help celebrate, and he wouldn't want to miss them.

Some friends from Westfield always teased him that he was a city boy now, and they arrived with a bale of hay, saying, "You should be out riding horses instead of the T." They placed the hay on the bar to make him "feel at home." Someone suggested the hay was going to waste and called a buddy who ran the carriages at Faneuil Hall, asking him to bring a horse to the Eliot. Coach Squires happened to be standing outside as a Boston Police horse arrived, and he brought the horse inside for a drink.

Getting a horse inside the Eliot was no small feat, as one first took a sharp right and then a left to get into the bar area. Doug Brown remembers the horse going straight to a waitress station where there was a big ice chest; he probably thought he was headed to a trough. Now the horse was wedged into a tiny spot that barely fit two people, and they had to reverse it back into the bar.

In his Globe article "It's Last Call at the Eliot Lounge," Michael Madden captured Tommy's retelling of the horse story as follows:

"It was my fiftieth birthday…They brought a horse in…." A chortle, a guffaw, laughter felt from the heart. "They brought the horse right down into the bar; I didn't know what to do with it," said Leonard, the laughter incessant. "So I gave the horse some White Russians and….This is a true story. Holy Cow! The horse came in and the horse had a personality. The horse acknowledged my birthday. He was a horse who drank White Russians. I never saw that before. He really tipped 'em up, the White Russians, but someone called the Health Department and said, 'There's a horse in the Eliot Lounge,' so we had to push the g.d. horse out of the bar.

"The horse had a personality. He didn't want to leave," said Leonard. "He kept shaking his head from side to side and going 'Neigh-heigghhhh,' and the horse's tail was wagging. But they had to push him out sideways. Geez, it was the most beautiful thing. I love animals. But this is a true story. No one is going to believe it."

Coach Squires noticed a guy with his head down on one end of the bar and worried that if he woke up and saw a horse in his face, it might kill him.

The next spring, Natalie Jacobson and Mike Lynch of Channel 5 TV asked Eddie Burke, who was serving as Chief of Security at the start of the Boston Marathon, to do a live interview from Hopkinton Common. Eddie was trying to relate the horse story on live TV. "We had a Boston Police horse in the Eliot and we were giving him a bucket of draught beer. The horse didn't want to leave. It was having a grand old time and now it wanted to sit down. Tommy was getting in a panic and the mounted officer was really in a panic. So there are six of us guys with our shoulders to the horse, who wasn't going anywhere. He wanted more beer. Finally about ten of us got the horse around the corner, down the corridor, and out the door. So, now the horse is leaning on the building with his front paws crossed...." Natalie was laughing so hard she had to hand her microphone to Mike Lynch.

Tommy's fiftieth was spontaneity at its best. Whenever Tommy talks about that night, he mentions how impressed he was that the horse stopped at each patron along the bar and acknowledged him or her. It was a zany and crowning moment to celebrate Tommy's life. Tommy would say of his life, "It was a constantly unfolding comic strip. It was never work. Every day I'd say, 'What interesting person am I going to meet today?'"

After the closing of the Eliot in 1996, Doug Brown would say, "I can't think of any other bar in Boston where on a night-to-night basis you could have so much entertainment that you didn't have to pay for as at the Eliot. We were always saying, 'That was too much fun!'"

On a cold gray day in March 1984, Tommy's dream of creating a "Walkway of the Running Stars" in Hollywood Boulevard style came to be on the sidewalk in front of the Eliot. Autographs and footprints were imprinted in freshly laid cement amidst considerable fanfare and media attention. Joanie Benoit Samuelson, Billy Rodgers, Johnny "the Elder" Kelley, Amby Burfoot, Bobby Hodge, Vin Fleming, Kevin Ryan, Patti Catalano, Randy Thomas, and Tommy Leonard all had their feet cast in front of this shrine to running.

May 12, 1984, was the day of the first-ever Women's Olympic Trials for the marathon in Olympia, Washington. Joan Benoit of Cape Elizabeth, Maine, who'd set a world record in Boston in 1983 with a time of 2:22:43, was the race favorite. Tommy put an ad in The Olympian newspaper, which read:

WE LOVE YOU
JOAN BENOIT
And the rest of the Greater Boston Runners
BEST OF LUCK IN THE TRIALS
Friends and customers of the Eliot Lounge
Boston, MA

He also placed a front-page article in that paper titled "Beantown bar's regulars follow their race favorite." Tommy told the paper, "We're the only bar in the world that has four major portraits of Joan Benoit. She's got that Maine toughness, like Betty Davis. We call her Joan of Maine. She's true grit."

The community of Olympia sent a state flag, a case of Olympia beer, and a five-pound salmon in ice to the Eliot. Jack Kearney happened to be sitting in the Eliot one quiet afternoon when the salmon arrived. An Irish delivery guy brought the package in, saying, "Hey, Tommy, I got something for you." Watching Tommy open the fish, Kearney started thinking, "Jesus Christ, I wonder if there really is an Irish mafia! Is someone trying to tell Tommy 'he sleeps with the fishes'?"

Tommy, of course, exuberantly exclaimed, "Oh, that's a beautiful fish. I'm gonna take it over to the Chinese restaurant. They'll bread it and cook it up for me." Then he absent-mindedly placed the fish behind the piano. A couple of days later, Jack came into the Eliot and his senses immediately informed him that the fish had not seen the inside of a refrigerator yet.

Joanie not only won the Olympic Trials but went on to become the gold medalist in the first Women's Olympic Marathon on August 4, 1984, in Los Angeles, with a time of 2:24:52. Tommy would have loved to be in LA to see Joanie win her gold, but long before, his good friend of Nantucket, the late Del Wynn, had asked Tommy to be in his wedding. Always loyal to his friends, Tommy felt it was most important to keep that commitment. However, on the afternoon of the wedding, the guests all watched Joanie win her Olympic gold on TV. Tommy flew out to LA the next day and attended the rest of the Olympic track and field events.

In 1985, Tommy and Joe Concannon made a point of traveling to Bowdoin College in Maine when Joanie was given the Bowdoin Prize. This prize is awarded "once in each of 5 years to the graduate or former member of the College, or member of its faculty at the time of the award, who shall have made during the period the most distinctive contribution in any field of human endeavor." The committee of award consists of the President of Harvard University, the President of Yale University, and the Chief Justice of the Supreme Judicial Court of the State of Maine. The prize is awarded to one who "shall be recognized as having won national and not merely local distinction."

1984 was a time in which the Boston Marathon was at a crossroads. Boston had stringent qualifying times, while other marathons began to offer prize money. The elite runners were following the money trail. The board of governors of the BAA opposed prize money and wanted the marathon to maintain the eighty-eight-year-old tradition of running a pure race in which nobody made a quarter. The elite runners viewed the future of the Boston race as being in jeopardy unless it joined the twentieth century.

Despite the admirable performances of winners Geoff Smith and Lisa Larsen Weidenbach of Michigan in the 1985 race, there was an embarrassing lack of talent in the field. Tommy would reflect, "It's a vintage wine that should and could have a delicate bouquet. It's becoming a race with a million-dollar audience and a 25-cent field."

The Boston Marathon had always been a source of great pride for the residents of Boston. For decades it was considered the showcase of marathons, and it was losing its luster. Mayor Flynn became aware the race was losing its distinctive reputation, and in July 1985 he proposed that the BAA offer $292,500 in prize money in the 1986 marathon.

Jim Sullivan, president of the Greater Boston Chamber of Commerce, said, "This is an important event for Boston's image, its economy, and the tourism industry. I feel we should do everything necessary to reclaim its status as No. 1."

Tommy, who by now was recognized nationally as the conscience of Boston's running community, said, "It's a great day for Boston. The city is waking up. I'll volunteer to be a one-man reception committee for the BAA and greet the runners at the airport. They're bringing a great event back from the dead."

In September 1985 the BAA and John Hancock Mutual Life Insurance Company entered into a 10-year, $10 million dollar contract in which $250,000 would be available for performance in the Boston Marathon and additional money for world, American, and course records.

Tommy's reaction was jubilant. "It's a day to rejoice," he said. "It's been comatose for five years. It's about time. John Kennedy always said you can do better. We had apple pie. Now we have apple pie a la mode. It's long, long overdue....The time has come when an athlete can go out and hammer for 26 miles at a sub–5-minute–per-mile pace with no substitutions, no oxygen masks, no time-outs, and no commercial breaks and be properly compensated. We're going to have five million people watching it. God bless John Hancock."

Even Fred Lebow, director of the New York City Marathon, was quoted as saying, "I think it's going to be a shot in the arm for the whole marathon world. When a big company like that puts up that kind of money, it helps us all. I think Boston overnight will regain its position as the world's No.1 marathon."

By Patriot's Day 1986, Tommy would be telling reporters at the Eliot Lounge, "We've been drenched by out-of-town phone calls. Whereas in the last couple of years the phone has been silent, all of a sudden there's an eruption of interest. It's been refreshing. They've restored the vitality.

"It's like taking a whaling captain's house on Nantucket that's fallen apart and restoring it. They've brought it back to life. They've given it luster and polish. I'd like to see John Hancock buy the Boston Red Sox. In all seriousness, there's going to be jubilation in Boston for a week.

"The Boston Marathon will make the Super Bowl seem like a sleepy affair in terms of excitement. The Boston Marathon is a tradition that should be cherished and preserved, and that's exactly what John Hancock has done. The Boston Marathon has the most informed spectators in the world. They've been weaned on it. The best audience in the world deserves the best field, and that's exactly what they're getting."

With renewed life and vigor in the marathon, the BAA approached Tommy and the legendary Jock Semple, trainer for the BAA and assistant director to Will Cloney, to be the official greeters for the race. Tommy commented, "I always wanted to do something like this since I was a little boy. I'll meet the runners at the airport and I'll make them feel comfortable. Jock's been doing things like that his whole life and I've done it informally, and now I'll be doing it formally. It's a big, big honor for me."

Tommy would often be seen walking around town in his role as official greeter, waxing philosophic with statements such as this, captured by Joe Concannon: "There's a burgeoning of bustle on Boylston Street The excitement permeates the atmosphere. You can hear the hammers banging. The dogwood is bursting on Commonwealth Avenue, and it all blends into a beautiful athletic symphony."

New life had been infused in the Boston Marathon, Tommy was now an official greeter for the BAA, and the Eliot Lounge had achieved international status as the official watering hole and "must stop" saloon for anyone with any kind of connection to running. Tommy's charm, warmth, and fun-loving nature combined with his genius for orchestrating events had created a unique and irreplaceable atmosphere.

That is why, at the end of the summer of 1986, Tommy would make a decision that would stun his patrons and co-workers at the Eliot Lounge.

The Shurtleff Mission—the orphanage Tommy lived in from 1940 to 1945.

The Shurtleff Mission—now the Barnard Rest Home in Westfield, Massachusetts.

TOMMY
"RAINBOW"
LEONARD

Tommy "Rainbow" Leonard

Tommy and George Kelleher
Westfield High graduation 1952

Westfield High School, now Westfield Vocational

"The Mugwumps" of Westfield *Front row:* George "Bardo" Kelleher, Maureen "Wren" O'Rourke, Connie Hammon, Ann "Pinky" McGowan. *Second row:* Sophie Zawada, Michael "Champ" Morris, Paul Meagher, John "Spiderlegs" Killips. *Standing:* Tommy "Rainbow" Leonard, Bruno "Hoot" Fioroni, June "Chunner" Graves, John "Jiggs" Morrissey.

Corporal Thomas Francis Leonard, U.S. Marine Corps,1952–1955.

(Photo courtesy of Enterprise Productions, Falmouth, MA.)

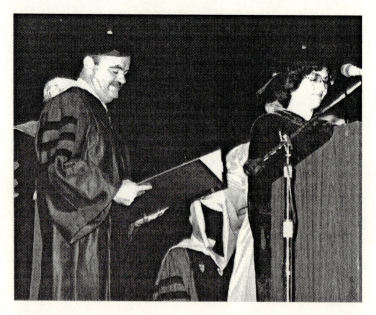

Receiving an honorary doctorate from Westfield State in 1985.

Flag-raising ceremony at the Eliot Lounge.

Tommy with pals at the Eliot: John Newton (retired, FBI), Eddie Burke (retired, Middlesex Sheriff's Office), Tommy, unidentified woman, and Brian Griffith of the Boston Police Force.

Joe Concannon, Gerry Vanasse (second place, Boston Marathon, 1984), Tommy, and Coach Bill Squires at the Eliot Lounge.

Tommy runs "like he has a suitcase in each hand."

Syracuse Citrus Society Band of Syracuse University plays the Eliot.

First Falmouth Road Race. *Front row:* Tommy Leonard, Giles Thread-gold, Bob Bensel. *Top row:* Mike Hyndman, Bob Kozok, Rich Sherman.

Tommy and the late Joe Concannon at the Falmouth Road Race.

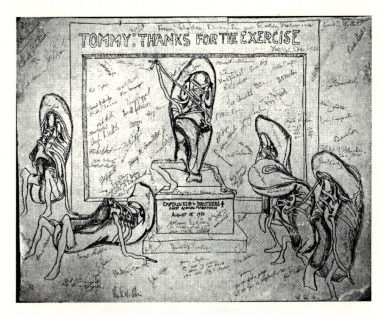

Poster of gratitude from first "Captain Kidd to Brothers 4 First Falmouth Marathon" signed by many of the runners.

Attention ◁◀ ◁◀

1st Annual Marathon

Captain Kidd's TO **Brothers 4**
WOODS HOLE   FALMOUTH HEIGHTS

A 7.3 Mile Race Open To All Serious Runners
TO BENEFIT THE FALMOUTH TRACK CLUB

**Wednesday, August 15th
at 12 noon**

Starts at CAPTAIN KIDD'S Woods Hole
Followed . . . by an afternoon of
gaiety and celebration at BROTHERS 4

— *featuring* —

The Ronnie Bill Tradtional Jazz Band
A MARK AKIN PRODUCTION

A SENSATIONAL BANJO BAND IN THEIR
MAJOR CAPE APPEARANCE OF THE SEASON

See The Race!   **Join The Fun!**

Tommy and Billy Rodgers under Old Glory at the Falmouth finish line.

T.L.'s friends at the *Herald* commemorate his fiftieth birthday with faux headline.

Always a twinkle in his eye, a poem in his soul, and an idea in his heart.

Senator John Kerry, Kenny Balducci, and Tommy with waiter at the
Hampshire House. (Photo courtesy of Hampshire House, Boston, MA.)

Eddie Doyle, "Norm," and Tommy at the "End of Cheers" party' at
Cheers. (Photo courtesy of Hampshire House, Boston, MA.)

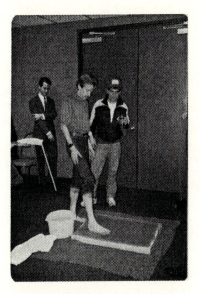

Billy Rodgers's paw goes into posterity at Pro's Bar and Grill in Houston.

Mayor Tom Menino of Boston with the late Johnny Kelley creating the "Walkway of the Running Stars" in front of the Eliot.

Tommy with Fred Lebow, Joe Concannon, and Japanese officials at Fukuoka Marathon.

Tommy and Yoichi Furukawa at the Bull & Finch Pub on Beacon Street, Boston. (Photo courtesy of Hampshire House, Boston, MA.)

Doug Brown and Tommy at the "Wall of Marathon Memories" at the Eliot. (Photograph by Kerry Brett Hurley for *Improper Bostonian*.)

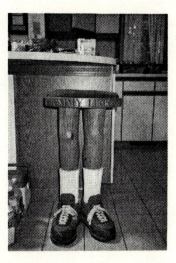

Wooden stool carved by New Balance for Tommy with inscription on the back: "For Making People Happy."

Tommy with Joan Benoit Samuelson at a BAA function at the Hampshire House, Boston.

Eddie Doyle, Tommy, and the late Johnny "the Elder" Kelley at BAA function, 2003.

Tommy on bench dedicated to him in Falmouth: "Thanks Tommy, for making people happy." (Photo courtesy of Enterprise Productions, Falmouth, MA.)

Four of the Falmouth Five with Tommy: Brian Salzberg, Tommy Leonard, Mike Bennett, Don Delinks, and Ron Pokraka.

Falmouth's twenty-fifth anniversary celebration at the Quarterdeck Restaurant. *Front row:* Toni Reavis, Michael Cleary, Craig Virgin. *Second row:* unidentified runner, Tommy Leonard, Kenny Gartner, unidentified female. *Back:* Brent "Hawk" Hawkins, Rod Dixon.

Billy Rodgers, Rod Dixon, Tommy Leonard, Craig Virgin, and Michael Cleary at the twenty-fifth road race anniversary.

Falmouth's thirtieth running celebration at Tommy's bungalow: Michael Cleary, Jeff Fumorala, Tommy, Steve Jones, Billy Harbilas, Rod Dixon, Richard Prior, and Scott Williamson.

Tommy enjoys a few pops with Westfield buddies John O'Connor & Don Foley at Chez Jay's in Malibu, CA

Tommy Leonard and Eddie Doyle with 2004 Boston Red Sox World Series trophy. (Photo courtesy of Hampshire House, Boston, MA.)

8

Houston

Hitting the Wall

"This cowboy is history."

—Tommy Leonard

The day before the 1978 Boston Marathon, a group of marathoners from Houston arrived at the Eliot Lounge in their cowboy boots, hats, and jeans. Tommy was presented with two cases of Lone Star beer by the group. Impressed with their friendliness and generous gift, he expressed an interest in visiting the Lone Star State. One week later, he found himself on a plane to Houston, where he was wined and dined by the Texas group headed by Tom Fatjo, founder of the Houstonian, an upscale fitness complex in Houston.

It seems Tom Fatjo had read the chapter about Tommy in Joe Falls's book *The Boston Marathon* and thought he was a colorful character. Thus began an eight-year courtship in which Fatjo and friends at the Houstonian would bring Tommy to Houston in an effort to lure him away from Boston to help create a sort of "Eliot South" at Pro's Bar and Grill in the Bayou Park Club complex. The Bayou is a private health club managed by the Houstonian, and Pro's was a pub in the complex open to the public.

The Texans could see that Tommy's infectious good humor and eagerness to please his customers could help create an atmosphere at Pro's where every-

103

one felt at home. They made him an Honorary Citizen and Goodwill Ambassador of Houston in 1983 and gave him the following documents:

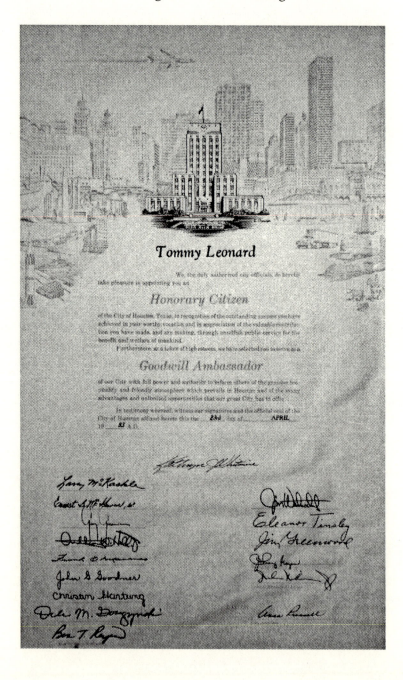

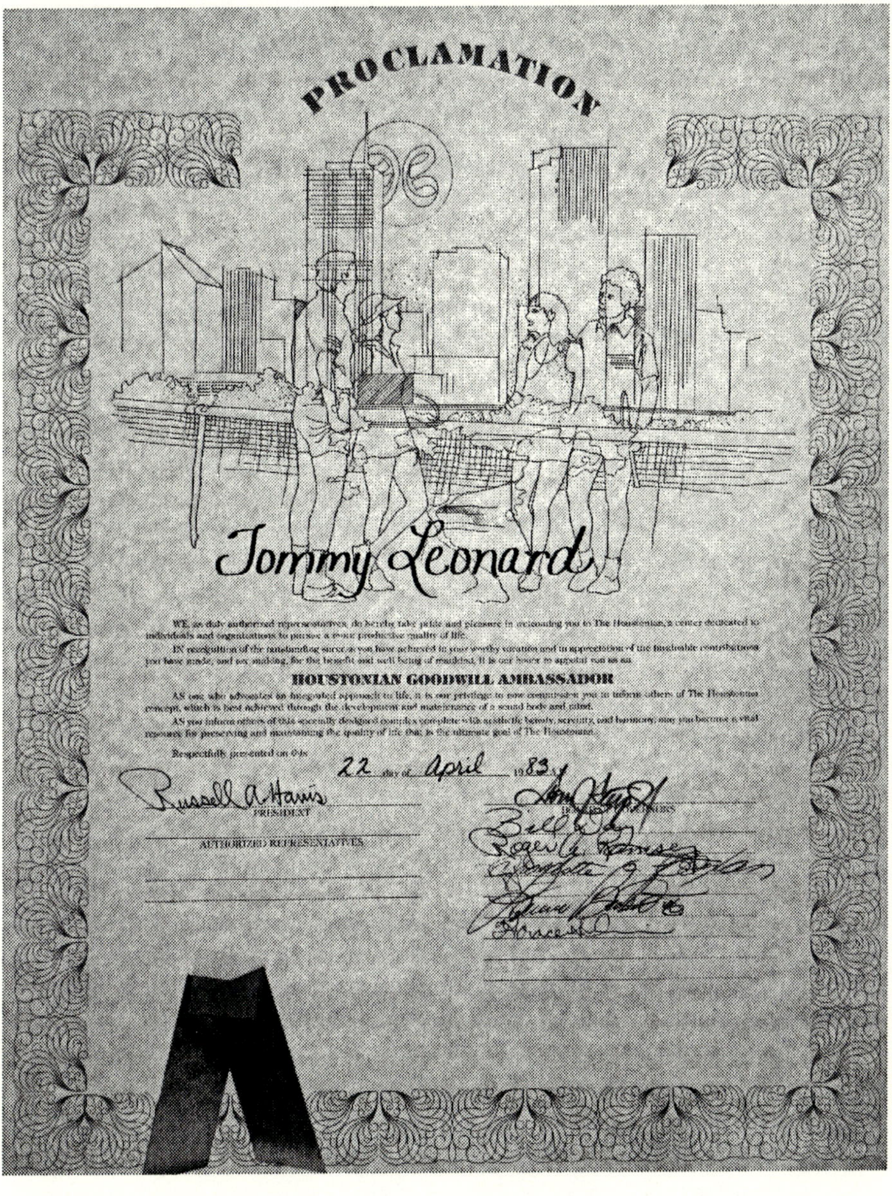
PROCLAMATION
Tommy Leonard
HOUSTONIAN GOODWILL AMBASSADOR
Respectfully presented on this
22 day of April 1983
Russell A. Harris
PRESIDENT
AUTHORIZED REPRESENTATIVES

They offered Tommy a newly furnished condo apartment, a percentage of the ownership of Pro's (in addition to his manager's salary), signing privileges for food and drink, membership in the health club, and two trips home per year.

Tommy met John Wing, an executive of Enron, through his friendship with Jim Koch, founder of the Boston Beer Company, brewer of Samuel Adams beer. Mr. Wing offered to fly Tommy home to Boston on several occasions on a private Falcon jet.

Tommy found himself eating shrimp cocktail, quaffing Sam Adams, and watching the "tangerine sunset" over Tennessee, and he considered the choices before him. After eight years of private jet flights to Houston, clam and lobster bakes, yacht outings, and parties, Tommy decided, "Nothing ventured, nothing gained," and he accepted their offer to come to Houston. "They extended me Texas hospitality with a capital H."

Tommy had struggled with his decision until mid-August 1986. He told sportswriter Mike Tempesta of the *Middlesex News*, "I have so many memories of customers…talking with writers…the more I talk about it, the more my heart breaks. You're stirring up all the sentiment in my bloodstream." He chuckled, "My foster father, Frank, says I'll be a fish out of water in Houston….Is the word incongruous?"

Tommy went to Houston in September 1986 with plans to host neighborhood parties over the holidays—Halloween, Thanksgiving, Christmas, and New Year's—as well as organize a 10K for the Special Olympics.

Doug Brown of the Eliot recalls that at first the customers and staff at the lounge didn't really believe that T.L. would ever go to Texas. Then everyone said, give him six months and he'll be back. But when Tommy would call and talk about his luxury apartment and running along the bayou with the robins "bop, bop, bopping along," people started to worry that he really would stay in Texas. According to Doug, the Eliot just did not have the same feeling without him.

Tommy's friends had sent him off with a gala party at the Eliot that included Boston Mayor Ray Flynn, Olympic gold medalist Joan Benoit, many members of the GBTC, and the many sportswriters, fans, and friends he had endeared himself to over the years.

Tommy made a great effort to create a welcoming atmosphere similar to that of the Eliot at Pro's, putting up photos of Ireland's John Treacy, the late Steve Prefontaine, and Billy Rodgers. There were Boston Marathon posters and articles on the walls. The obligatory national flags hung in an alcove, and

T-shirts from many races, cities, and bars were stapled to the ceiling. Billy Rodgers even traveled down and had his footprints once again framed in cement. Several of T.L.'s friends from the Eliot traveled down to see him, including Michael Gee, who was writing for the *Boston Phoenix* at the time. Tommy made new friends and welcomed such Houston athletes as Carl Lewis and Earl Campbell to Pro's.

The place, with neon lights running along the ceiling, was more open and contemporary and less cozy than the Eliot. There were no decaying deer heads or stalled clocks like those that gave the Eliot its "Grandfather's Attic" charm and sense of history. Although the people were friendly despite the oil glut depression at the time, Tommy missed the New England passion and enthusiasm that had been part of daily life at the Eliot.

Coach Squires mailed a packet of weekly newspaper clippings written by Mike Barnicle to Tommy. "I miss the Coach's Corner at the Eliot. My pleasant memories became activated every week when Coach sent me all those clippings," Tommy told Joe Concannon of the *Globe*.

Hard as he tried, he could never quite get comfortable in his new digs. By February Tommy made the choice to follow his heart back to Boston. It seems his Eliot friends had him pegged pretty well. He told Joe, "You have to be where your heart is, and my heart is hanging on a bridge on the corner of Mass Ave and Commonwealth Ave.

"I wanted to add a chapter to my life...to expand my culture. It was a challenge coming down here, where there's a sluggish economy. I don't think I've given it my best shot, because I left my heart and soul in the Back Bay.

"I think the customers here sensed it....Ten years ago I would have made a longer go of it. I'm at the 3 o'clock stage of my life....What I miss is walking along Commonwealth Avenue in the springtime and a quiet run in the Sunday morning stillness of the Freedom Trail."

Tommy returned to Boston in time to be the official greeter for the Boston Athletic Association at the 1987 Boston Marathon. The owners of the Eliot hired him back, and customers were delighted to have him back behind the bar, miscalculating their change, listening to their tales of woe or gladness, and spreading his goodwill and cheer.

Tommy, however, was haunted all summer by a sense that he had not left a positive legacy and that he had let Tom Fatjo and all the people at the Houstonian down after all their generosity to him. He arranged to return to Houston in the fall of 1987 to give it another go.

He wanted to give something back to the people of Texas who had been so good to him, so when he settled back into Pro's, he began planning a road race that had him more excited than any of his previous adventures.

The "Texas Tom Trot" would be held in February. Tommy sent invitations to Tom Brokaw, Tom Cruise, Tom Selleck, Tom Hanks, Tommy Lasorda, and the Eliot's bartender, Tommy Sullivan, to participate. Tom Selleck sent a photo, as he was busy shooting *Magnum P.I.* Tommy Lasorda sent a note explaining that spring training was soon to start for the Los Angeles Dodgers.

The race would be open to the public, and the proceeds would benefit, of course, St. Thomas High School in Houston. Tom Fatjo would wear number 1. Each product sponsor would be "Tom"-related. Tommy contacted Thomas's English Muffins, Thom McCann shoes, Tom's Toothpaste of Maine, and Tom's Texas Snacks, among others. He was working on a deal with Continental Airlines to offer a round-trip ticket to St. Thomas.

The race would start at Pro's Bar and Grill and finish with a loop around the running track at St. Thomas High stadium, while the musical score of *Tommy* by the Who played over the loudspeakers. Former GBTC star Randy Thomas was invited in the hope that he could guarantee a Tom would win the race. Naturally, a large post-race bash was planned.

Tommy told John Connolly of the *Herald* that pulling the race together had its hurdles, both political and administrative. "Falmouth was easy because I knew everyone. Here I'm like a carpetbagger." But his infectious good spirits and impassioned enthusiasm found people lining up to help. Dave Odom of the Hit and Run Sporting Goods store agreed to be the race director. Father Gaelens and Gerry Donoghue of St. Thomas High offered a huge support system. Enron gave Tommy a check for $2,000 to cover the traffic expenses. Tommy was generating the same kind of excitement as he had back home for numerous races—Falmouth, Litchfield Hills, the Holyoke Turkey Trot, and the Holyoke St. Patrick's 10K.

Then the ownership of Pro's changed. The new owners pulled the plug on the race and wrote it out of the budget. Tommy was truly devastated. "The Texas Tom Trot has been tomahawked. I feel as if I was tossed into the tempestuous seas of the Gulf of Mexico during a raging hurricane in a rowboat without any oars," he bemoaned.

He went to Father Gaelens and offered to face the student body, staff, and administration of St. Thomas to apologize. Putting his arm around Tommy's shoulder, Father Gaelens thanked him for all his concern and efforts.

Tommy did arrange for a check to be sent to St. Thomas High from his friend Don Facey, whose Falmouth in the Fall road race has a scholarship fund in Tommy's name. But his bubble had burst. He told his friend Joe Concannon of the *Globe*, "I tried to make a triumphant return and I ended up with egg on my face. I'm like Goldilocks. I'm always trying to find the right bed."

By early 1988, Tommy was back in Boston for good, admitting, "You can't make a cowboy out of this Irishman."

Once safely ensconced behind the bar at the Eliot, this true-blue New England barkeep declared, "I'm never going West of the Berkshires or South of Cape Cod again!"

9

The Eliot Lounge, Part Two

Second Wind

"It's a Noah's Ark of life, a bouillabaisse of humanity."

—Tommy Leonard

With Tommy back at the stick at the Eliot, the ambience reacquired the passion and zany flavor of the days before the Houston sabbatical.

Throughout Tommy's twenty-four-year career at the Eliot, he had quietly helped people to make enormous lifestyle changes. He had a way of teasing and cajoling people into believing in themselves. If he had a smoker in the bar, he'd say, "Ah, you don't want to be smoking. Try running around the block. You'll feel so good." He'd encourage people to go longer and harder. "How far did you go today?" he'd ask. "Wow! That's great! Next time try going to the next bridge. If you can do 3 miles, you can do 5."

Tommy was always having so much fun and he made the running scene seem so interesting that people would want to get involved. *Sports Illustrated* writer Leigh Montville says, "I never even ran for the bus and Tommy convinced me to run the marathon." He asked Coach Squires what he had to do to be able to run the marathon, so Squires scratched out a daily training program on a cocktail napkin and said, "Do this for a month and then call me." Eventually, Squires offered to run with Leigh and helped him train for the race.

No matter where anyone finished in a road race, Tommy was always very supportive, "That was great! You are out there doing something to help yourself," he'd say. He cajoled both Doug Brown and Don Aiken to run in the Falmouth Road Race. Don finished dead last, and Tommy was waiting for him at the top of the hill in Falmouth Heights near the finish line. They ran down and across the finish line together.

Tommy encouraged Eddie Doyle, his bartending buddy at the Bull & Finch/Cheers, to give running a try. A hockey and baseball player who suffers with asthma, Eddie took to running and in 1979 formed the Barley-hoppers Running Club, whose motto was "We run for fun...We roam for foam." It would become one of the first running groups to raise money for charitable causes.

Tommy and Sharpless Jones shared an apartment in Coolidge Corner for a while. When Tommy sensed that Sharpless was ready, he encouraged him to try running. Surprised by how much he enjoyed running, Sharpless became the manager of running stores for several years.

Sharpless, Tommy, and their friend Don Facey, who owned a printing business and printed the numbers for countless road races, traveled to many road races together. Sharpless had somehow picked up the nickname "Sharp-Who," and Tommy was often described as the running "Guru." When they traveled together, they would be referred to as "the Who, the Do, and the Gu." Whether they were in Greenwich, Connecticut, New York City, or San Blas, Puerto Rico, people would look at Tommy and ask, "Aren't you Tommy Leonard?" His fame as the Guru of New England running had indeed stretched far and wide.

In the early 1960s, Sharpless's mother had begun the tradition of hosting a New Year's Day party with friends and neighbors to watch the Rose Bowl. Over the years, the party grew and grew with guests of every age. The Pete Collins Jazz Band, a six-piece Dixieland band, still plays today at this annual event. The first year Tommy went to the party, he declared that the following year he'd run the 26 miles from the Eliot to the party in Scituate. Tommy garnered great enthusiasm for the idea, and the following year a large group gathered at noon to run to the Jones house. Since so many people were now attending the party, runners could run 5, 10, or 20 miles and be picked up by someone at the end of their run. The Jones's neighbors opened their homes for the runners to shower and spruce up.

One year, six of the top ten finishers in the Boston Marathon attended the party, including Bill Rodgers, Bobby Hodge, and Vinnie Fleming. Rodgers somehow missed the North Scituate cut-off and ran almost 10 miles further to the Grog Shop. Recognizing him as "Boston Billy," the owner gave him some beer, which, after a run of nearly 35 miles, didn't help Billy to stay on his feet. The annual party continues today with a 3-mile run/1-mile walk and a celebration at the Scituate Harbor Yacht Club.

Living with Tommy had its moments for Sharpless. While Tommy worked days, Sharpless had the night shift and dreaded the question "Hey, Sharp, can I have your keys to get home? I forgot mine." Sharpless knew it would be a challenge to wake Tommy up at 3 AM to let him in. One cold and snowy morning, Sharpless knocked and knocked so long that three girls who lived in the building let him sleep on their couch. On another occasion, Sharpless took a cab home after work, and when they arrived at his building the cabbie said, "I've got some keys from a guy I once drove here." Sure enough, he handed over Tommy's keys.

Sharpless was accustomed to coming home to the scent of Chinese food, Tommy's usual midnight snack. He didn't expect the putrid odor that accosted him the night Tommy forgot to turn off the burner under the little skillet he'd used to heat his Chinese. The bottom of the pan had burned entirely off.

Doug Brown describes Tommy as the most "peripatetic" person he knows. He has a strong aversion to being in one place for any length of time and needs to keep walking about from place to place. Whether he had a free ticket to the Beanpot (the annual hockey tournament between Boston University, Boston College, Harvard University, and Northeastern) or a Red Sox game at Fenway, a mechanism seems to kick in, and he wanders away. Perhaps those early years he had spent constrained at the orphanage with no shoes led to a powerful desire to come and go as he pleases.

When Joe Concannon learned that Tommy had never been to his beloved Beanpot, he got tickets for Doug and Tommy. They went together, and after a while Tommy said, "I'm going to walk around. I'll be back." Doug watched a terrific hockey game and hoped T.L. had seen it, as Tommy never returned. About 1 AM, Tommy called the Eliot, saying he was at the "Purple Plume or the Blue Onion or something," so Doug asked him to put someone else on the phone. The person said he was at the Red Hat, a bar near the Garden. Tommy said, "I couldn't stand it. It was too crowded. I had to get out of there."

Doug and Tommy traveled to the Marine Corps Marathon with a group for a week one year. Doug barely saw Tommy that week, as he was off in museums or talking to Marines involved with the race. A voracious reader, Tommy has a true joy of learning and an intellectual curiosity, yet he carefully avoids the appearance of being studious.

Several of Tommy's friends interviewed for this book commented that they were sorry he had never found that one special woman to settle down with. His peripatetic nature would drive most women insane. It precluded the chance for him to make a true relational commitment that would keep him anchored. Even during the course of a night's socializing, Tommy would be bouncing around faster than a Mexican jumping bean. Sharpless recalled an evening out at Copperfield's when Tommy met a woman from Ireland and proclaimed, "Holy Jeez! The forty shades of green! Will you marry me?" When she gave him the nod, he shouted, "This is the happiest day of my life! I'm getting married!" Shortly after that interchange, he met a woman from Springfield and said, "Holy Jeez! Right near my hometown! Will you marry me? I'm getting married!" Although his friends recall several women who had a sincere interest in Tommy, whenever they'd ask, "Any future Mrs. Leonard's coming along?" Tommy would respond in his high-pitched singsong, "Never you mind. Never you mind...."

In 1988 Tommy was inducted into the Bartender Hall of Fame, which was developed by *Bartender* magazine and supported by the House of Seagram Tour. The Hall of Fame was created to "salute the otherwise unsung men and women behind the bar who play so large a role in On-Premises atmosphere and conviviality. In everything from *New Yorker* cartoons to the old radio show, *Duffy's Tavern*, from the plays of Eugene O'Neill to the stories of O Henry, the Bartender is as much a cheerful philosopher of life itself as well as a key ingredient to any successful establishment's ambience." The honorees in the Hall of Fame have all met the qualifications of not only "pouring with personality but also conveying good taste and high professionalism behind the bar."

There are countless customers from the Eliot who no doubt would agree that Tommy met these qualifications, as long as nobody asked him to pour a mixed drink or return accurate change. As he has often said in his self-deprecating way, "I'm the world's worst bartender. I just happen to love people."

For his recognition in the Hall of Fame, he was given an Official Citation of the Massachusetts State Senate signed by then—Senate President William Bulger:

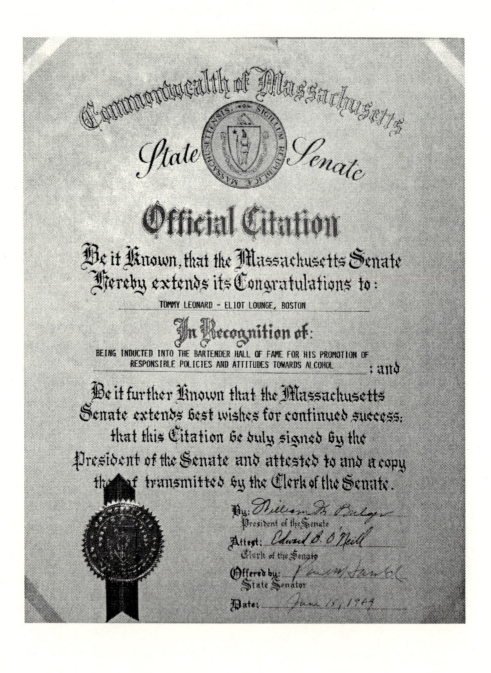

Commonwealth of Massachusetts
State Senate

Official Citation

Be it Known, that the Massachusetts Senate
Hereby extends its Congratulations to :

TOMMY LEONARD - ELIOT LOUNGE, BOSTON

In Recognition of :

BEING INDUCTED INTO THE BARTENDER HALL OF FAME FOR HIS PROMOTION OF
RESPONSIBLE POLICIES AND ATTITUDES TOWARDS ALCOHOL   : and

Be it further Known that the Massachusetts
Senate extends best wishes for continued success;
that this Citation be duly signed by the
President of the Senate and attested to and a copy
thereof transmitted by the Clerk of the Senate.

By: _William M. Bulger_
President of the Senate

Attest: _Edward B. O'Neill_
Clerk of the Senate

Offered by: _____
State Senator

Date: _June 15, 1949_

In November 1988, while a group of running friends sat together in Coach's Corner at the Eliot, Paul Fetscher of the Warren Street Running Club in New York City challenged Coach Squires to run a time less than his age in the 440 for his next birthday, his fifty-sixth. Paul had heard that Coach Percy Cerutty had run 400 meters in less than 60 seconds shortly after his sixtieth birthday.

For a pint of Sam Adams (Squires's risk) versus $100, Coach agreed to attempt the quarter-mile in less than 56 seconds the following April. He set to hard training and lost 15 pounds.

Tommy saw this as an opportunity to pay homage to Coach and jumped on the idea with pizzazz. The wheels of imagination and organization were set in motion, and arrangements to use Boston College's Jack Ryder track, where Coach had developed the fledgling GBTC to marathon fame, were put in place. Mayor Ray Flynn and the City of Boston proclaimed Sunday, April 16, 1989, the day before the Boston Marathon, as "Billy Squires Day" to acknowledge his achievements as a runner, a coach, and a person.

Tommy arranged for twenty-eight gold and twenty-eight green balloons. Many of Coach's former runners were invited to run the Squires Stroll, a fun mile before Coach met the challenge. The Notre Dame fighting song played while he warmed up. A tape of the McGuire Sisters singing *You Gotta Have Heart* played while Coach ran the quarter. That was the song he used to listen to as a Domer while training for the elusive win over Wes Santee of Kansas University. Tommy tried to track Santee down for the event but was unable to find him.

The Wednesday before the race, Kenny Balducci, owner of Balducci's Pizza in Quincy, gave Coach fifty-six slices of pizza to go with the fifty-six Sam Adams he'd been given to enjoy while reading his fifty-six issues of the *New Yorker*.

Tommy predicted he'd do it in 64 seconds. "That's not even the point....I mean, I don't want to kill the guy," Tommy said. "He's just a beautiful human being. Everybody is a friend of Billy's." With the number 56 on his chest, Coach ran the distance in a valiant 66 seconds. Billy Squires Day was acknowledged in the Congressional Record of the U.S. Senate on May 2, 1989.

Many runners have reported approaching Squires with an ache or pain after a 3- or 4-mile run, and he would tell them what to do, generously dispensing free advice. Billy Squires Day gave everyone a chance to say thank you to this man who'd been such a help to runners of any talent, not just the great ones he developed.

Coach's advice was often the kind runners are quite happy to receive. Such was the case with Billy Harbilas, director of the Holyoke Talking Turkey Road Race. Billy went to meet Tommy at the Back Bay Brewing Company in the late 1990s, the day before the Boston Marathon. Upon arriving, he saw Tommy sitting with Coach Squires and Marty Liquori. Billy was feeling awed by these running legends before him when Tommy turned around and saw him. "Billy Harbilas! This is one of the best race directors I know!" After introducing Billy, Tommy asked the bartender, "Would you give Billy a 16ounce Freedom Pale Ale? Do you have any frozen glasses?"

Billy resisted. "Oh, no, no, Tommy. I'm running tomorrow. I don't want to drink today, really."

"Oh, you could have one, Billy."

"No, no, Tommy, really. I'm going to run tomorrow," Billy replied.

"Okay, Billy. I'm not going to argue with you. You know, you've got the best distance running coach here in the history of the world. He coached Billy Rodgers, Alberto Salazar, Dick Beardsley. Coach Squires, would it be detrimental to Billy's performance tomorrow if he had a beer?" Tommy asked.

Coach looked at Billy and asked, "What are you looking to do for time?"

"Well, between 3 hours and 3:10, I hope."

"Son, have four or five," Squires advised.

Tommy then had a phone call from Japan, asking about his predictions for the race. When he returned about a half hour later he said, "I really couldn't understand what they were saying." The group around the table laughed, saying, "Don't worry, Tommy. If you were talking about the 'powder puff clouds in the cerulean blue skies,' you were a puzzle to them, too!"

Dr. Charles Tifft, a cardiologist at Boston University Medical Center and a regular member of Coach's Corner, recalls going to run in the "Horse of a Different Color 10-Miler" in Portsmouth, New Hampshire, with a crowd from the Eliot. The race was a fast course held annually in late August. The course passed Wentworth-by-the-Sea, the resort Tommy worked at during his Marine service, and was named for a bar on the waterfront.

One year, Dr. Tifft and Coach Squires decided to run the race as close to 60 minutes as possible. It didn't matter who ran the fastest; the goal was to come closest to 60 minutes. Tommy had traveled to the race with Doug Brown, Bernie Corbett, and Mike King. All the way up, Tommy debated, while sipping a beer or two, whether he would run the race. Upon arriving in

Portsmouth, they stopped into the Horse of a Different Color Tavern, where the owner gave Tom a beer. One moment, he would take off his sweats and say, "Yeah, I think I'll run." Shortly afterward, he'd put his sweats back on, saying, "No, I'm not gonna run." His traveling buddies were laughing so hard they worried about not being able to run themselves. By the fourth beer at the tavern, he decided to sit it out.

Later, everyone was enjoying the post-race festivities. At some point, they realized that Tommy was in need of a rest, so they gave some money to a cab driver to take Tommy to where he was staying. About 45 minutes later, the frustrated cabbie returned. Tommy couldn't remember where he was supposed to stay and had been knocking on all sorts of doors trying to figure out who was putting him up for the night.

Over the years, most of the winners of the Boston Marathon made their way to the Eliot Lounge on the night of their victory. A bottle of champagne and a hero's welcome were always waiting. Some came quietly, such as Ingrid Kristiansen of Norway, winner in 1986 and 1989, who stood in line with her husband for 45 minutes in 1986 until she was recognized and let in. Joanie Benoit also stood in line the night she had broken the world record.

In 1990 Gelindo Bordin of Italy, the only runner to win both the Boston Marathon and the Olympic Marathon, arrived in a limousine. His intention was to stay a few minutes. After a couple of hours, he was hoisted on the crowd's shoulders and given a Red Sox cap, which he took off and replaced with an Eliot Lounge cap. With tears in his eyes, speaking in broken English, he told the crowd he had always heard of this place but never really understood what it was. Looking around at all the historic marathon pictures on the walls, he said he was proud to be a part of its history. Doug Brown recalls the moment as "utter adulation and unbelievable camaraderie—a truly great moment."

There was one Boston Marathoner who did not consider his race finished until he was inside the Eliot Lounge. For twelve years, John Gorman would end the 26.2-mile race literally runing through the finish-line barricades to the Eliot, where he would click off his watch.

The spaghetti dinners continued off and on at the Eliot for almost twenty years. Doug Brown recalls that when Don Aiken sold the Eliot in 1982 and moved the Medieval Manor, they did not have a kitchen for a while. Owner Mike King's brother lived in the Back Bay and would cook vats of pasta at his home and drive them over to the Eliot. The doormen looked like a bucket brigade, doling out the pasta as quickly as it arrived.

Throughout the years, all the major shoe companies got involved with the Eliot—Nike, New Balance, Reebok, Puma. Many had private parties with sushi, shrimp, burgers, and other fare on or near race day. One year, Nike was having a private party at the Eliot, and the Eliot was catering a pasta dinner for Reebok on Newbury Street. "It was nuts," Doug Brown recalls.

Tommy's influence in Boston was so widespread by the early 1990s that Mayor Ray Flynn sent him the following Certificate of Recognition:

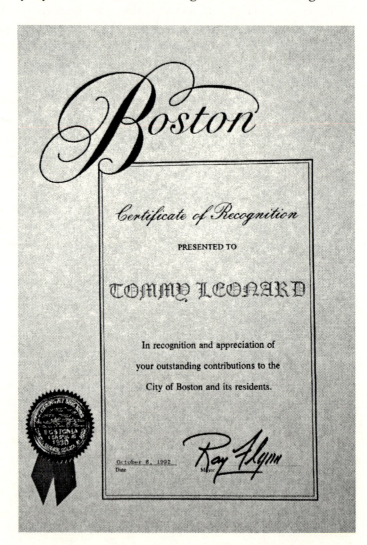

Boston

Certificate of Recognition

PRESENTED TO

TOMMY LEONARD

In recognition and appreciation of
your outstanding contributions to the
City of Boston and its residents.

October 8, 1992
Date

Ray Flynn
Mayor

The "Walkway of the Running Stars," created and dedicated on a cold day in March 1984, was accidentally ripped up by the Boston Department of Public Works in July 1993 as part of a routine resurfacing job. The autographs and footprints of Billy Rodgers, Joan Benoit, the late Johnny "the Elder" Kelley, Amby Burfoot, Patti Catalano, Vinnie Fleming, Kevin Ryan, Bobby Hodge, and Randy Thomas, along with those of Tommy Leonard, were dumped in a truck and carted off to a Dorchester landfill.

Tommy said, "It brought tears to my eyes. I saw Bobby Hodge go into the back of the truck upside down." The *Globe* ran a small blurb about the desecration, and reaction was swift. Although the Walkway was not a major tourist attraction, it was a conversation piece and a bit of Boston history related to the most famous of marathons.

Tommy received a phone call from Frank O'Brien of the Mayor's office offering to help the Eliot replace the Walkway. Tommy got the OK from the owners of the hotel and set to recruiting the paws for posterity. On July 16, 1993, the "Walkway of the Running Stars II" was dedicated, with the prints of Boston winners Billy Rodgers, Johnny Kelley, Geoff Smith, Olympian Lynn Jennings, Coach Bill Squires, and Tommy Leonard. Rodgers commented, "I think this is nice because this is the oldest marathon in the country, and this marathon played a big part in developing other aspects of the sport." Mayor Tom Menino signed the plaque, which read "To those who have contributed significantly to the success of the Boston Marathon."

Tommy received his first proclamation from Governor William Weld in 1995, proclaiming August 2, 1995, as Tommy Leonard Day with the following certificate (stains on the document compliments of Tommy):

The Commonwealth of Massachusetts

A Proclamation

By His Excellency

GOVERNOR WILLIAM F. WELD

1995

WHEREAS: Tommy Leonard is a proud native son of the Commonwealth of Massachusetts who served our state and nation proudly in the United States Marines; and

WHEREAS: Tommy Leonard has long attended to the thirsty needs of the people of Massachusetts by offering them good cheer, an open ear, and an ice cold beer; and

WHEREAS: Tommy Leonard, with his fellow bartending great Mr. Eddie Doyle, has always been ready, willing, and able to reach out and help those down on their luck when they needed help the most; and

WHEREAS: Tommy Leonard shares my great affection for amber-colored liquids, and yet, has been honored with a distinction that no Weld of the last three centuries has enjoyed—the naming of a bridge after him; and

WHEREAS: So many of his friends and admirers are coming together on August 2, 1995, to honor him at the historic Eliot Lounge;

NOW, THEREFORE, I, WILLIAM F. WELD, Governor of the Commonwealth of Massachusetts, do hereby proclaim August 2nd, 1995, as

TOMMY LEONARD DAY

and urge all the citizens of the Commonwealth to take cognizance of this event and participate fittingly in its observance.

Given at the Executive Chamber in Boston, this twenty-eighth day of July, in the year of our Lord one thousand nine hundred and ninety-five, and of the Independence of the United States of America, the two hundred and twentieth.

William F. Weld

By His Excellency the Governor   WILLIAM F. WELD

GOD SAVE THE COMMONWEALTH OF MASSACHUSETTS

1996 was the year of the one hundredth running of the Boston Marathon, which was greeted with great fanfare and media attention. Tommy fielded phone calls for over a year with pleas and bribery offers for help in getting into the race. The New England Cable News show *Talk Around the Globe* was filmed from the Eliot on April 4, 1996.

On April 12, the *Boston Globe* published a list of one hundred people who had made significant contributions to the history of the Boston Marathon. Tommy Leonard was listed at number 92 under the title "Hundreds Worked Behind the Scenes to Ensure That the 100th Will Be a Success." His listing read "Tommy Leonard: By profession, a bartender at the Eliot Lounge. By passion, an ardent supporter for years."

Over 38,000 runners participated in the historic event. Moses Tanui of Kenya won the men's race, and Uta Pippig of Germany won the women's race.

The day after the one hundredth Boston Marathon, Tommy took the Reebok marathon countdown clock that had helped to build the excitement leading up to so many marathon celebrations at the Eliot Lounge, and put the number 138 on the board. It was the final countdown to the closing of the Eliot on September 30, 1996.

The Eliot was falling prey to the wheels of change and progress. The owners of the Eliot Hotel had transformed it from a somewhat seedy, almost welfare-style hotel with decades-long residents to a chic and upscale luxury hotel. In 1996 they chose not to renew the Eliot Lounge's lease so that they could convert the space to a symbiotic chic and upscale restaurant, Clio's.

For Eliot Lounge patrons, none of whom had any tolerance for airs, yuppiness, or pretension, it was salt in an already painful wound. They braced themselves for the sad and inevitable change that was coming to their inveterate, patterned lives.

Eddie Doyle of the Bull & Finch/Cheers pub told Michael Madden of the *Globe*, "Tommy is the epoxy that brought together the Eliot Lounge, the Boston Marathon, and the City of Boston and just being a regular good guy to a lot of people. I can't believe that bar is closing....October 1 is going to be a very sad day in Boston."

Storytelling and reminiscence became the order of the day, as everyone who'd been fortunate enough to be involved with the Eliot Lounge knew the experience was irreplaceable.

Robin Young filmed her last segment of *Evening Magazine* at the Eliot, highlighting the cops, mailmen, plumbers, doctors, and the homeless who had made the Eliot their favorite spot. Eddie Burke reflected that the "Eliot

Lounge brought people together—open-heart surgeons, truck drivers, all sitting next to each other." Another dream of Tommy's come to life.

Bernie Corbett loved to sit in Tommy's warmth at the end of a busy workday. "Nothing would make me feel better than being able to go to the Eliot. It had such spirit." As he entered the lounge, Tommy would cry, "Bernardo! How ya be, laddie? Can I interest you in a cold Heineken?" And then Tommy would make a comment about something that Bernie was currently involved in, saying perhaps, "Bernardo, you're becoming quite the celebrity, lad. I saw you last night on Channel 7. I had the game tuned in at the Beanpot." Bernie felt that Tommy was always right in step with whatever was going on, and always so proud of the accomplishments of his friends and customers.

Since he first came to the Eliot as a very young man, Bernie feels that the relationships he formed at the Eliot have had a significant impact on the development of his career as a sports broadcaster and owner of his own production company, Giant Sports Associates. Like the book title *All I Really Need to Know I Learned in Kindergarten*, Bernie feels he can say, "All I Really Need to Know I Learned at the Eliot," acknowledging his many lessons from the media representatives and athletic patrons who loved the bar and mentored him along the way.

Bernie fondly recalls how "Appalled at Society Tommy" would always make him laugh. Tommy would turn on the evening news and something particularly bad would be reported, prompting Tommy to cry, "It's not the 6:00 news! It's the 6:00 blues! I've had it up to my mustache with this bad news! I can't take it anymore!" And the first cold one would be popped in disgust as he came off his shift.

Tommy taught Bernie and countless others that you can keep your child-like enthusiasm and love for fun no matter what age you are. One of Bernie's all-time favorite lines of Ray Fitzgerald was that he'd had the "opportunity to make a living in life's toy department" (as a sportswriter for the *Globe*), and that's exactly where both Tommy and Bernie aspire to be. It is where most of us aspire to be and why the lucky few who knew the Eliot Lounge intimately will forever hold on to the memories.

Coach Squires, along with Bernie's father, Mitchell Corbett, Joe Concannon, Don Facey, and Tommy loved the youthful exuberance of the Eliot. Squires recalls doing lots of zany things like sliding down the banister and seeing who could land the farthest out. Being of the same generation, this group once shared a house at the Litchfield Road Race. Bernie remembers it being like a bunch of twelve-year-olds sharing a cabin at a campground. "Talk about the blind leading the blind leading the blind!" he chuckled.

Coach remembered a day in 1980 when Arthur Lydiard, one of the world's outstanding coaches, came into the Eliot. The winner of the New Zealand Marathon from 1953 to 1955, Lydiard produced many Olympic medal winners and world record breakers, especially in middle distance. Squires and Lydiard decided to pull one over on Tommy, so as they were talking in Coach's Corner, Squires raised his voice, saying, "You call yourself a coach? You think you know what you are doing? What did you say your name was?" As the visiting coach said, "I'm Arthur Lydiard," Squires thought Tommy was going to jump over the bar in excitement and disbelief as he said to him, "Oh, God! Coach! What are you doing?"

One of the nights Tommy will never forget wasn't actually an Eliot Lounge night, but it had its beginning there. The cast of the TV show *Cheers* came to Boston to celebrate the final episode of their eleven-year sitcom. The celebration was held at the Bull & Finch Pub on Beacon Street, which had been the inspiration for the show's setting. Its cast was modeled on those who worked for or frequented the Bull & Finch.

U.S. Senator and 2004 Democratic presidential candidate John Kerry was in the Eliot prior to going to the Bull & Finch for the celebration. Knowing that Tommy was also going to the function, he offered Tommy a ride in his waiting limousine. The phone rang in the limo and Tommy sat sipping his Sam Adams while Senator Kerry spoke with Ted Koppel about Operation Desert Storm. It was one of the hundreds of moments when Tommy would reflect, "I'm not doing too bad for an over-the-hill bartender."

By the end of Tommy's twenty-four-year career at the Eliot Lounge, he had a bridge in Boston and a bench in Falmouth dedicated to him for his selfless and tireless efforts to promote health and fitness as well as help others in his community. He was mentioned or quoted in over seventy *Boston Globe* articles and at least a dozen *Boston Herald* articles, and had profiles and interviews in *GQ*, *Sports Illustrated*, the *New England Monthly*, the *Waterbury Republican*, the *Middlesex News*, the *Falmouth Enterprise*, the *Cape Cod Times*, the *Olympian*, the *Springfield Union News*, the *Patriot Ledger*, *USA Today*, *Runner's World*, the *Westfield Evening News*, the *Miami Herald*, the *New York Times*, the *Metro West Daily News*, the *Houston Post*, the *Hartford Courant*, the *Baltimore Sun*, the Chicago *Sun-Times*, and the BAA Boston Marathon Program.

He was even the subject of a *Waterbury* (Connecticut) *Sunday Republican* "Sportstester" cartoon on July 6, 1980, which asked, "Can you name the well-known Boston barkeep who is known as the Guru of New England marathon running?" accompanied by a picture of a runner passing a bartender behind the bar who is saying, "Give ya a beer if ya finish!"

Tommy Leonard, who has an aversion to being in the spotlight or receiving accolades; who is the first to credit anyone but himself for the success of events he orchestrated; who is viewed by friends around the globe as the most selfless person they know; whose biggest dream as a child was to have a family he could call his own, found his way into the hearts and minds of people around the world. The world became his family. He helped those who came across his path feel better about themselves than they had ever thought possible.

On September 18, 1996, Tommy's friends and fans organized the "Tommy Leonard Wicked Awesome Hampshire House Happening" in his honor. Tommy arrived in a white limousine wearing a red "Eliot Lounge—End of an Era" baseball cap, blue sports coat, and white polo shirt. With several TV and video cameras trained on him, the Boston Police bagpipe band broke into a medley of Irish tunes as Tommy kissed all the ladies in the foyer while exclaiming his trademark, "Holy Cow! Holy Cow!" The band segued into the Marine Corps Hymn as he entered the room full of waiting guests.

John Henning of WBZ Channel 4 TV and Toni Reavis served as emcees for this night of fun, laughter, and memories. Henning, an "irregular regular" patron of the Eliot, had shared the stage with Tommy in 1985 when they both were given honorary doctorates at Westfield State College.

Mayor Tom Menino of Boston kicked off the evening with the reading of the following proclamation celebrating another "Tommy Leonard Day" in the City of Boston:

♦WHEREAS: For the past twenty-five years, Tommy Leonard has been the chief greeter, philosopher and Father Confessor at Boston's Eliot Lounge, the Mecca for runners around the world; and

♦WHEREAS: Runners across the continents know Tommy through his role as official greeter of the Boston Marathon; and

♦WHEREAS: Tommy Lenoard put Cape Cod on the runners' map when he founded the now world-famous Falmouth Road Race; and

♦WHEREAS: Over the years, Tommy has been a true friend to the young people of Boston, raising funds for The Jimmy Fund and leading the pack to "Bring Back Mac," the duckling statuette taken from the Public Garden; and

◆WHEREAS: Among his numerous titles, Tommy Leonard has become known as the "Good Samaritan of Massachusetts Avenue" for coming to the aid of scores of people and projects in need over the past twenty-five years; and

◆WHEREAS: If retirement doesn't suit him, Tommy can always fall back on his fundraising and public assistance skills, which, fortunately, have always surpassed his bartending skills;

NOW

THEREFORE, I, THOMAS M. MENINO, Mayor of the City of Boston, do hereby proclaim Wednesday, September 18, 1996, to be

TOMMY LEONARD DAY

in the city of Boston, and, on the event of his retirement from the Eliot Lounge, I urge all my fellow Bostonians to join me in acknowledging his many contribution to our city.

Thomas M Menino

Mayor of Boston

Mayor Tom Concannon of the City of Newton then read his city's proclamation:

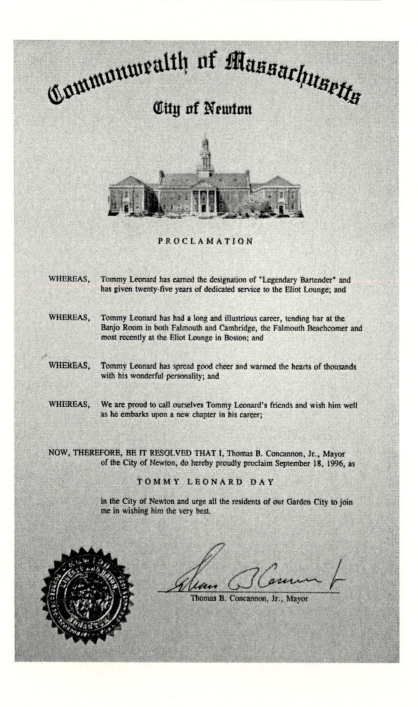

Commonwealth of Massachusetts

City of Newton

PROCLAMATION

WHEREAS,   Tommy Leonard has earned the designation of "Legendary Bartender" and
has given twenty-five years of dedicated service to the Eliot Lounge; and

WHEREAS,   Tommy Leonard has had a long and illustrious career, tending bar at the
Banjo Room in both Falmouth and Cambridge, the Falmouth Beachcomer and
most recently at the Eliot Lounge in Boston; and

WHEREAS,   Tommy Leonard has spread good cheer and warmed the hearts of thousands
with his wonderful personality; and

WHEREAS,   We are proud to call ourselves Tommy Leonard's friends and wish him well
as he embarks upon a new chapter in his career;

NOW, THEREFORE, BE IT RESOLVED THAT I, Thomas B. Concannon, Jr., Mayor
of the City of Newton, do hereby proudly proclaim September 18, 1996, as

TOMMY LEONARD DAY

in the City of Newton and urge all the residents of our Garden City to join
me in wishing him the very best.

Thomas B. Concannon, Jr., Mayor

The Mayor then jokingly pondered how the staff managed to keep Tommy on for so many years "since you can't mix a drink if you tried," causing an eruption of understanding laughter.

Frank Connolly of Senator John Kerry's office then read the following acknowledgment of the closing of the Eliot, which was entered in the U.S. Senate Congressional Record, thanking Tommy for "providing an essential social service":

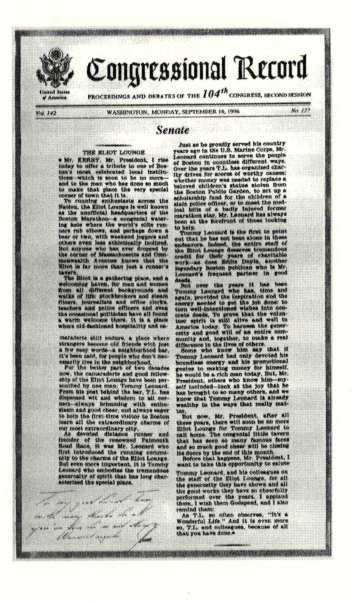

Charlie Manning, Republican consultant to Governor William Weld, read a proclamation signed by the Governor acknowledging the second Tommy Leonard Day in the City of Boston on September 18, 1996:

The Commonwealth of Massachusetts

A Proclamation

By His Excellency

GOVERNOR WILLIAM F. WELD

1996

WHEREAS: Tommy Leonard is a true son of the Commonwealth: born, bred, and educated in our Bay State, a home he proudly served as a member of the United States Marine Corps; and

WHEREAS: For many years, Tommy Leonard has served the citizens of the Commonwealth from behind the bar of the world-famous Eliot Lounge, whence he has dispensed good cheer, wisdom, and nice, cold beer, with legendary bartending skills that serve as the textbook example of what not to do in the hallowed halls of Bartenders College; and

WHEREAS: Tommy Leonard, together with his good friend Eddie Doyle, has shown a commendable commitment to numerous charities and causes, raising money to help countless numbers of people; and

WHEREAS: The lore and legend of Tommy Leonard continues to grow—witness the latest tale in which Tommy, banned as a high school student from the campus of Westfield State after applying his legendary charm a bit too generously in the company of a certain comely co-ed, makes his triumphant return to that same institution to accept an honorary degree; and

WHEREAS: With his trademark saying, "It's a wonderful life," Tommy Leonard imparts to all, by word and by deed, his upbeat philosophy on the joys of life, a true illustration of—to quote the late, great George Frazier—a man with duende.

NOW, THEREFORE, I, WILLIAM F. WELD, Governor of the Commonwealth of Massachusetts, do hereby proclaim September 18th, 1996, to be

TOMMY LEONARD DAY

and urge all the citizens of the Commonwealth to take cognizance of this event and participate fittingly.

Given at the Executive Chamber in Boston, this eighteenth day of September, in the year of our Lord one thousand nine hundred and ninety-six, and of the Independence of the United States of America, the two hundred and twenty-first.

William F. Weld

By His Excellency the Governor   WILLIAM F. WELD

GOD SAVE THE COMMONWEALTH OF MASSACHUSETTS

Jack Kearney, Tommy's radio exec friend, then read the following piece, which he had written a couple of years earlier and is reprinted here with permission of the author:

Leonard versus Clemens? It's No Contest

Does Roger Clemens have a bridge *and* a bench named after him? No way! Tommy Leonard does. Tommy Leonard, for you few unknowing souls, is the high priest of running/philosopher/bartender-in-residence at Boston's Eliot Lounge. He is also, in no particular order, consigliore to the high and mighty and the "not so" high and mighty, world expert on…tap beer, Joni James, Stan Musial, "Night Train" Lane, The Four Freshmen, crispness of Chinese fried rice after 11 PM, first-class espouser of the traditional values of the United States Marine Corps…and the author of perhaps the most meaningful statement I have ever heard in my life—"Without dreams, life would be intolerable." (It escapes me now if he made that statement while standing on his bridge or sitting on his bench.) Oh yes!…the bridge and the bench. The Tommy Leonard Bridge is located on Massachusetts Avenue at Commonwealth and is commemorated by a wooden marker. The reverential dedication was held in 1982 during a summer mist. Appropriately, his beloved Boston Marathon directly passes the site (yearly homage, if you will). The bench is located on the sound at Falmouth Harbor. It bears a plaque with appropriate words from the running community to their leader, prophet, visionary and founder of the Falmouth Road Race…It is a physical beacon to "The tired, the poor and the masses."

As for Roger Clemens. He can throw a baseball ninety-seven miles per hour but is rapidly becoming the "Don Newcombe of the American League," i.e., he can't win "the big ones." He is also arrogant and charges eight dollars and fifty cents for his autograph to all comers…although he is paid in excess of one million dollars per year. Furthermore, he does not have a bridge or a bench named after him!

Leonard vs. Clemens? It's no contest. As a matter of fact, one of these days, just to prove the point, I am going to give Tommy a check for nine dollars for his autograph. Undoubtedly, he'll donate the money to the Jimmy Fund.

Michael Gee of the *Boston Phoenix* and the *Boston Herald* thanked Tommy for creating the "best environment for people who like to idle, to be idled in."

Former mayor and then ambassador to the Vatican Ray Flynn wrote:

"Boston is a remarkable city with a rich history and tradition. The Boston Marathon, The Pops, Swan Boats, Red Sox, and all the many great colleges and universities. But I've learned over the years that it's the people that make it special. Down to earth, straight-talking, nobody is important but everybody is special. Or, where everybody knows your name. Tommy Leonard fits Boston like a beat-up old pair of comfortable running shoes you just don't want to throw away. They are not good-looking and have a lot of miles on them, but you like them.

"Winston Churchill once said in toasting the Royal Air Force, "Never was so much owed by so many, to so few." We can honestly say the same thing tonight in Boston about Tommy Leonard."

Ron Della Chiesa of WGBH radio's *Classics in the Morning* and *The Jazz Songbook* delivered a signed photo of Tony Bennett, whose "heart left San Francisco to be with Tommy Leonard tonight." Ron had always thought of the Eliot as a kind of "Duffy's Tavern," the fictional Third Avenue saloon that came to be loved by thousands listening to the radio between 1941 and 1951. Written by Ed Gardner, each episode would begin with *When Irish Eyes Are Smiling* playing. Then a ringing telephone would cut through the music, and Archie, played by Gardner, would answer, "Duffy's Tavern, where the elite meet to eat. Archie the Manager speaking. Duffy ain't here…"

Many people thought that the Eliot was Tommy's place because of the atmosphere Tommy created there. Ron recalled that Tommy kept his cassette collection behind the bar, and when he walked in, Tommy would always go over to the music and select something that he knew Ron would enjoy. Ron said, "Tommy was to Boston what Louis Armstrong was to jazz and Sinatra was to the Great American Songbook….It was uplifting to be around him. What comes to mind is the song *The Sunny Side of the Street.*

Toni Reavis commented that the "Wall of Marathon Memories" at the Eliot had taken on a life of its own. Any runner of talent aspired to have his or her photo mounted on the wall. Only months earlier the wall had been refurbished with new frames, layouts, and a dedication ceremony. Now the photos and banners were coming down, the flags folded and removed, the CBS and ABC marathon and Olympic banners dropped from the ceiling, the various items of memorabilia stored. Even the "Walkway to the Running Stars" cement footprints were dug up and now sit in the basement of a friend in Natick, Massachusetts. Tommy, of course, has promised several different people that he'd give the memorabilia to them. So numerous people expect someday to adorn their recreation rooms with these treasures.

Charlie Pierce of the *Boston Phoenix* and *Boston Herald* and current co-host of NPR's *Only a Game* read from his soon-to-be-published *GQ* article "The Last Sports Bar," which lamented, "Tommy Leonard found the Eliot so he wouldn't be an orphan anymore. Alas and goddammit, that can no longer be said for the rest of us."

Guy Morse, race director of the Boston Marathon, thanked Tommy for adding "character, charisma and compassion" to Boston.

Bob Ryan of the *Boston Globe*, discussing the institutions of Boston, such as the Pops, the Swan boats and the Red Sox, acknowledged that Tommy represented Boston to the entire international running community. Reflecting that writers like Pierce, Gee, and himself would be thrilled to be big in Boston, he said, "Jesus, Tommy, you are big in Bisbane!"

Tommy's longtime friend Eddie Burke thanked him for "taking the best of everyone and making us better."

John Henning remarked that Tommy was "more than a character—he's an icon. The word "laughter" comes to mind. You laugh with him, you laugh at what he says, and you laugh at the people he brings in—the Stanford band, the horse...." He then commented, "Tonight, Tommy will be giving a demonstration on how to make a perfect Rob Roy, followed by a Brandy Alexander and an Old-Fashioned. Then he will autograph copies of his book, *Preparation of the Bar* (which elicited more raucous laughter), "which brings me to Doug Brown, who followed Tommy, checking on dirty glasses, making sure everything was cold, and serving as a great backdrop to Tommy's notions, motions, and legerdemain in the Eliot Lounge."

Eddie Doyle, who together with Tommy was responsible for raising thousands of dollars for charities, once paid a customer at the Eliot who was down on his luck $15 for the following poem he had written, which Eddie then read:

> When you walk into his bar
> He will greet you with a smile
> Be you workers dressed in overalls
> Or bankers dressed in style.

Be you Irish, English, Dutch, or French
It doesn't matter what
He'll treat you like a King or Queen,
Unless you prove you're not.

Should he sit down to read the "Running News"
Some fool with half a jag,
Pulls up a chair beside him
And begins to chew the rag.

Though Job they say had patience
A more patient man by far
Than Job could ever hope to be
Is the man behind the bar.

It matters not the aches and pains
The hardships he endures;
He doesn't tell you his troubles
Though you always tell him yours.

He deserves a lot of credit
For the way he stands the strain
For the bump he has to swallow
Would drive most of us insane

Tommy and the Eliot
Seem to go hand-in-hand
Especially that night when in marched
The entire Stanford band

Now I have quaffed a few beers in many a pub
And he's the best I've seen thus far
His charm, his wit, his welcoming smile,
This man behind the bar.

Eddie then handed Tommy a mounted piece of the Bull & Finch bar with "all the chili you spilled on it over the years." Accepting the gift, Tommy turned to the crowd who had been so genuinely thankful for the countless ways he had affected their lives and made his trademark remark: "It's the good life....I'm a man of few words. This is the greatest moment of my life and I've had many, many highlights and great moments."

Then, with the purity of heart and childlike innocence that everyone found so endearing in Tommy Leonard, he looked at the crowd and said, "If this is Heaven, I am going to be a good boy."

The Eliot Lounge closed its doors for the final time on September 30, 1996. As Tommy closed up the tavern, his friend Glenn McKinnon was with him. The only two people in the pub at the time, Glenn served Tommy the very last drink in the Eliot Lounge.

10

The Road Races

The Thrill of Victory

"Let the race begin and the dance to follow."

—Tommy Leonard

Tommy's visionary and starry-eyed creation of several road races combined with his passionate involvement and influence has led to the development of some of the nation's most successful road races. While bartending has been his profession, running and road racing have been his avocation, his signature, and a life-enriching force. Tommy's outlook on participating in a road race is that you are "going to a moving street party."

In the acknowledgments of Billy Rodgers's book *Marathoning*, written with Joe Concannon, Billy thanked Tommy, calling him "perhaps the most inspirational force in New England road racing."

John Stifler, columnist for the *Northampton Gazette* once wrote an article in his "On the Run" column titled "Cyber-evolution has no answer for Tommy Leonard." He wrote, "What Tommy does is immeasurable and irreproducible. There's no job description for it and his name does not appear on the master list of assignments. But whenever he shows up at a running event, the event is a success.

"A big part of his contribution is that he's very good at talking with and listening to people. At the Eliot Lounge, he met and greeted every runner, spectator, and journalist who walked in the door and they became friends.

"So, when he asks for a favor, they say yes."

Tommy has often been quoted as saying, "I've never met a long-distance runner I didn't like. They are all low-key happy people. I really believe if everybody ran, the crime rate in this country would be reduced about 60 percent."

Following is a summary of some of the road races that have benefited from the Tommy Leonard touch.

The Litchfield Hills Road Race

"The History of the Litchfield Hills Road Race"

—(written by and reproduced with permission of Brent Hawkins, "the Hawk")

The Litchfield Hills Road Race is more than a race. It is a homecoming, a reunion, a wedding of all people fast and slow, rich and poor, black and white. It was just a pipe dream of Litchfield-born, *Boston Globe* sportswriter Joe Concannon. He wanted to have a race in his beloved hometown of Litchfield, Connecticut, in order for his world-renowned marathoning friends in Boston to meet his life-long friends at home.

Joe was the lead writer for the *Boston Globe*'s coverage of the Boston Marathon. Through his writings and his interviews he made "fast" friends in more ways than one.

Concannon dearly wanted his running friends to come to Litchfield, but there really was no good reason for them to come, until he thought up the idea of having a race through the quiet colonial town. He approached his longtime friend Billy Neller with the idea. He imagined the Litchfield race patterned after the Falmouth Road Race, founded by yet another friend, Tommy Leonard.

Selectman Dave Skonieczy took the idea of the race before his fellow selectmen of Litchfield. He was all for it; however, there were some dissenting voices. If the selectmen said no to the race, then Litchfield would not have one. Concannon and Neller called upon the visionary Tommy Leonard, known as the "Guru of Running" and as "The Official Greeter of the Boston Marathon" among other titles.

Leonard promptly "wowed" the selectmen with his colorful prose. "The church bells will ring. There will be bands playing happy music. That cannon on the green will roar for the start of the race. The town will be packed with runners, friends, relatives, spectators, and curiosity seekers all dancing to the music until the sunshine wanes to a tangerine sunset!"

Tommy Leonard's smile lingered in the office of the selectmen like that of the Cheshire Cat. His speech won them over, and to their surprise, he was right! The Litchfield Hills Road Race was born in the mind of Joe Concannon and was nurtured by the care of Billy Neller, Tommy Leonard, and numerous members of the newly formed Road Race Committee. The coming-out party was on June 12, 1977, when Dennis Meltzer played *The Call to the Post* on his trumpet. Then promptly at 1:00 PM the First Litchfield Artillery fired the Civil War cannon, and the race and tradition began.

There were 234 runners in the first race. One of those entries was Concannon's friend, Billy Rodgers, the best distance runner in the world at the time. His victory literally put the Litchfield Hills Road Race on the runner's map. Now it is 2003, and the race is *limited* to 1,300 runners. It could easily be 13,000 if this little town could handle that many runners. It has become that popular.

The seven-mile race of Litchfield mirrored that of Falmouth, complete with downhill finishes to delight runners and spectators alike. Litchfield and Falmouth became "sister" races, with each town sending many representatives to the other's race. The same happened with races in Boston; the Boston Marathon and Freedom Trail races. Each race mingled friends from Europe, Africa, Asia, New Zealand, Ireland, England, and every state in the Union.

Litchfield grew in numbers and respect over the years. All this packed into one heck of a weekend celebration because a Litchfield boy wanted to invite his Boston friends to his hometown to meet and befriend some of the local characters. And Litchfield is full of characters and character. We can never thank you enough, Joe.

So when the time comes for the running of the Litchfield Hills Road Race, that special feeling overtakes the town and all the people in it. It is an indescribable "happy feeling" that everyone wishes would last all year long. Maybe it *is* some sort of extremely contagious runner's high that is passed on to everyone.

The Litchfield Hills Road Race is much more than a race. It is a special feeling of joy and friendship. To paraphrase Dorothy Gale from *The Wizard of Oz*, "There is no place like Litchfield!"

And there is "no race like Litchfield" either.

One of the unusual traditions of the road race committee is to throw a small pre-race party in the local cemetery to honor Joe Concannon (who died too young in 2000) and other departed local heroes. Bagpipers and a folk singer attend and the participants come with beer and whiskey in hand. They stop at each designated gravesite to make a few memorial comments. One year someone reverentially began to sing, "Schaeffer is the...one beer to have...," and everyone joined in, "...when you're having more than one."

In 2004, at the Cemetery Walk, one of Tommy's pals, Ed Pas of east Falmouth, placed a walkie-talkie under an Irish tweed cap like the one Joe always wore in front of Joe's gravestone. Someone suggested that Tommy say a few words, so he stepped forward. "Joe, you were one of my closest friends and one of the finest writers who've ever lived. You pushed running to a new level. I can't thank you enough. Here's to you, Joe Concannon!" As Tommy raised his glass, a voice from under the Irish cap said, "Tommy...Tommy" The astonished Leonard looked at the cap, exclaiming, "Holy Cow, Joe, is that *you*?" He nearly had a heart attack on the spot but enjoyed a good laugh when the gig was up.

As Ken Gartner pointed out in the Falmouth Track Club newsletter in 2003, Joe had laid out the course for the road race. It passes the cemetery twice, so each June more than 1,000 smiling faces pass him as they run down Gallows Hill at mile 1, and then more than 1,000 somewhat grimacing faces pass him as they struggle up Gallows Hill at mile 6.

The eclectic group of runners from Litchfield have a few other unique annual events. Easter is celebrated with an "Easter shot and beer hunt." Little 7-ounce beers are hidden throughout a designated yard, and participants are given baskets to go and hunt for their liquid treasures.

They unofficially "seceded" from the town and created their own little town so that they could give out proclamations and other official documents. One of their most popular events is the annual run across the "Tommy Leonard Bridge." Once a year, they hang a "Tommy Leonard Bridge" sign on an 18-foot-long bridge and have a run across it. The road is closed and an off-duty police cruiser leads the group. At the halfway mark, or 9 feet, they hold a beer stop. This run generally takes about two hours and is tremendously enjoyed by all who participate.

When the Litchfield Road Race began, Tommy once again used his friend-ships and influence to bring in Billy Rodgers and the talented runners from the Greater Boston Track Club, giving the race instant credibility.

When Joan Benoit accepted an invitation to run in the road race, Tommy enthusiastically said, "We need to show Joanie how much we appreciate her and make this a classy welcome since she is such a classy lady. Let's get a Win-nebago; we'll wear tuxedos and serve quiche when we pick her up at Bradley Airport."

So Billy Neller, Tommy, and three or four others from the race committee donned their tuxedos, put quiche in the oven of Dave Eisenhower's Win-nebago, and set off to Bradley. They chose to park in what Billy describes as a "quasi-illegal" spot so they could pick Joan up with some style.

Joan knew only Tommy among the tuxedoed entourage waiting excitedly, beer in hand, at the gate. As she approached the group, an announcement came over the loudspeaker: "Will the owner of the illegally parked Winnebago please return to your vehicle? It is on fire!"

After looking quickly at Tommy, the rest of the group turned and furiously darted back to the Winnebago. Unfazed, Tommy stretched out his hand to Joanie, saying "Geez, Joanie! Welcome to the beautiful state of Connecticut! How was your flight?" as if nothing unusual had occurred.

When the group reached the Winnebago, they discovered that the quiche had started to flame but was now only smoking. Everyone decided to have a beer before leaving, except Joanie, who was growing a bit leery of her traveling partners. As the vehicle pulled out of its spot and went through an underpass, the ladder ripped off. Once again, Tommy turned to Joanie and, with his eter-nal optimism, said, "Don't worry, Joanie. It's just a minor problem. We'll be fine in a few minutes." Joanie did trust Tommy, and about halfway back to Litchfield he convinced her to have a Bud Light, and she began to relax and enjoy her new friends.

In an article written by Gus Martins for the *Boston Globe*, Tommy calls Litchfield "New England's prettiest town...the race is not only accepted, but the entire town embraces it with a passion. The outpouring of affection is incredible. Every runner is put up in a private home, and that is unprece-dented."

On many occasions, the road race committee members would decide to jump into their cars in midweek and drive to the Eliot (160 miles away) to visit with Tommy for a few hours and then drive home. Sometimes they would relay-run, starting at their local pub and official race committee headquarters, the Village Restaurant. As they arrived, Tommy would announce, "The Litchfield runners are here! All the way from northwest Connecticut! Let's welcome them to our little pub!" The Eliot became a sort of "unofficial headquarters east" for these zany runners.

Billy Neller and Hawk both credit Tommy with being the conduit to many, many new friendships. Whether at the Millrose Games, the New York or Boston Marathon, Falmouth, Holyoke, Westfield, or elsewhere, they have always found themselves at terrific parties and meeting great people because of Tommy's connections in the running world.

Billy and his wife, Allie, like many others, have been guests at Tommy's bungalow in Falmouth. Unlike many others, they actually managed to sleep in his bed while Tommy slept on the couch, as they had expected to. Many folks have arrived at the bungalow upon Tommy's heartfelt invitation, only to find the entire living room strewn with bodies, pillows, and sleeping bags of people who thought they were going to sleep in Tommy's bedroom that night.

Billy recalls trying to tiptoe back into the bungalow with his wife well past midnight, only to step onto Tommy's Marine Corps area rug, which played a rendition of the Marine Corps Hymn whenever anyone stepped on it. Tommy jumped off the sofa, saying, "Hey guys! Have a beer with me!" Now rested, Tommy and Billy sat up chatting, drinking, and calling Tommy's California friends into the wee hours of the morning.

One of Litchfield's colorful characters, Brent Hawkins, DJ extraordinaire, King of Karaoke, Coach of Litchfield High girl's track and cross-country teams, and road race announcer beyond compare, recalls another invitation that Tommy once made from the heart. It was during a visit Tommy paid to Uniontown, Pennsylvania, Hawk's hometown. Hawk and Don Norman invited their favorite Irish bartender from Boston to be the Grand Marshal of the second annual Twilight 5K, being held in association with the town's Italian festival. It was the week of Tommy's fiftieth birthday, and he sprinted through the road race in his usual bar-side manner, making friends along the way.

That evening, the two main streets of Uniontown, Main and Beeson, were shut down for the Italian festival's food and craft booths. Hawk and Don invited Tommy to the stage set up at this intersection to say a few words.

Looking out into the crowd of 30,000-plus, Tommy said, "You know...I was in the Marines with people from Pennsy...and people from Pennsy are the greatest people in the world!" (Cheers and applause.) "I'm just a bartender from Boston. But if you come in the Eliot Lounge in Boston and tell me you are from Uniontown, Pennsylvania, your first beer is on me!"

Amidst the cheering and pandemonium that ensued, Tommy walked off the stage, saying, "I can't believe what I just said. But I meant it!"

The Holyoke Elks Talking Turkey 10K

Tommy has returned to the Tierney family for the holidays and the traditional Thanksgiving football game between Westfield and Cathedral for most of the years of his adult life. While traveling home in 1978, Tommy's simmering mind got to thinking how everyone is home for the holidays enjoying extra food and drink. It was the perfect weekend to promote a road race to work off the holiday imbibing and enjoy some running camaraderie.

Tommy spontaneously visited the press box the morning of the game and asked the announcer to invite runners to an informal run on Saturday morning. He also called the *Morning Union* sports department to see if he could get a plug for the run. He expected a small blurb but got a headline.

As Dick Osgood recorded in the *Springfield Sunday Republican* years later, Tommy said, "Just write that everyone is invited. Tell them to show up at the Tierney homestead on Old Holyoke Road in Westfield." And for good measure, Tommy added, "There will be free wine and cheese for the finishers!"

There was one small problem with Tommy's brilliant idea for a Thanksgiving road race. His spontaneity kept him from running the idea past his adoptive brother, Michael, and his wife, Robin, who lived at the home on Old Holyoke Road, which had just become the starting line as well as post-race reception hall of the new road race.

Thanksgiving dinner that year lacked the warmth that Tommy was accustomed to, as his invitation, though heartfelt, infuriated the family, and he endured their frosty silent treatment for quite a while.

About ten or fifteen runners did show up for the first road race and followed Tommy on an approximate 5-mile course he improvised through the streets of Westfield where he had run so often as a child.

The next year the race was moved to Ashley Reservoir in Holyoke when Tommy asked John Kane, former Holyoke High track coach, and the Holyoke Elks to get involved. The race drew eighty-three runners in its second year.

Tommy recalls looking out at the course on the morning of the race and realizing it was full of potholes. He thought of an old track buddy who ran the mile with him at Westfield High, Hank Lane. Hank now owned the nearby Lane Quarry. Although he had not seen him since 1952, Tommy called him, asking if he could bring over "some of that fine stone that looks like dust." Hank showed up with two trailer dumps of stone and another trailer with a front-end loader. "I'll never forget it," Tommy told Osgood of the *Sunday Republican*. "Hank was dressed in a three-piece suit and wingtip shoes. I guess he had somewhere to go. But he drove the bulldozer over and scraped the entire course. It was remarkable."

Tommy had tried to recruit a quarter horse, Poco-King-Rhoden, to set the pace for the 10K around the reservoir, but the environmentalists kicked up a storm and the idea was nixed. Tommy reluctantly agreed to have the pack led by a Jeep, which promptly got stuck in the mud early in the race. The race was won that year by Mark Duggan, a national Division III steeplechaser.

The course is actually a cross-country course through the woods, which Tommy once described to Joe Concannon in this way: "It's a pollution-free race. You'll be listening to a symphony of nature. You'll be running on pine needles. All you'll hear is the ripple of the reservoir and all you'll smell is the scent of hemlocks."

In its third year, Tommy talked Billy Harbilas, a former high school sprinter who later became a marathoner, into directing the Thanksgiving road race. Billy had just finished the New York City Marathon and was walking in Central Park with 18,000 runners and spectators, when he looked up to see Tommy Leonard walking toward him with a cooler of beer. "So we were sitting on a park bench having a couple of beers," said Harbilas, "and Tommy began telling me how he started this informal little race in Westfield during the Thanksgiving break."

Billy, who has completed thirteen Boston and four New York City marathons, has been the race director of the Holyoke Elks Talking Turkey 10K ever since. He has created a class event with the assistance of seventy-five to eighty volunteers from the Elks, who are very dedicated to the race's annual success.

They cook up pounds and pounds of ziti, clam chowder, and other dishes for the post-race celebration, and then throw quite an evening party complete with band and dancing. One year, a bridge covering a 40-foot span along the course was out and some of the Elks built a new bridge the day before the race. An ice storm once covered the course, and Skip Clayton plowed the entire course with his Jeep.

The race has grown into a favorite annual event for many families, drawing runners from as far away as California and the Virgin Islands. For several years, the race was capped at 750 to 775 runners. Most of the participants and their families want to go to the post-race party at the Elks Lodge, which has limited capacity. They have upped the numbers in recent years and have been able to accommodate between 1,100 and 1,200 runners. It remains a highly successful and much anticipated annual event.

Although it is primarily a fun, family-oriented event, it does bring in some decent competition. There are usually 60 or 70 runners who complete the course under 40 minutes. Brent Coon holds the course record at 30:37, and Nancy Conz holds the women's record at 35:01.

Holyoke St. Patrick's Day Road Race

It was 1975, and Tommy's adoptive brother, Michael Tierney, was serving his first year as a member of the Holyoke St. Patrick's Day Parade Committee. It was also a period of growing interest in running and fitness in general.

Tommy and Michael, along with friends Paul Lunney and Dr. Fran Baker, a podiatrist, went before the Parade Committee to try to sell them on the idea of having a road race to enhance the annual St. Patrick's festivities. The committee, at the time, was quite content to focus on the parade.

Tierney credits Dr. Baker with having the most influence on a number of the older committee members and eliciting the support they needed to put on a road race. The first race had 197 runners, and the organizers remember barely pulling it off. Then John Kane, the former cross-country and track coach at Holyoke High and then the Associate Athletic Director for Operations at Boston College, joined the committee in time to give the 1976 race stability.

Michael told Dick Osgood of the *Union News*, "Myself, Tommy, Doc Baker, and Lunney were nothing more than promoters. It was Kane who gave us a person with technical knowledge on the dos and don'ts when it comes to putting on a road race the size of ours. It's a lot of work.

"What we started with was an insurance man (Tierney), a foot doctor (Baker), a bartender (Leonard), and a steamfitter (Lunney)," said Tierney. "But in Kane we finally got someone who knew what actually had to be done."

The 1976 road race was called the Bill Keating Spirit of '76 Road Race, commemorating both the former *Holyoke Transcript-Telegram* sports editor Keating's seventy-sixth birthday and the nation's bicentennial. It was a 7.6-

mile course; the distance would be adjusted between 7.5 and 8.3 miles until 1986, when the committee settled on a certified 10K course.

Over the years, Tommy used his promotional skills and drum beating to bring in such world-class runners as Billy Rodgers (who won in 1975, 1976, and 1977) as well as Olympian Frank Shorter, Gary Bjorklund, Mike Slack, and Irish star athletes, many of whom hailed from Providence College, such as John and Ray Treacy, Jimmy Fallon, Mick O'Shea, Paul Maloney, Brendan Quinn, Andy Ronan, John Doherty, Richard Mulligan, and Randy Thomas. World-class runners who have competed over the years include Charlotte Lettis, Nancy Conz, Janice Cataldo, Lisa Welch, Leslie Lehane, and Geraldine Hendricken.

John Treacy commented on running the race: "This race came at an ideal time. It's a great course—a miniature Boston. There were a lot of people out there considering the weather. I guess this town goes crazy for St. Patrick's Day."

Today the Holyoke St. Patrick's Day Road Race is the largest race in western Massachusetts, with over 2,000 runners. It celebrated its thirtieth anniversary in 2005. It is held the Saturday before the famous St. Patrick's Day Parade in Holyoke and brings much celebration and business to the city. Michael Tierney and Mike Zwirko are now co-chairpersons of the race, and John Kane is the director.

The Nantucket 10-Miler

In the early 1970s, the late Del Wynn was running 4- or 5-milers regularly. He read in the *Boston Phoenix* that Tommy Leonard was the contact person for the Falmouth Road Race, so Del called Tommy, explaining that he was calling from Nantucket. Tommy immediately started to wax poetic about the beauty of Nantucket and how "even the birds sing prettier on the island." Once Del met Tommy, he would say, "I realized he was one of the most extraordinary people I would ever meet. Tommy was born with a smile on his face, and his goal in life is to infect everyone else with that smile."

Del told Tommy he was interested in starting a road race on Nantucket, and Tommy offered to help in any way he could. Tommy brought in his friends from the Greater Boston Track Club to run and a "special surprise" for the first Columbus Day 10-Mile Road Race on Nantucket in 1976. The weather was fierce, with piercing wind and rain. The "special surprise" turned out to be "old" Johnny Kelley, who said he "felt like he was running in place for 10 miles, the winds were so strong."

In Tommy's treasure trove of letters from friends and fans around the globe is a letter from the 1976 winner, GBTC runner Mark Duggan. He comments, "Let me say that you continue to amaze me with your unceasing dedication and devotion to fellow runners. I have never been treated as good as in the races you have promoted. The Nantucket race was the ultimate....Not only was the race successful from the runners' viewpoint, but you could see the success in the eyes of the people of the island.

"The biggest thing I got from the weekend was not that I won the race, although that was a tremendous award, but the friendship I experienced and developed through you and your friends."

Del would later be sitting in the Eliot next to George Kimball of the *Herald,* and he told him he understood why Tommy was called the "Guru" of New England road racing. "Everybody laughs at that, but when I asked him for help in putting together a road race after reading what he had done at Falmouth, he gave me all the help in the world. I needed to make it a success. I looked it up, and 'guru' in Sanskrit means 'one who points the way.' That is Tommy."

Del recalled one year when Tommy got so caught up in the pre-race planning and parties that he exhausted himself before the race. About one mile into the race, Tommy noticed an appealing thicket by the side of the road, and he crawled in for a power nap. Later in the race, Del watched as Tommy went flying past, and he finished ahead, nap and all!

Tommy was an usher for Del's wedding on August 4, 1984. This was the day of Joan Benoit's gold medal win in the inaugural women's Olympic Marathon. Several of the guests were staying at the lovely Anchor Inn. The third floor of the inn was being used by the owner's kids and had the atmosphere of a college rental house. After the wedding, there were wall-to-wall people sleeping on the floor, so Tommy made up a bed in the bathtub and slept there all night.

Del and the owners of the inn wrote up the following proclamation on the inn's letterhead:

PROCLAMATION

Not to be outdone by the City of Boston, we the members of the Anchor Inn Society do hereby resolve that Tommy Leonard, beloved friend, in recognition of his flowering show of kindness, his buoyancy to the sinking spirits of others, and his flush of generosity, not to mention that he has slept in our bathtub, is forthwith honored by this Society by having the third-floor john at the Anchor Inn, Nantucket Island, Massachusetts, known from this day forward as the "TOMMY LEONARD MEMORIAL* BATHROOM."

*You don't have to go to be remembered.

Del Wynn succumbed to Lou Gehrig's disease in the summer of 2004, never having had the opportunity to read this book about his beloved friend, which he had so looked forward to reading.

The Westfield Road Race

For many years, Tommy thought about starting a road race in Westfield to give back to the community in which he'd grown up and to benefit the Westfield High School track and field program, which had always remained close to his heart.

In 1993 Tommy decided it was time to do something about his dream before his "big road race in the sky." So he began to talk up his vision of what the race could be and elicited help from friends and family from Boston and the Cape, Holyoke, and the Berkshires.

Tommy wanted to create a fun, informal race that friends and family could enjoy. He also wanted to create an event that would pay tribute to and celebrate the various ethnic groups that helped to "make Westfield the great city that it is...and put the Whip City on the running map."

For almost a decade the Westfield 5K was held, each year honoring a different ethnic group from the city. The first race was held on Mother's Day, May 9, 1993. The start and finish of the flat course was at the Air National Guard's 104th Tactical Fighter Group base at Barnes Municipal Airport. The runners finished on the runway under a banner that was strewn between two A-10 fighter jets.

Tommy acquired donations of Sam Adams beer from the Boston Beer Company and got them to sponsor the event, paying for the T-shirts, race numbers, and banners. His friend Arthur Campagna of Seafood Rich donated 300 pounds of swordfish, and Trio's, the gourmet pasta company, donated tons of tortellini salad. Poland Springs supplied water and merchandise for the runners. Tommy's foster brother, Michael, and cousin, Jimmy Tierney, were recruited to take charge of the picnic lunch. Each year, the gourmet picnics were available to spectators with advance purchase, in addition to the runners.

All kinds of prizes were solicited, ranging from Irish crystal to tickets to a Boston College football game. "There's an endless list of folks who are helping out. Everyone's being overly generous," Tommy said. When asked why, he replied, "I don't know. Maybe I gave them a beer once in awhile."

U.S. Olympic bronze medalist in the 10,000-meter, Lynn Jennings, agreed to run in the first Westfield 5K in exchange for a beer, giving Tommy a huge thrill. In February 1994, *Runner's World* mentioned the Westfield 5K as one of the races Jennings had completed in 1993.

The Italian community was honored that first year, and over 200 runners participated. The money raised went to BOOST (Boost Our Outstanding Sports Tradition), the fund raising group for city school sports.

The 1994 race honored the Polish community and drew close to 400 runners. A Tiny Tot Trot of 1K was added, and all the kids were given the number 1 to wear. Members of the Polish Women's Alliance cooked the post-race meal of golumki, lazy pierogi, kielbasa, and rye bread.

Members of the Dozynki dancers from St. Joseph's Polish National Catholic Church were recruited to perform, wearing flower wreaths on their heads and beaded vests and flower-patterned skirts. The girls ranged from nursery to college age. Although they perform frequently at festivals and other Polish National Churches, they considered performing at the road race a special honor since it was a tribute to the Polish community in their own city.

By the second year, sponsors included Nike, Poland Spring, Sam Adams, Stanhome, WNNZ, SportsSmith, Westfield Savings Bank, and the 104th Fighter Group.

Among the athletes competing in the second road race were two-time Boston Marathon winner Geoff Smith and State Representative Michael Knapek of Westfield. Proceeds of the race went into the Tommy Leonard Scholarship Fund for the three high schools in Westfield: St. Mary's, Westfield High, and Westfield Vocational Tech.

The third road race honored the town's Irish community. Art Campagna donated 300 pounds of salmon filets to be served with potatoes O'Brien and broccoli. Irish dancers and music entertained the crowd. The vice principal of

Westfield Middle School, Janet Larese, recruited scores of teens to volunteer and help with the community event.

In 1996 Hispanic Americans were honored at the post-race festivities. Ballet Folklore International performed Puerto Rican and Caribbean folk music and dancing. Rafael Fernandez of the Fernandez Family Restaurant in Holyoke presented a picnic of banana salad, marinated pork shoulder, and Spanish rice to a background of salsa music.

The theme of the 1997 Westfield Road Race was All-American. Jimmy Tierney cooked up pounds of hamburgers and hot dogs. The race was moved from May to September, and three categories of competition were added, giving special awards to finishers from the Sons of Erin, Westfield Air National Guard, and Westfield State College.

The eighth Westfield Road Race was run in September 2000. It was run entirely on the airport grounds at Barnes. The race never grew to 500 runners, yet the participants and volunteers who loved the community spirit that the race elicited enjoyed it enormously. Quite a few young runners from the local high schools have benefited from the scholarship money they received from the race.

Scheduled for September 2001, the ninth race never occurred, as the tragic attack of September 11 on the World Trade Center and the Pentagon changed security in this country forever, and the air base could no longer be used. Thus, the Westfield Road Race met its demise due to the 9/11 tragedies.

Tommy was influential in assisting a number of other races to get off the ground, including the GBTC Freedom Trail Classic and the Riverside Park 5 miler.

The Falmouth Road Race

The jewel in the crown, the race that would grow to become one of the most well-known races around the globe, the race that was born and nurtured through Tommy's inspiration and determination, is the Falmouth Road Race. Although it was actually the first road race that Tommy started, there is so much to say about the Falmouth Road Race that it has been left as the final race in this chapter.

The inspiration for the Falmouth Road Race actually began while Tommy was bartending at the Brothers Four in Falmouth Heights in 1972. The Olympic Marathon in Munich, Germany, was on TV, and out of principle, Tommy refused to pour a drink or ring the register until Frank Shorter crossed the finish line, thus becoming the first American in sixty-four years to win the gold medal in the Olympic Marathon. George Robbat, owner of the Brothers Four, told Amby Burfoot in 1978 in an interview for *Runner's World* that he could see the humor in being a dry bar. "I didn't mind. Nobody minded. We were happy having such a good time watching Tommy. Shorter wasn't nearly as interesting. Tommy can put on an incredible show when he's excited, and was he ever! Watching, analyzing, empathizing, so involved."

Tommy does have a tendency to get excited and to identify with the athletes he admires. Brent Hawkins of Litchfield once watched Mary Decker in the World Cup Track and Field Competition with Tommy. As the race came to a finish, Tommy had sweat on his brow and his face was bright red. Grabbing his heart with both hands, he said through his twinkling and inspired eyes, "Boy, that race took it all out of me!"

Shortly after Shorter's win in the Olympic Marathon, Tommy came off a busy night at the Brothers Four. Several years later, he would tell Toni Reavis, who was writing a running column for the *Boston Herald*, "I was sitting in the bar with my feet up on a chair having a cold one. I'm looking out over Martha's Vineyard Sound. The sound was shimmering under the moonlight. In the background, there was a little Roberta Flack softly singing, *The First Time Ever I Saw Your Face*. I was with Captain Red Kavanaugh of the Captain Kidd Restaurant, and it all came into being.

"I'm a little bit of a romantic. With all this background I said I'd really like to do something for the Falmouth Track Club. And I began putting it all together. The conception was right there at the Brothers Four."

Falmouth had hired its first recreation director in the spring of 1973, Rich Sherman. Rich had just acquired his master's from Springfield College after a three-year stint in the Navy. Rich had run the Boston Marathon that year, and Tommy heard that he was a runner. So Tommy walked into the old recreation center, introduced himself, and welcomed Rich as the new recreation director.

Tommy told Rich he was thinking of having a road race, and Rich classified that as a recreation program, so he let Tommy know he'd be happy to help in any way he could.

Entry forms were available at the recreation center, and Rich provided some help but recalls that the first year Tommy pretty much organized everything.

Tommy also went to John Carroll, coach of the Falmouth Track Club and Falmouth High School track team, and asked if he could help put on a road race. Joe Concannon recorded Carroll's response in the *Globe*: "Sure. How many do you expect? 50? 100? I'd been race director for track meets with 400, 500, and 800 people." John served as starter, timer, and finish-line judge with the assistance of his wife, Lucia.

The first "Woods Hole to Falmouth Road Race" was scheduled for Wednesday, August 15, 1973, which was Tommy's fortieth birthday. Rich remembers it as being a celebration and birthday party that happened to incorporate a road race

The race would begin in front of one of Tommy's favorite watering holes, the Captain Kidd in Woods Hole, near the drawbridge on Water Street, and followed a strikingly beautiful course past the Nobska Lighthouse and Vineyard Sound, ending 7 miles later in front of another of his favorite watering holes, the Brothers Four, where he worked.

McDonald's had donated a double-decker bus to take the runners out to Woods Hole, but Tommy objected to the cigarette ads on the bus and refused to use it until the ads were removed. Captain Red Kavanaugh, who was the chef at the Captain Kidd, prepared a huge tub of clam chowder at Tommy's request. Red said, "Tommy felt Boston gave beef stew, we ought to have clam chowder, so I mixed 85 gallons, just in case we ran short."

The weather was like a baby monsoon on the 15th of August, with fierce winds and piercing rain. Tommy managed to miss the bus to the start and nearly missed the race itself. George Robbat gave him a ride toward Woods Hole, but the car stalled halfway there. They thumbed a ride in an already overcrowded Volkswagen, barely arriving for the start of the race.

Ninety-eight runners, many bartenders, waitresses, and locals, showed up for the start of the race, wearing numbers donated by Don Facey's printing business. Tommy finished thirteenth in 46:18, and "old" Johnny Kelley, age 65, finished seventeenth at in 47:30. The winner was a college senior at Central Michigan University, Dave Duba, who had only heard about the race the day before. He finished in 39:16, his first win in distance running. The first woman was Jenny Taylor of Cambridge, Massachusetts, who was fifteenth overall and finished in 47:23.

There were small clusters of cars along the route with people inside offering cheers and applause to the rain-soaked runners. Selectman John DeMello presented Duba with his laurel wreath and 36-inch trophy at the finish.

Although ninety-two runners finished the race, several hundred packed into the Brothers Four for the post-race party, which went to 1 o'clock in the morning. Tommy had gotten a banjo band, and runners feasted on warm Schlitz beer, bologna sandwiches, and Captain Red's Clam Chowder.

Tommy, beer in hand, was ecstatic and exuberant as everyone sang *Happy Birthday* to him. He grabbed a cigar box and raised $473 for the Falmouth Track Club.

"I can still remember Johnny Kelley jitterbugging with his wife. Not too many made it to work the next day. It wasn't the race that did them in, it was the boogie," Tommy would tell Kenny Gartner of the *Falmouth Enterprise*. "Everyone was singing *I Believe in Music*. Geez, it was beautiful." Tommy says, "Life is too short. There are too many takers and not enough givers. I wanted to be a giver and wanted to start something that promoted fitness and physical exercise."

In the second year of the race, Tommy began to solicit the town's merchants for donations to be given as prizes to the runners, and it became a very focused function for him. Tommy pushed an old cart down Main Street going from business to business. Most were supportive, although Steve Hamel, one of the early runners, told Ken Gartner that he felt many store owners weren't sure whether Tommy was a homeless man, a carpetbagger, or a race director.

Tommy remembers Eleanor Smith, owner of 'Malchmans' clothing store, initially turning him down, saying she was always being solicited. Then she chased him down the street with a handbag for the first female finisher. She even bought an entry to the race for $2, although she had no intention of running. She told Gartner, "I just thought it would be a good thing for Falmouth. I don't imagine it's easy to go in cold with something new and persuade somebody. He was very enthusiastic; a dynamo."

Runners would draw for their prizes in the early days, long before the appearance of prize money. Tommy would get dinners for two, toasters, rain slickers, and fishing poles. Dick Stone, owner of the local barbershop, gave a free haircut and recalls that a bald guy happened to draw it. Years later, Frank Shorter would humorously paraphrase Amby Burfoot, saying, "In those days you ran (Falmouth) to outfit your kitchen. You'd win a toaster, a blender...."

In 1974 Tommy recruited Marty Liquori, one of the best milers and 1,500-meter runners in the country in the early 1970s, to run Falmouth through his friendship with Marty's brother, Steve. A quiet, unassuming, relatively unknown conscientious objector and Boston College graduate, Billy Rodgers, beat Liquori in 34:16. This was eight months before "Boston Billy's" first win in the Boston Marathon and his first real ink on the running circuit. Several members of the Greater Boston Track Club ran the 1974 race, including Randy Thomas, Bobby Hodge, Vinnie Fleming, and Greg Meyer. When

Marty arrived at the awards ceremony to pick up his second-place award, Tommy had already given away all the prizes.

Rodgers told Jack Perry of the *Cape Cod Times*, "I remember Tommy telling me about this new race. He was using all sorts of wild embellishments. They all turned out to be true. Said there'd be girls in bikinis handing out water....That guy could promote a race on the moon. It's still one of the most beautiful courses in the country."

Tommy predicted early on that the race would be a big event, telling Joe Concannon, "If I don't get 5,000 runners for the Falmouth Road Race, I'll do a swan dive off the Bourne Bridge." Rich Sherman recalls that no one could really see it getting that big, but when over 400 runners showed up the second year, they began to think that Tommy was on to something.

The Brothers Four had a mileage chart on the wall with over 30 jogger-drinkers recording their daily and weekly mileage for seven weeks prior to the race. Four hundred and forty five runners registered for the second road race, which was fairly large by 1974 standards. The runners in the 1974 race ranged in age from five years old to seventy-five. The weather was hot and humid. Twenty-three of the finishers beat Dave Duba's winning time of the year before. Tommy would tell Joe Concannon, "For one solid year, I slept, ate, and drank this race. It's the greatest day of my life. People from all over came up to me and said they've run all over the world and they never received treatment like this. It wasn't me. It was everyone here."

Tommy put together the original VIP gatherings at the Oar 'n Anchor on Main Street, now a Peking Restaurant. It was owned by Billy Crowley and holds many happy memories of fun times together for Rodgers, Shorter, the GBTC, Tommy, Rich Sherman, John Carroll, and others.

Billy Crowley, who also owned the Captain Kidd, put up Billy Rodgers at his home that year. This was the start of a tradition of local families hosting elite runners, which continues to this day, with over seventy families volunteering to host the runners. Billy won a Waring blender in his first Falmouth victory and had his car towed, although the town did rescind his ticket when they discovered who he was.

Back in 1972, while watching Frank Shorter win his Olympic gold, Tommy had reflected, "Wouldn't it be great if we could get Frank Shorter to run in a race on Cape Cod?" Of course, no one thought it was really possible, but by 1975, Tommy had chased Shorter around the globe with phone calls and recruited him, through his friendship with Rodgers, to run in the third

Falmouth Road Race. "I was tired of people doubting my abilities," Leonard would say.

Frank Shorter, running in a McSorley's Ale singlet, defeated Billy Rodgers and 850 other runners in 1975 and set a new course record of 33:24. Tommy's dream of bringing Olympians, especially Frank Shorter, to Falmouth became reality in three short years. Rodgers and Shorter quickly put the Falmouth Road Race on the national radar for top-quality races.

Tommy recalls being so pumped up about the race that when he ran the Mt. Washington Road Race in 1976, he spent the entire race going from runner to runner, encouraging them to come to the Falmouth Road Race. Mt. Washington is a 7.6-mile footrace up the Mt. Washington Auto Road to the summit at 6,288 feet. Tommy had traveled to the race with Bobby Hodge and Vinnie Fleming. The conditions at the start were somewhat humid and about 64 degrees, but as they climbed above the tree line, hailstones began to fall, the winds grew fierce, and there was no level ground for secure footing. As Tommy promoted his race to every runner he passed, someone finally said, "Leonard, why don't you shut up and you'll probably get more people to come to your race?" Bobby Hodge won the climb to the summit, one of seven victories on the mountain between 1976 and 1987.

In 1976 Tommy secured Perrier as the first major sponsor of the Falmouth Road Race. Putting on his best pair of slacks and a sports coat (i.e., wrinkled khakis with pizza stains and a blue blazer with two buttons missing), Tommy boarded the shuttle to New York City to meet with Perrier CEO Bruce Nevins. As he sailed into his soliloquy in the boardroom about the beauty of running in the road race and the 35,000 spectators offering cups and hoses to the runners, Nevins cut him off, saying, "Enough, I'm sold." Nevins handed Tommy a check for $5,000.

"Holy Cow! That was the happiest day of my life," Tommy would once again claim. (T.L.'s happiest days last only twenty-four hours, until he moves on to the next happiest day.) "I didn't know what to do, so I ran across the street to PJ Clark's and had a burger and beer. Then I flew home."

In 1975 the finish line of the race had been moved from the crest of Grand Avenue, in front of the Brothers Four, to the bottom of the hill by the ball field opposite the flagpole. Shorter and Rodgers both returned to Falmouth in 1976 along with 2,090 other runners. The race's notoriety was certainly growing, and back-of-the-pack runners saw this as an opportunity to actually compete alongside the world's top athletes. Frank had just won the silver medal at the Montreal Olympics, and Rodgers had established himself as one of the best marathoners in the country. Once again, Shorter won the 1976 race, setting another course record of 33:13. Joan Benoit of Cape Elizabeth, Maine, took the women's title with a course record of 43:08. This would be the first of six crowns Joanie would win at Falmouth.

The field in 1976 included three former Boston Marathon winners (Rodgers, Burfoot, and Johnny Kelley) in addition to Olympic gold and silver medalist Shorter. No fewer than ten runners were within two minutes of Shorter's course record time.

Rich Sherman ran in the Falmouth Road Race from 1973 through 1976. Then in 1976, the crowds stopped him 150 yards from the finish. "There was no real organized system to process the runners, and we had grown so fast we didn't have sufficient awareness of what a challenge this would be. I decided I wouldn't run this race again. I would try to help get a better-managed finish line."

The race was growing at an enormous rate. Race organizers Sherman and Carroll began to think about having medical technicians stationed in the crowd with ice, fluids, oxygen, and ambulances. After the finish-line chaos and lack of coordination in 1976, Rich suggested they give finishing times to the first 500, and the rest of the runners could be given index cards with their order of finish, which they would then take to a recorder. At the time, three or four runners were finishing per second and there was no technology yet to record those times.

Since the participant numbers were more than doubling each year, they considered capping the race at 2,000, worried that in the following year there could be 4,000 runners.

Community support for the race had also grown exponentially. Entire committees now solicited the merchandise prizes from seventy businesses, and over two dozen trophies were given to the winners in different categories. The spectator crowds were now estimated at 50,000 people watching the race on the roads and rooftops and from boats along the shore.

Rodgers brought one of the first charities to the Falmouth Road Race as a representative of the "Athletes vs. MS" committee. He requested permission from the race organizers to write to runners asking them to find sponsors to raise money to help in the fight against multiple sclerosis. Sherman, Carroll, and Tommy all signed the letter, which went out to the registered runners.

In 1977 Rich Sherman left the Recreation Department and took a job as a first-grade teacher, but chose to continue co-directing the road race with his wife, Kathleen, and John and Lucia Carroll.

There were now 3,500 runners, including a vastly talented field, and huge interest from the media. Channel 7's Bob Gamere, Boston College's Sports Info Director Reid Oslin, the *Christian Science Monitor*'s sports editor Larry Eldridge, UPI sports scribe Gil Peters, the *Globe*'s Joe Concannon, and *Springfield Union*'s Dick Osgood were all present to witness the race, now considered a world-class event.

Alberto Salazar chased Billy Rodgers for 6 miles before Rodgers shattered Shorter's course record by 50 seconds, running 32:23. In seven years, there were seven new course records set. Kim Merritt took 4 minutes off of Joan Benoit's record, set the previous year. This was the first year that a runner from Kenya would participate in the event, Hillary Tuwei, finishing sixth at 33:07. 1977 also saw the first wheelchair competition, with Bob Hall of Belmont, Massachusetts, winning his first of six victories.

Toni Reavis interviewed many runners after the race for his *Runner's Digest* radio program in Boston and said, "The spirit is the thing that counts. Of all the people I interviewed the most common words were 'unbelievable,' 'fantastic,' 'never better.'...I concur wholeheartedly."

George Kimball wrote an article, "Guru on Tap" for the 1977 New York City Marathon program, in which he quoted Tommy as saying, "When the phone calls start coming in so heavily that I can't wait on customers and I have to start telling people there's no more room in the race, I start thinking what a monster this whole thing has turned into and I don't want any part of it.

"Then I get to Falmouth and I see everyone working so hard and thousands of runners there and WOW! I mean, I see everyone so happy and geez, it's beautiful. It's the most wonderful feeling in the world."

"Give Tommy Leonard all the credit," insists race co-director John Carroll. "After all, this was his fantasy."

"Not really," corrects George Robbat. "A fantasy is something you conjure up in your imagination. This isn't fantasy. Tommy made his dream come true."

The Falmouth Road Race had become so popular that the 1978 registrations closed nineteen days after the entries were mailed out. Some runners even drove down from Maine to ensure that their entries were received. "Number wanted" signs began to show up at the recreation center, with requests coming from as far away as California.

Four thousand runners woke on the day of the 1978 race to find conditions very hot and humid. Seventeen runners would end up in the hospital with heat prostration, dehydration, and shock, including Alberto Salazar, whose body temperature of 108 degrees at the finish line induced the medical volunteers to quickly put him in a tub of ice before sending him to Falmouth Hospital.

The 1978 field included thirteen sub–4-minute milers, sixteen individual NCAA and AAU champions, and nine Olympians. Despite the heat, Billy Rodgers set a new course record of 32:21. Tommy would say, "Billy Rodgers took on the strongest field of runners you could gather, from 1500-meter men to steeplechasers to marathoners. And he put them in his back pocket and he destroyed them."

Besides Salazar, who finished tenth, the top ten included Mike Roche, Craig Virgin (who flew in overnight from Belgium to run the race), Mike Slack, Greg Fredericks, Hillary Tuweii of Kenya (who finished sixth for the second year in a row), Bruce Bickford, Bobby Hodge, and Greg Meyer.

Of the weather, Rodgers would say, "It was just awful. It was just damned unpleasant." Nevertheless, he sat in the ball field after the race for an hour and a half holding court for the press and signing autographs for fans.

Amby Burfoot, Rodger's former college roommate and his colleague as a former winner of the Boston Marathon, ran the race for *Runner's World*. He wrote an article titled "The Race to Decide the King of the Road," in which he said, "Judging by the excellence of the world-class field, Falmouth has become probably the most important non-marathon road race in the country."

Kenny Moore ran the race for *Sports Illustrated* and wrote an article in which he called the 1978 race "the best-organized race of this size I have ever seen."

The *Boston Globe* and Perrier both had photographer helicopters hovering above the road race; the *Boston Herald American* gave the race two front-page stories, and two Boston TV stations covered it.

Perrier offered a trip to France for two to be chosen in a drawing limited to those who finished the race *and* completed their post-race cards. This probably inspired quite a few people to finish the race despite the heat.

Tommy veered off course near the Brothers Four (about 200 yards from the finish line) to avoid the ovation that undoubtedly would meet him as he crossed the finish. He'd say, "I just couldn't deal with all those people. It was just too great a day for stuff like that."

In 1979 the weather gave the runners a break, with a light rain falling. Five thousand runners now participated in the road race, and Tommy no longer had to be concerned with his promise to "do a swan dive off the Bourne Bridge." Craig Virgin set a new course record of 32:19 and Ellison Goodall set a women's course record of 38:14.

In 1980 the road race truly went international, with Rod Dixon of New Zealand and Grete Waitz of Norway taking the winner's titles. Grete, who at the time was the most dominant long-distance female in the world, set a new course record and became the first woman to run under 38:00 with a time of 37:12. Lorraine Moeller of New Zealand and Jacqueline Gareau of Canada both finished in the top ten, giving the women's field true international status. Dave Duba, winner of the very first race in 1973, returned and marveled at the growth of the race. And world middleweight boxing champion "Marvelous" Marvin Hagler ran the race in sweat pants and heavy construction boots.

The *Falmouth Enterprise* published a special road race supplement with the names of all the runners, details on the top contenders, photos from the 1979 race, an article on where the money that is raised goes, and a history of the race itself.

The race organizers limited the entries to 4,000 since the previous year's 5,000 runners were somewhat difficult to manage. Temperatures were moderate, humidity was low, the sun shone, and the race went off without a hitch.

Dr. Arthur Crago and Dr. Richard Adams supervised a volunteer medical team of thirty physicians, twenty-five nurses and paramedics, and more than fifteen EMTs stationed at eleven checkpoints along the course. The medical teams were prepared for everything from heart attacks to heat-related injuries. The Army National Guard provided tents as field hospitals and two ambulances along the course. Two more ambulances were at the finish line and town ambulances were on alert. Falmouth's amateur radio club provided communications between the field hospitals.

Bill Dougherty, owner of Road Race Caterers, volunteered his services as race food director for the first twelve years of the race, taking responsibility for the Friday night spaghetti feed for 4,000 as well as the post-race picnic, which served 12,000 people in 1980. He never accepted money for his work at the road race, saying, "Falmouth has built my business. It is my hometown. I love it." For the last twenty years race co-director Kathleen Sherman has taken full responsibility for the management of the pasta supper, volunteer parties, and the post-race picnic.

The men's club and the Falmouth Track Club provided the manpower to serve the food at these two events. The pasta supper includes music and entertainment. In 1980 Perrier donated 30,000 bottles of water, Dannon provided 12,000 cups of yogurt, and over 10,000 hot dogs, rolls, chips, and watermelons were prepared for the picnic.

Perrier donated $25,000 to the 1980 road race. Adidas put on the pasta supper, flew in its national team of thirty-six runners, took care of the prize structure, and gave out 500 T-shirts and hats to race officials. Tommy would reflect, "Isn't it funny that the Great American Road Race is sponsored by a French fizz and a German shoe company?"

At the time, talks were just beginning about prize money in open road race competition. John Carroll told Joe Concannon, "I think it is going to come about but I don't know if we'll be part of it. We're well established as a race. Whether or not the prize money would be a draw, I don't know. I don't know if the town fathers would be as responsive to the race if it was run for pay. It's a good concept. I just don't know where we will fit in."

Just as Tommy had dreamt in 1972, proceeds of the race, after paying for all the expenses, went to the Falmouth Track Club. Many runners have been sent to the National Junior Olympics as well as other championship meets across the nation and in Canada. Over the past decade, proceeds have been donated to a wide variety of local sports teams and nonprofit groups.

In addition to the pasta supper and post-race picnic, there was now a question-and-answer clinic with some of the top runners on Saturday evening, a showing of the 1978 race film *Falmouth, the Great American Road Race*, and a Sunday morning non-sectarian prayer service before the race.

The 1980 race went so smoothly that co-director John Carroll said, "Everything was very, very positive. After the race, we could have skipped out for coffee and donuts, and everything would have come off just fine. It was all made possible by volunteers. There was so much enthusiasm. We had people call and say, 'I can't run. Can I help out?'"

Tommy spewed accolades everywhere and said, "I can't say enough about Rich and John. Their efforts are what makes Falmouth the class event that it is." Rich and John and their wives, Kathleen and Lucia, have been the co-directors of the race since its inception. Race day for them starts at 4 AM and doesn't end until after 6 PM. The day after the race is also consumed with returning items that were used for the race.

In an interview for the *Falmouth Enterprise* Road Race Supplement, Kathleen reflected, "I think the feeling I like best is after the race, when we receive letters from spectators and runners alike. It gives us a sense of pride to know that all our hard work and efforts are appreciated.

"If all the Falmouth people who oppose this race (due to the influx of crowds into the town) were to read the post-race mail, they would see what a good name Falmouth is getting for it. It's a wonderful method of free advertising." A teacher by profession, Kathleen would be named Massachusetts Teacher of the Year in 1996, and she enjoyed a visit to the Oval Office at the White House to meet the President for this honor.

By 1980 the Falmouth Road Race had become quite an annual event for friends and families and had taken on a "class reunion" feeling, with people looking forward to the annual picnics and parties. Many spectators faithfully spray their water hoses at the runners and work the water stations set up along the course.

Charlie Pierce wrote a 1980 article for the *Boston Phoenix* titled "Watch on the Brine: Observations on the Sport of Observing Falmouth," in which he noted that Falmouth had developed a reputation as an event that was twice as much fun to watch as to run. To ensure that one actually sees the race, he suggested not arriving until race day, as there was just too much fun to be had on Friday and Saturday before the race.

His tongue-in-cheek article offered some sound advice on places to view the race, gear to bring (for the only two types of weather the race gets—hot and lousy), and diversions to consider. In summary, he wrote, "In few places is fun as persistent as it is in greater Falmouth."

In promoting his races, Tommy has often said, "An afternoon of merriment and gaiety will be had by all." In Leonard parlance, that afternoon generally starts on Wednesday and stretches to the following Tuesday.

George Robbat, owner of the Brothers Four, published the following letter to the people of Falmouth in the 1980 *Falmouth Enterprise* Road Race Supplement:

My brothers and I would like to extend our thanks again to all of Falmouth for supporting and adopting the Falmouth Road Race and making it the single greatest event to happen on Cape Cod all summer.

Little did we think 8 years ago when our bartender Tommy Leonard came to us with an idea for a road race that it would grow to such proportions. What started as a Road Race for the bar people has grown to be what most runners consider the finest field ever assembled for this type of race anywhere in the world.

Much of the credit for this must go to John Carroll, Rich Sherman, and others whose genius for organization and promotion made it possible for the race to become what it is. We at the Brothers 4 remember the first race with 87 runners finishing in the wind and rain and Tommy Leonard telling us that someday there would be more than 3,000 runners, including the best in the world. No one believed Tommy, of course, but we decided to humor him and continue contributing the manpower and financial support needed to keep the infant race alive. We all know the result.

I'd like to thank Tommy for showing me that the only difference between a dream and reality is belief and desire.

I'd like to invite every one of all ages to the Official Road Race party starting Sunday noon at the Brothers 4 and continuing until one in the morning.

Sincerely,

George Robbat, Proprietor

Brothers 4 Hotel

The bartenders at the Brothers 4 and at the Casino, a large club just down the hill past the Brothers 4, were always happy when road race weekend arrived. The Casino was on the coast side of the road with decks overlooking Vineyard Sound. In one small corner bar of the Casino, two bartenders split $600 for a single shift during race weekend in 1981. The Casino would go through 800 cases, or roughly 19,200 bottles, of beer on race day alone.

Craig Virgin, three-time Olympian in the 10,000-meter run, finished in the top five at Falmouth four times between 1978 and 1982. Virgin recalls that the year he won, 1979, he decided to go back to his host house, which was near the start, for a shower before the awards ceremony. Not familiar with the gridlock that saddles Falmouth roads over race weekend, he never dreamed he would miss the entire ceremony, but the event was held without the victor making it back in time to receive his laurel wreath and trophy. "I felt so embarrassed to miss my own award ceremony!" Virgin recently recounted.

The 1981 race saw Alberto Salazar become the first runner to go under 32:00, defeating title defender Rod Dixon with a new course record of 31:55 amidst 4,345 runners. *Runner's World* magazine named Falmouth winner of its prestigious Nurmi Award as the "Best USA Road Race."

While the 1973 Woods Hole to Falmouth race had a budget based on friendship, the tenth running of the race in 1982 had a budget of $77,500. Runners needed to enter by May 1, and 500 slots were reserved for local Falmouth runners. For an $8 entry fee, runners now received their number, a key chain and belt, Friday pasta supper, free bus transportation to the Woods Hole starting line, and a picnic for two at the finish. Various shoe companies set up exhibits in the gym at the rec center. Perrier was now donating $32,000 as well as $12,000 in water bottles. The cost to actually put on the race was now approximately $100,000, with the largest budget item being the cost of bringing in the invited athletes.

During the tenth running of the race, George Robbat reflected back to the first race, telling Joe Concannon, "I didn't know if anyone would even show up for the first race. When I saw the weather the morning of the race, I figured they'd call it off. I didn't know then what runners are like."

For the tenth, Rich Sherman, a member of the Air National Guard, lured the 567th Air Force Band from Otis Air National Guard to salute the winner with a rendition of *America the Beautiful,* which was written by Falmouth native Kathryn Lee Bates.

Tommy announced his retirement as a viable force in the race, telling Joe Concannon, "I'm more or less involved in a spiritual way but there's some kind of a magnetic force that compels me to come back. There's too many positive ramifications for me to say it's over. I might as well stop living. It's my life."

Tommy remained grateful that Sherman and Carroll would call in the winter months asking for advice or information. "It's all theirs now," Tommy said, "but it's a nice feeling when they call me asking about the nuts and bolts. Thoughtfulness is the best measure of a man."

Just four months after Alberto Salazar defeated Dick Beardsley by 2 seconds in 1982 in the Boston Marathon, he cruised to the fastest Falmouth record yet in 31:53, a record that would stand for ten years. Joanie Benoit had her fourth win at Falmouth and posted a new course record of 36:33. CBS aired a same-day 17-minute segment on the race, commentated by Frank Shorter. Eighty-one-year-old Ruth Rothfarb completed the race, becoming the oldest competitor to ever run the race.

In 1983 Joseph Nzau and Simeon Kigen became the first Kenyans to take first and second places at Falmouth. It would be another eight years before the Kenyans would start to become the most dominant force at Falmouth. Joanie had her fifth win, setting another course record of 36:21.

The *Boston Phoenix* newspaper published a "Guide to the Falmouth Road Race" in its August 21, 1984, issue. Jeff Wegenheim wrote an article on the history of the race, "As Time Goes By." At the end of his historic narrative, he noted, "Though the field of runners has become more world class and perhaps less down to earth, the race itself hasn't. It's still plain old Falmouth, a week-long event that parties right up to race time and takes up right where it left off as soon as the race is over. And as the winning times of the Falmouth front runners get faster, that means the race itself takes up less of the weekend's valuable party time. That's incentive for a personal best, Falmouth style."

Puma-Energizer agreed to sponsor the race in 1984 for $80,000, nearly double the amount that Perrier was contributing. Rich Sherman explained to Joe Concannon for a *Globe* article, "We've been trying to get through to them for two years that we needed more money. The split (with Perrier) was building up. We told them we couldn't attract the best field in the United States with the money we had. It was a difficult decision because we've had a good relationship."

The split with Perrier caused some bruised feelings between Tommy and the race co-directors. Tommy felt that loyalty to Perrier should have entered into it, saying, "I'll be eternally grateful to a French mineral water company for the financial underpinning of the race and to Bill Crowley and George Robbat, who were the original angels."

John Carroll commented, "We were always $10,000 short of being able to bring in the top athletes. This year we were able to talk about bringing in Carlos Lopez, Alberto Cova, and Joan Benoit after we had already assembled a fast field."

Tommy claimed he was severing his ties with the race. "I watched it grow from a seedling to a giant redwood. I loved it with a fiery passion. It's been a large part of my life. It's like going through a divorce."

Of course, Tommy could never really sever his ties to Falmouth, and the move to Puma helped the race continue to grow and prosper, drawing great running talent from around the globe.

Although financial inducements and compensation had been a part of the running scene for quite a while, 1984 was the first year that prize money was officially given to the runners. The prize structure included $6,000 each to the first man and woman. A total of $46,000 was awarded to the top 20 men and top 15 women of the more than 5,000 starters. This was also an Olympic year, and Joseph Nzau and Joanie stayed home to recuperate from the Olympic marathons they had run in Los Angeles just weeks earlier.

In August 1985 the race directors and the friends and organizers of the Tommy Leonard Scholarship fund gathered at the corner of Central Park Avenue and Grand Avenue by the finish line of the race to dedicate a park bench to Tommy. John D. Oser, director of the scholarship fund, said the purpose of the dedication was to "honor him [Tommy] for all the things he has done in the past and the continuous spirit he exudes." The bench is inscribed with the trademark quote of gratitude found also on the "running leg" stool given to T.L. by New Balance, various T-shirts, and elsewhere: "Thanks Tommy…for Making People Happy. Tom Leonard, Founder Falmouth Road Race 1973." In his usual poignant way, Tommy commented, "Geez, first the bridge, now the bench. I feel like I'm among the Faithful Departed."

The 1985 road race saw one of the strongest fields ever assembled, with the top ten men finishing under 33:00. Dave Murphy of England, Steve Jones of Wales, and Rob de Castella of Australia took first, second, and third with 32:02, 32:06, and 32:09. Joan Benoit had her sixth and final winning crown at Falmouth with another course record of 36:17, and would always be considered the Queen of Falmouth by the fans and spectators who so enjoyed watching her victories.

Tommy said, "Joanie, to me, has always represented the true grit of the Maine lady. When I think of Joan Benoit, I think of Bette Davis. Toughness. She has that aura of invincibility. She just lends incredible stature to any race or anywhere she goes. If you're looking for a hero or heroine, we've got one in our backyard."

The fourteenth running of Falmouth in 1986 was held just one month before Tommy left New England to try his hand bartending in Texas. He began to get nostalgic, reflecting on the development of the race with several writers. To *Boston Globe*'s Ron Indrisano, Tommy said, "It was the little race that grew and grew. I used to run the course myself and I was struck by its beauty. It's been my big rush. At the time, I wanted to encourage other people. It was the post-Vietnam era and people were frying their brains with drugs. I'd say, 'If you want to try a high, try running into a tangerine sunset at Chapoquoit Beach.' I wanted God to look down and be happy to see all those people taking good care of their bodies. I wanted to create something that brought happiness to people."

The day before the 1986 race, Joe Concannon captured this quote from Tommy: "It almost seems like the twinkle of Vineyard Sound is beckoning the runners for the race. Don't you hear the twinkles out there? It has a dazzling effect. I guarantee it will fire up the juices of anybody who sits here. This is a very happy peak in my life. The best things in life are free." This was the largest field of runners yet assembled for this race—5,500.

In 1987 Tommy heard that the race sponsorship might be a bit shaky, so he and the race directors approached John Hancock, already the sponsor of the Boston and New York City marathons. "I wanted to have some enduring insurance, and no one does it better than John Hancock. It was no hard talk at all."

John Hancock Financial Services joined Puma/USA as major sponsor of the 1987 road race, and Perrier returned as a minor sponsor. Dave D'Alessandro, Senior Vice President of Corporate Communications at John Hancock, told Joe Concannon, "It was good for us because it was one of the top road races in the country. It's an event that is well run and well respected."

John Hancock offered $60,000 to combine with Puma's $90,000-plus as well as $15,000 in goods and services and $30,000 to advertise on ESPN's telecast. The prize money that was disbursed now totaled $70,300.

In celebration of the fifteenth running of the race, one of the largest flags in the nation, the Mount Rushmore flag, hung from a fifteen-story crane above the finish line. The flag has hung at the finish every race since. It was first commissioned to fly over Mount Rushmore for its fiftieth anniversary in 1987. A road race volunteer, the late Jim Gehris, heard about the flag and invited the organizers to come to the road race as the flag tours the world each year.

After the Kenyans began to dominate the race, winning in a single day more money than they could earn in almost a decade at home, Elizabeth Sherman wrote an article in the *Official* magazine on her thoughts about the flag, in which she reflected, "I came to understand that in the sight of our flag lay a promise that we as Americans often take for granted. I discovered that the incredible athletes who flock to our race every year came here to find and make a better life than they could find elsewhere. Our country, for so many, represents a chance for success, freedom, and expression—three things denied to millions every day....Many of the athletes know that it [the flag] is a symbol of a place where they can reach for their dreams and beliefs."

The 1987 race was dominated by foreign runners, with Rolando Vera of Ecuador and Aurora Cunha of Portugal taking the men's and women's titles. Seven of the top ten men were foreigners that year. Runners also traveled from New Zealand, Australia, Mexico, Kenya, Great Britain, Ireland, Italy, Belgium, and Tanzania to run in the Falmouth Road Race.

That year Rich Sherman had had a cancer removed, and it gave him pause to stop and think about what is important. He and his wife, Kathleen, decided that the monumental task of putting on the road race was worth the effort for the community, and they have continued as co-directors to this day.

Sherman commented in another Concannon article for the *Globe*, "As long as the race remembers it is important to serve all the runners and preserve good relationships, the established races will survive....It's all the little things.

It's making the athletes feel at home....Before John Hancock came in, we were trying to figure out ways to cut down costs. Should we cut the prize money? I argued we couldn't. Not only have we maintained our position, we added Hancock and maintained Puma. We also added five sponsors."

By 1988 the Brothers Four had been razed for luxury townhouses. "When the runners had crested the final hill of the road race, it loomed into view on your left and you knew you were home. It was Falmouth's Citgo sign" wrote Joe in the *Globe*.

In 1988 the *Falmouth Enterprise* Road Race Supplement was a 28-page publication with local merchant advertisements wishing the runners luck, a list of all the local runners, schedules of the weekend's events, and articles on the top contenders, as well as running advice.

Woods Hole is a charming and quaint fishing village and home of the Oceanographic Research Institute as well as ferry service to Martha's Vineyard. Its narrow streets cannot accommodate cars for over 5,000 runners, and the race organizers have always provided free transportation to the start for the runners.

The shuttle buses leave Lawrence School in Falmouth between 7:30 and 9:00 AM. The operation is a sight to behold. The buses are lined up in rows across the parking lot, and there are strings of runners lined up in front of each bus all the way to the port-a-potties at the other end of the parking lot. Years ago, Tommy had recruited former Marine and retired Middlesex sheriff's officer Eddie Burke to be head of transportation ("Eddie, I've got a real simple job for you..."). So Eddie and his crew of volunteers—many state troopers, FBI agents, and police officers by profession—load up the buses, which head out one after another filled with happy, anxious, nervous, chatting, and delighted runners on their way to their designated starting corrals on Water Street in Woods Hole.

During the race, boats fill the sound close to shore jockeying for position to watch the race, so Coast Guard boats patrol Vineyard Sound to ensure the safety of swimmers and boaters alike. Safety zones 300 feet out from shore are established for swimmers where boats cannot go. In years past, many people would swim in from their boats to watch the road race, putting them at risk from passing propellers. The Coast Guard also keeps an eye out for "over-loaded" conditions and violations of federal drunk boating laws.

The 1988 race was the last one that U.S. runners dominated, with seven of the top ten finishers being Americans. Mark Curp of Missouri took the title in 32:22, becoming the first American to win the men's division since Alberto

Salazar's win in 1982. Anne Hannam of New Zealand won the women's division in 36:36. Rodgers and Shorter, both now forty years old, returned to race in the young end of the master's division. Rodgers not only won in 33:50, but finished twenty-third overall and ran 26 seconds faster than he did when he won his first Falmouth in 1974 at age twenty-six.

In 1989 Puma and John Hancock pulled out as sponsors, but Pilgrim Health Care stepped in with $75,000, enabling the prize money to remain at $67,050. Pilgrim organized a health fair at the new $2.4 million Gus Canty Community Center.

Before the 1989 race, Tommy once again got reflective with Joe, saying, "I lose sight of the fact that the race is a world-class athletic event. I get more wrapped up in the social side, the rejoicing and frolicking in the friendly confines of Falmouth....It's like all the summers of my life come to a beautiful summit.

"There aren't enough hours in the day to see your friends and acquaintances. I wish there were some kind of divine intervention to extend the daylight hours a little longer.

"I'm happy that people have gotten off their fat bums and stopped cigarette smoking, the way they are out doing it. That's the greatest gratification I've had out of this. Watching lifetime cigarette smokers losing weight and getting into some kind of exercise program. If I can be a small part of promoting longevity, I'll be a happy man. I am a happy man. I'll do it until the cows come home. Until that road race in the sky.

"I always felt like I was receiving a kickoff and I ran it back to the 35-yard line and Rich took over at quarterback and threw a touch down pass to John.

"Even though I'm no longer involved, people still ask me to get into the race and I can see the excitement in their eyes. I hope it lasts as long as I'm alive and beyond that. I say this with all my heart and soul. I'll never try to get people into the race again. It's not fair to Rich and John. I have to make a public statement. People get me in a weak moment."

To this day, Tommy Leonard is annually inundated with requests for numbers for entry into the Falmouth Road Race. He is given a certain amount of numbers each year, his "founder's privilege." My husband and I were the recipients of two of those numbers the first year we ran Falmouth. Michael, being a 2:23 marathoner, expected to start fairly close to the front, while I, being an 8:00-plus per miler, expected to be in the middle of the pack. As we approached Water Street and began to make our way to our assigned corrals, a volunteer stopped Michael soon after we started going through the crowds. I, on the other hand, was pushed ahead corral after corral until I found myself in the front pack. There I stood in my bright pink shorts and fluorescent yellow cap, chosen so that Michael could find me at the post-race picnic. Feeling like I had just crashed an exclusive runners' party I tried desperately to melt inconspicuously into the back of the corral with my very non–world-class-looking runner's hips amidst the many slender Kenyan and international female athletes surrounding me. While Michael had to run through hundreds of pregnant women, weekend joggers, and runners wearing knee braces before joining other 6-minute milers, I endured having virtually every runner pass me for about 2 miles until I fell in with other runners of my pace. It was the one race Michael ran in which not one runner passed him the entire distance. Tommy's generosity knows no bounds, but the details often get lost in the process...

Falmouth now had one of the largest prize money totals of any race in the world except for marathons. Foreign domination returned to the race, with only one U.S. runner in the top ten in 1989. Salvatore Bettiol of Italy took the men's title, and five of the top ten men hailed from Mexico. Aurora Cunha of Portugal had her second victory. Ruth Rothfarb, now eighty-eight, and Johnny Kelley, eighty-one, both completed the race that year. It was Johnny's seventeenth Falmouth; he had run in every one since the start.

For many years, Rich Sherman would shoot the starting gun at the race and then jump into an orange Porsche driven by John Carroll as the pace car, until the Porsche went out of commission in 1981. In 1989 Mazda provided a Miata to use as the pace car, and it got stuck in reverse at the start. Rich and John had to push it off to the side of the road and drive to the finish in a borrowed pickup truck. For the first time ever, they did not see their own event.

The 1991 race was held one day before Hurricane Bob furiously blew onto Cape Cod with sustained winds over 100 miles per hour. Perhaps an omen of things to come, the press truck lost a wheel and broke down, and the bouncing wheel just missed the lead runner. Part of the course along Surf Drive would be washed away by the hurricane.

Tommy's cousin, Jimmy Tierney, was in Falmouth for the race and recalls that on the day of the hurricane, he brought a thirty-pack over to Don Facey's house, where Tommy, Joe Concannon, John Connolly of the *Herald*, Bernie Corbett, and Coach Squires were riding out the storm. The winds were howling, the windows were rattling, trees were bending in two, and branches were flying past. Bernie remembers that as they sat there having a few brews and talking, Tommy kept going to Facey's back porch and opening the door saying, "I've never smelled the air so clean! I've really *never* smelled the air so clean!" At this point, "Jocko" Connolly recalled, Tommy took out his harmonica and proceeded to play the "only two songs he knows": the Marine Corps Hymn and *When the Red Red Robin Goes Bob-Bob-Bobbin' Along.* The group inside could only shake their heads in wonder.

Then Tommy hunched over the phone book looking at the Yellow Pages. "Tommy, what the hell are you doing?" Jimmy asked. Tommy looked at him, surprised he wouldn't know that Tommy was doing the most natural thing he could at that moment, and retorted, "I'm looking for a bar with structural integrity."

"Jocko" recalled another occasion when the same group stayed at Facey's and had just finished their morning runs. While sitting around in their shorts without T-shirts, Don's niece, Susan, happened to come over. Joe felt he should have a shirt on, so he went upstairs and came down wearing a beautiful silk kimono. Tommy asked, "Joe, where'd you get that, laddie?" which led to tales of their trip to Fukuoka in 1977. Tommy dubbed him "Kimono Joe" that day—a nickname that stuck.

Over 7,000 runners competed for $77,050 in prize money at the twentieth running of the road race. When asked about the birth of this race, which had become such an institution, Tommy said, "There was a multitude of factors....I saw a grand slam home run. It had all the ingredients and all the parts of the equation. You had the aesthetic beauty. You had the course. You had the social nature of the competitors."

Reflecting on the support that the Carrolls and Shermans gave, Tommy said, "They handled all the logistics. If they didn't, it probably would have been a disaster because I am probably the most disorganized person on the face of the earth."

Apparently Billy Rodgers agrees with that assessment, as he once told George Kimball for his "Guru on Tap" article, "I can't think of anything I would not do if Tommy Leonard asked me to...but the predilection of the media to refer to him as a 'race organizer' constitutes a misnomer of the first degree.

"Nobody's done more for running than Tommy. He created this race, he's promoted it, he's publicized it, and he's made it go," chuckled Rodgers. "But organize? There's absolutely nothing organized about Tommy Leonard."

Records fell at the 1992 road race as Benson Masya of Kenya broke Salazar's ten-year-old record by running 31:52, and Lynn Jennings, just off her bronze medal win in the 10,000 meters at the Olympics in Barcelona, ran

36:13, breaking Joan Benoit's 1985 record. They each earned $11,000 that day, including $1,000 bonuses for their records.

Hillary Tuwei was the first Kenyan to compete in Falmouth in 1977. In the ensuing years, there would occasionally be two or three Kenyans in the top ten until the twentieth running, when four of the top ten slots went to Kenyans. This was the beginning of domination by the Kenyans, who have taken at least seven of the top ten slots since 1994. In 1996, all but one of the top ten went to Kenyans. Seventh place went to Phillimon Hanneck of Zimbabwe.

Tommy's perspective in 1994 was "To see the majestic presence of the Kenyans who run with a hurricane force and an ever-present smile on their faces has to do damage to the other runners. It's just a delightful scene. It's something you can't buy. The essence of Falmouth is pulling people together in a positive way."

With growing domination by the Kenyans of most of the prize money races in the United States, the race organizers decided to join other major road races and offer an added incentive to U.S. runners, with significant money earmarked for the top U.S. finishers. They explained that their intent was to afford American runners the opportunity to earn some money from their racing efforts, to enable them to continue to train and compete on an international level. Without these incentives, it was feared the top American runners would be forced to drop out of road racing entirely to seek full-time employment in other fields.

The prize structure in 1995 for U.S. runners looked like this:

	Men	Women
1.	$2,000	$2,000
2.	$1,500	$1,500
3.	$1,000	$1,000
4.	$ 750	$ 750
5.	$ 500	$ 500

The first-place finishers overall, for both the men and the women, received $10,000.

In 1992 the Falmouth Road Race Committee established the Michael Denmark Award in memory of Michael Denmark, who died that year at the age of twenty-four of cystic fibrosis. The award is given annually to the runner in the race who has demonstrated significant achievement despite extraordinary personal challenges. Despite his cystic fibrosis, which ravages the respiratory system, Michael ran high school and college cross-country and completed the Falmouth Road Race with his Dad in 1982, and again a couple of years before he died.

Michael's parents, Jay and Cheryl, had been former road race finish-line volunteers with their family, and now live in North Carolina. They travel to the race each year to present the award at the post-race ceremony to honor their son. Michael's dad explained, "Running was a very important part of Michael's life. He never used his condition as an excuse. He was a spirited competitor and he never quit." The award is very important to the Denmarks, as it "keeps Michael's memory alive in the town that he so loved."

The extraordinary stories of the past recipients of the Denmark award are reported in the Falmouth Road Race Official Magazine each year. The first recipient was Frank Niro, an outstanding high school and college distance runner in the mid-1960s. As a teenager, Niro completed twelve marathons, including a 2:57 time in 1967 at Boston. Three days before Christmas that year, he was hit head on by a drunk driver while on a training run. The accident left him with a smashed kneecap, a shattered right leg, and a pelvis broken in three places. He spent 760 days in Hartford Hospital enduring nineteen operations. The doctors considered amputating his leg at one point. He spent three years in a wheelchair and seven in leg braces. Frank watched the Falmouth race from his wheelchair in the 1970s and promised himself that someday he would complete the course. Twenty-one years after his near-fatal accident, he entered the race and completed the course by running a bit and walking a bit, finishing last. He did the same in 1989, running more, and in 1990 he ran the entire course. He commented, "What happened to me gave me strength and taught me how to deal with adversity....I learned never to give up."

Ray McNamara was a former Newton firefighter who had run about twenty Falmouth Road Races before a near-fatal accident on October 23, 1993. As he was responding to a call at the Newton Highlands chemical plant, a barrel of metallic sodium exploded in his face. His fire-retardant coat and mask were of no use against the 2,000-degree droplets, which scorched more than 90 percent of his body. After a year in a coma and six more months in the hospital, Ray had lost his sight and some of his hearing, and his face was disfigured. One of his darkest moments came when he again lost his sight after it had returned to him in December 1994. Against all odds, he returned to Falmouth in 1997 because "Running it makes me feel more complete." Ray's wife, son, sister-in-law, and brother surrounded him and kept a steady stream of water spraying onto his body while they walked and jogged the entire course.

Jennifer DiMartino had her first open-heart surgery at age three, another one at seventeen, and a valve replacement at twenty-three. In 1992 a pacemaker was inserted beneath her breast. After the pacemaker, she decided to give running a try and amazed even herself by training up to 5 miles. Then, ten days after coming home following the birth of her son, she experienced life-threatening bleeding and hemorrhaging due to complications from a change in the blood-thinning medication required because of her replacement valve. She had five blood transfusions and two packs of plasma, and nearly died when the nurses issued a code blue. After recovering, Jennifer ran her first Falmouth Road Race in 1999 and was the recipient of the Denmark Award.

In June 1994 Frank Shephard was a healthy, athletic forty-nine-year-old. While stretching before a training run for the Falmouth race, he felt a "fiery white hot pain." Within minutes, he was completely paralyzed and without sensation from the waist down. The doctors were baffled and discovered that arterial blood flow to the spinal cord had been interrupted. They didn't know if he would be able to walk again. They later came to realize that the initial injury occurred a week earlier, when Frank was loading a canoe on top of his car and slipped. He hyperextended his back, fracturing a lumbar disk. One day in rehab, he was able to move his big toe, which brought him to tears, as he then knew he would walk again. While watching the 1994 road race at the finish line in his wheelchair, Frank resolved to complete the race in 1995. Then a woman with multiple sclerosis who had completed the New York City Marathon on crutches inspired him. He decided to train for Falmouth on forearm crutches. His training helped get him out of the wheelchair, and he has run the Falmouth Road Race on crutches every year since 1995.

In 1987 Woods Hole resident Kevin Lehy was traveling in his car when it crashed through a guardrail at Nobska Lighthouse and careened over 150 feet into the air, landing on the rocks below. In addition to fracturing multiple ribs, facial bones, and his collarbone, Kevin lost his vision. "At that point, I had a choice. I could run from myself and become depressed, or I could face my fears and find the lesson that was buried in my misfortune." Kevin began daily walks to the library with his guide dog, Orwell. When Kevin's friend Daniel "Pup" Gould was diagnosed with cancer and underwent extensive chemotherapy, he began to go on lengthy walks with Kevin to regain the strength in his heart and lungs. "We would just talk and talk and talk," said Lehy. "It was our time to spill our guts about the things we were going through, be it blindness, cancer, or just a bad day." One day Gould showed up with a contraption made of rope and suggested they do the Falmouth Road Race. The duo learned to walk together and trust each other, using a harness and bells on Gould's shoes. Seventeen years after his auto accident, Kevin and his friend "Pup" completed their first road race. "It was the freest I have felt since I lost my sight. No cars to worry about, no dog to follow, just me, my best pal "Puppy," and seven miles of open road." Kevin received the Denmark Award in 2004. Annually, he goes to Gould's English class at Falmouth High and discusses his blindness and the lessons he has drawn from his experiences.

These are just a few of the remarkable stories of the people who have been honored with this award, all of whom demonstrate a passionate faith in Michael Denmark's favorite motto: "Do not quit." The 1992 article about the first award recipient included this poem:

> Success is failure turned inside out,
>
> The silver tint of the clouds of doubt,
>
> And you never can tell how close you are,
>
> It may be near when it seems so far,
>
> So stick to the fight when you're hardest hit,
>
> It's when things seem worse,
>
> That you must not quit.

The Denmark Award's recognition of courage displayed against adversity toward the accomplishment of great things is another element of the Falmouth Road Race that gives Tommy great pride and satisfaction in being associated with the annual event.

The first Falmouth Invitational Mile was organized by the race committee and took place in 1995 at the Falmouth High School track. The event is held on Saturday night before the road race. The 1995 winner won $500. Today, over 1,000 spectators attend the mile event, and the winners take home a cool $1,000 and a bonus of $500 if the men run under 4:00 and the women run under 4:33. Three-time Olympian Suzy-Favor Hamilton from New Glarus, Wisconsin, ran the fastest female outdoor mile in the world in 2002 at Falmouth, in 4:25:27.

In the twenty-fifth-anniversary issue of the *Falmouth Road Race Official Magazine*, John Manners, a former Peace Corps volunteer in Kenya, wrote an article titled "Kenyan Runners Challenge the World to Keep Up." Amidst his explanations of the history of Kenyan dominance, he cited the facts that the per-capita annual income in Kenya was $1,170 and unemployment is very high. The prospect of earning $10,000 for winning a road race is a very powerful lure for Kenyan runners.

The prize structure for the twenty-fifth Falmouth Road Race in 1997 looked like this:

Open:

	Men and Women	USA: Men and Women	Masters
1.	$10,000	$4,000	$3,000
2.	$ 5,000	$2,500	$1,500
3.	$ 2,000	$1,500	$ 750
4.	$ 1,000	$1,000	$ 500
5.	$ 750	$ 750	$ 250
6.	$ 700	$ 600	
7.	$ 650	$ 500	
8.	$ 600	$ 400	
9.	$ 500	$ 300	
10.	$ 450	$ 200	
11.	$ 400		
12.	$ 350		
13.	$ 300		
14.	$ 250		
15.	$ 200		

Wheelchair division:

Men	Women
1. $1,000	$1,000
2. $ 750	$ 500
3. $ 500	$ 250
4. $ 250	

The domination of the Falmouth Road Race by foreign runners has spawned many international friendships between the families of Falmouth and the elite runners from around the globe. Since the beginning of the race, local families have continued to host the top runners in their homes.

Dr. Arthur Crago, medical director of the race, and his wife have hosted several Kenyan runners as well as Moroccan Khalid Khannouchi (four-time winner of the Chicago Marathon) and his wife, Sandra. Several Kenyans have been taught how to play tennis by their hosts' children, a sport they are not familiar with, and many hosts go out for runs together with their foreign guests (at least for the first warm-up miles!). Ninety-five percent of the runners ask to return to their host families in subsequent years.

Regina Poff, a respiratory therapist at Falmouth Hospital who has worked the respiratory tent at the finish line, has also been a frequent host. Catherine Ndereba, winner of the 1996, 1998, and 1999 road races, has been her guest and invited Regina to her wedding in Kenya. Catherine has returned to the Poffs' with her husband and daughter as guests.

The hosting program provides a wonderful change from hotel rooms for the elite runners, and many prepare meals of their native lands for their hosts to show their appreciation.

Mr. Robert Gusmini, who has vacationed in Falmouth Heights for over forty years and has run in more than fifteen Falmouth races, has also hosted many Kenyan runners. He told Kate Tetreault of the *Falmouth Enterprise*, "You learn how really simple it is to communicate with people from an entirely different culture and a different part of the world. When you first meet them you have that bit of anxiety whether it will be a quiet weekend and no one will talk, but you have that common bond because of running."

The twenty-fifth-anniversary race and *Official Magazine* were dedicated to Tommy Leonard and Bill Crowley. Bill, the owner of the Captain Kidd Restaurant at the starting line of the race, had personally subsidized the expenses of several of the top runners who brought the race national attention, including Billy Rodgers and Frank Shorter. Bill had passed away the previous November at the age of 63. His children still operate the Captain Kidd Restaurant.

About 20,000 people make requests for numbers and over 9,000 lucky runners are chosen in the lottery annually to answer the bugler's call in Woods Hole. Falmouth taxpayers who choose to take advantage of their guaranteed entry into the race now number approximately 1,500. The race directors annually hear enough dubious sob stories from runners seeking a number to fill a book. The classic appeal is, of course, "But I'm a friend of Tommy Leonard."

The 1997 race had 9,558 runners competing for the $88,000 in prize money. The temperature was over 90 degrees with high humidity. Khalid Khannouchi took the men's division in 31:58, and Colleen de Reuck of South Africa took the women's in 36:19.

There was an aura of excitement in town for the twenty-fifth. Tommy, now a bartender at Rob and Rita Pacheco's Quarterdeck Restaurant on Main Street in Falmouth, could barely contain his excitement, acknowledging everyone who came into the pub with "Welcome to Race Week!"

The *Cape Cod Times* ran a front-page article titled "Tommy Leonard's Dream" by Jack Perry, in which T.L. was quoted: "I'm like a little boy under the Christmas tree getting my first flexible flyer or first pair of ice skates. When it's over on Monday, I get kind of depressed, like after Christmas or the Fourth of July."

Every past winner the organizers could find was invited to return to Falmouth. They held a clinic at the Gus Canty Community Center, emceed by Toni Reavis. Runners were treated to an afternoon session with Dave Duba (1973), Billy Rodgers (1974, 1977, and 1978), Frank Shorter (1975 and 1976), Craig Virgin (1979), Rod Dixon (1980), Alberto Salazar (1981 and 1982), Joseph Nzau (1983), Dave Murphy (1984 and 1985), Arturo Barrios (1986), Mark Curp (1988), Salvatore Bettiol (1989 and 1990), Joseph Kamau (1995), Jenny Taylor Tuthill (1973 and 1975), Debbie Ritchie Oberbillig (1974), Joan Benoit Samuelson (1976, 1978, 1981, 1982, 1983 and 1985), Joan Nesbit (1984), Lorraine Moeller (1986), Colleen de Reuck (1993 and 1997), Delillah Asiago (1995), and Catherine Ndereba (1996, 1998, and 1999).

Many everyday joggers and back-of-the-pack runners were rubbing elbows at the Quarterdeck and other pubs with many of the most talented distance runners in history. Rod Dixon was known to keep the Quarterdeck bartenders working the sticks until the latest possible last call. The town was filled not only with past winners but many, many talented runners who had finished in the top ten over the years and came to enjoy the celebrations.

The runners on the stage at the "past winners" clinic were joined by a group that has come to be known as the Falmouth Five. They are a group of runners who have participated in every Falmouth Road Race since its inception in 1973. Until 1996, the late Johnny Kelley was a member of this group. Ron Pokraka, Dr. Don Delinks, Michael Bennett, Brian Salzberg and Tom Brannelly first became aware of one another about ten years into the race.

In 1973 Ron had just moved to Falmouth and talked his tennis buddy, Dr. Delinks, a Falmouth veterinarian, into joining him to run the first race. Brian Salzberg was working at the Marine Biological Lab in Woods Hole with Michael Bennett and entered the race. Salzberg, eleven years younger than Bennett, figured if his older buddy could run the race, there's no reason why he couldn't also. Tom Brannelly was working at the Landfall Restaurant and had just taken up running to ward off the pounds that beer and ice cream tend to put on.

These are athletes who take running in general very seriously and maintaining their streak at Falmouth with the utmost passion. Ron, a college athlete at Worcester Polytechnic Institute, was known as "the Tank" in school. He has run sixty marathons, including twenty Bostons, and seven 50-mile runs. Over the years, Ron has had a friendly rivalry with Ron LaFreniere to see who could outdo whom in ultra-running. LaFreniere ran 40 miles on his fortieth birthday and then 82 miles on a track for his forty-first. Pokraka then decided to run from his hometown of Webster, Massachusetts, to Falmouth on his forty-second birthday, a distance of 105 miles.

In 2000 Ron had prostate surgery but didn't let that "little bump in the road" stop him from running Falmouth two months later. Then a week and a half after the 2001 road race, he had two hip surgeries that damaged a sciatic nerve and left him with a partially paralyzed leg. The doctors told him he would never walk again, but he found that unacceptable, saying, "I'm a very determined person."

Ironically, in a 1998 interview with the *Falmouth Enterprise,* Ron had said, "Injuries are not an issue. I think all of us (runners) feel the same way. If one of us had a broken leg, he'd do it on crutches. If he had two broken legs, he'd do it in a wheelchair." After training in a wheelchair, Ron walked the 2002 road race with two canes at age 63. In 2003, he used no canes and did the race at a fast walk. Ron won the Denmark Award in 2002 for his determination and courage, becoming the second Falmouth resident to win the award. Ron and his wife host over 250 people each year at a party at their home over race weekend.

Michael Bennett had run the Earth Day Marathon in 1973 and then entered the Falmouth Road Race. He has since run in over fifty-six marathons. He once flew from Japan to the Cape before traveling to Hawaii so that he would not miss the Falmouth Road Race.

Brian Salzberg now teaches neuroscience and physiology at the University of Pennsylvania and makes the annual pilgrimage to Falmouth for the race. He once ran seven weeks after breaking his arm in a bicycling accident, and in 1987 he ran only three months after back surgery. Says Salzberg, "I've run twenty marathons and I love Boston, but Falmouth is my favorite race. The setting is gorgeous and there's still a small-town flavor even though you have top talent 20 or 30 runners deep." Between the ages of thirty-five and fifty Dr. Salzberg averaged 44:07, and he estimated in 2003 that he had run almost 43,450 miles since July 3, 1973.

Dr. Delinks ran the 1974 Boston marathon and four New York City marathons. His son, Don, first ran the Falmouth Road Race at age five and has run in every single race since. He is now thirty-eight years old and returns from Florida each year to keep up the tradition with his father. Don recalls running in the New York City Marathon with his son when he was only eight or nine years old. His son was starting to struggle when Tommy Leonard happened to come upon them in the race. He encouraged him to keep going and really helped him to finish the race.

No one in the group wants to be the first runner who fails to complete the road race, and they will go to great lengths to keep participating. Brannelly admitted to John Powers of the *Globe* that "we're looking over each other's shoulders now....It takes me as long to stretch now as it does to run. They tell me that's what getting old is all about."

The Falmouth Five have another tradition that is less taxing to maintain annually. The night after the road race, they enjoy a meal with their wives and Tommy at the Captain Kidd Restaurant in Woods Hole.

After an eleven-year relationship with Harvard Pilgrim Health as sponsor, and one year with Breakaway Solutions, Savings Bank Life Insurance signed on as principal sponsor in March 2001. Reebok is the footwear sponsor, and there are many, many contributing and supporting sponsors as well.

SBLI CEO Robert Sheridan has been thrilled with the success and magnitude of the Falmouth Road Race. Sponsorship has grown to $150,000 plus medals and T-shirts to 300 runners in the Junior Road Race.

The weekend now has a full calendar of events, including:

- Friday night pasta supper for 3,000, with jugglers, face painting, DJ, and entertainment

- Saturday morning 5K walk for charity

- Running Expo and Health Fair, with displays, information, and product samplings as well as physical therapists and athletic trainers offering advice on safe and healthy training, flexibility, nutrition, and related topics

- "Meet the Olympians" hour, which has often included Rodgers, Shorter, Joanie, Uta Pippig, and Kate O'Neill

- Junior Road Race at the Falmouth High School for five- to thirteen-year-olds

- Volunteers meeting to coordinate the activities of over 2,000 volunteers

- Falmouth Invitational Mile at the high school track on Saturday evening

- Special Mass and non-sectarian blessing at St. Patrick's Church on Saturday

- Band concert at the Falmouth Harbor Band Shell on Saturday evening

- Post-race picnic and awards ceremony attended by over 9,000 people

In 2004 the race had its largest registration, with 10,200 runners. "Champion Chip" microchips laced on the runners' shoes sent a signal as the shoes cross a transmitter mat at the start and finish, sending data into a laptop with each runner's precise time.

With cool temperatures and low humidity, Gilbert Okari of Kenya demolished the course record by 24 seconds, winning in 31:08. Kenyans have won twelve of the last fourteen men's titles at Falmouth.

It is estimated that 70,000 spectators watch the race along the course. Those at the finish line can now view live coverage of the race from the start, Nobska Lighthouse, Surf Drive, and the last hill on a huge video screen. A total of 80,000 cups of water are distributed at five water stops along the course.

Families, friends, and co-workers annually challenge one another, sending e-mails and phone calls to update one another on their training and weight loss progress. There are many, many runners who have done fifteen, twenty, twenty-five, or thirty Falmouth races, collecting their commemorative posters and mugs each year. Many run to be cheered on by friends and for the community atmosphere, camaraderie, and friendships that develop each year. Groups of friends and families run in memory of loved ones lost to disease, 9/11, or accidents. Many come together for family reunions, and hundreds run to raise money for their chosen charities.

The Falmouth Road Race initially raised money to support the Falmouth High girl's track club. Today, the SBLI Falmouth Road Race, like the Boston Marathon and most of the major marathons in the country, raises hundreds of thousands of dollars, which benefit a wide array of community, sports, and charitable organizations.

The Falmouth race committee and its principal sponsor, Savings Bank Life Insurance, make guaranteed entries available to many diverse charities. These charities award the entries to runners who pledge to raise at least $750 for their cause. In 2003 these groups received over $325,000 from the Falmouth Road Race.

Although Falmouth has always drawn elite runners who are able to run spectacular times, the "fun bunch" comes to run and enjoy "the moving street party," some sporting outlandish outfits—shark fin hats and grass skirts, lobster hats, Superman shirts, Statue of Liberty costumes, and many other creations. Spectators along the course amplify the themes of *Rocky* and *Chariots of Fire*.

The thirty-second *Official Magazine* in 2004 was a 136-page publication filled with articles and special stories of participants in the race. It is also filled with many, many e-mails that the race organizers have received, which are glowing testaments to the quality of the Falmouth experience.

Among the e-mails received by the organizers was the following: "Every step was scenic, every spectator was encouraging, and every breath was easy...the music, the panoramic views, the crowds, the blue skies made you forget everything but the absolute enjoyment of being alive and continuing to put one foot in front of the other."

The race was featured in a two-page color photo in *Life* magazine in November 1991. *Sports Illustrated* published "Sports Illustrated 50 Years, the Anniversary Book" in 2004, which included a two-page photograph of the start of the Falmouth Road Race that was first published in the August 18, 2003, issue. It has been rated one of the top fifteen American road races every year since 1977 by *Runner's World* and *Running Times* magazines.

Olympic athletes who have run in the Falmouth road race include Marty Liquori, Billy Rodgers, Frank Shorter, Craig Virgin, Alberto Salazar, Abdi Abdirahman, Dan Browne, and Paul Cummings of the United States; Rod Dixon of New Zealand; Arturo Barrios of Mexico; Joseph Nzau, Mike Musoyki, and Simeon Kigen of Kenya; Rolando Vera of Ecuador; Mike McCleod and Dave Murphy of England; Rob de Castella of Australia; Salvatore Bettiol of Italy; Joan Benoit, Jan Merrill, Lynn Jennings, Libbie Hickman, Judi St. Hilaire, Kate O'Neill, and Jennifer Rhines of the United States; Grete Waitz of Norway; Utta Pippig of Germany; Jacqueline Gareau of Canada; Aurora Cunha of Portugal; Elana Meyer and Colleen de Reuck of South Africa; Ann Audain, Lorraine Moeller, and Dianne Rogers of New Zealand; Svetlana Zakharova and Valentina Yegorova of Russia; and Catherine Ndereba and Lornah Kiplagat of Kenya.

The SBLI Falmouth Road Race commissioned a survey in 2003 to look at the economic impact of the road race on the community of Falmouth. An article about the results was published in the thirty-second *Road Race Official Magazine,* and copies of the survey are available in all branches of the Falmouth Public Library.

The survey found that the race brings over $5 million into Falmouth, including $4.5 million from non-residents who are there for the road race. While 44 percent come just for the race, 56 percent come also to vacation, spending for lodging, restaurants and bars, package stores, supermarkets, retail outlets, and car rentals. The average spending is about $847 per person. The residents average about $396 per person in shops and restaurants and markets. Fifty-two percent of the resident respondents reported having between one and five guests during road race weekend who did not run in the race.

One respondent wrote, "Since (coming to) the race, I have visited Falmouth at least twice a year and have run thirteen of the past fifteen races. If not for the road race, I probably would not have found out what a wonderful place Falmouth is for a great vacation."

The survey clearly showed that the race provides a substantial boost to many of the town's businesses and dispels the notion that the race is a transient event in which people come to run and then leave without spending money. As Tommy pushed his cart down Main Street in the early 1970s, no merchant could have imagined how his dream and determination would affect their lives as the race grew and developed.

As Tommy Leonard sat on that bar stool in 1972 at the Brothers Four watching the moon glisten over Vineyard Sound, he wanted to help the Falmouth Track Club. He wanted to create a race that the top Olympic and world runners would come to. He wanted to inspire people to become healthy and fit while having a good time. He wanted to give back to the community of Falmouth.

Every hope and dream Tommy had for the Falmouth Road Race has been fulfilled in a most gratifying way. A vision, a belief in the possibilities, a desire to see it come to life crystallized into an event that annually touches the lives of hundreds of thousands, whether running, watching, volunteering, or being the recipient of the many charitable dollars that are now raised in the race.

As this book was going to press, plans were being developed for a finish-line park with a carved boulder, walkways, and benches surrounded by plantings and flowers. The walkway will include engraved pavers, and the first to be set will have Tommy's name on it.

"The Lord can take me now" is Tommy's oft-quoted sentiment when he feels gratified by the good he finds around him. Those who know and love him hope that the great "road race in the sky" is many years in the distant future. When that day does arrive, the Lord will have a very lengthy list to consider of the many people who have benefited from the one life He blessed us all with on August 15, 1933.

11

The Charities

The Charity Challenge

"Thoughtfulness is the best measure of a man."
—Another favorite Tommy Leonard expression

From an early age, Tommy was always looking for any way in which he could help people. While working at the Banjo Room, he often arranged for the Gaslight Gang to play at fundraisers with which his adoptive father, Francis X. Tierney, was involved at Blessed Sacrament Church in Westfield.

In 1974 Tommy happened to walk into the Bull & Finch Pub in the lower level of the Hampshire House on Beacon Street in Boston. This is the pub that would later become the inspiration and outdoor setting for the TV sitcom *Cheers*. Eddie Doyle was the bartender that day. Tommy had not seen Eddie since the monumental brawl at the Banjo Room on Eddie's last night of work there in the late 1960s.

This chance meeting led to the beginning of a unique relationship in which these fast friends would raise literally hundreds of thousands of dollars to help those less fortunate.

Tommy began to frequent the Bull & Finch around 11 AM and say, "Hey, Eddie, you got any Sam Adams?" or "Hey, Eddie, let me have one of those red, white and blue puppies" (Budweiser). After a while he'd ask, "Eddie, do you have any chili today?" They'd read the paper together and talk about people who they thought needed some help. Tommy would generally come up with an idea and look at Eddie, saying, "Hey, Ed, do you think *we* could do that?" Thus, T.L. the Visionary and Eddie the Facilitator would put their heads together and dream up ways to help people.

Then Eddie would ask, "You working today, T.L.?" "Yeah, yeah. I gotta be there at 1 PM. What time is it, Eddie?" "Oh, about 2:30," Eddie would respond. "Geez, I better get down there!" Tommy would exclaim. Eddie fondly recalls that if Tommy happened to be talking to a lady, it could be 3:30 before he asked what time it was.

These Boston barkeeps felt that their jobs as bartenders put them in the heart of the Boston community, where they would hear or read about what was going on and who needed help, and then come up with someone among their contacts who could be a resource for that help.

Mike Barnicle, a patron of the Eliot and writer for the *Boston Globe*, often wrote stories about people who had had a setback or tragedy, and he inspired Tommy to start a Friends of the Eliot club to raise money for such folks. He solicited $5 each from a bunch of bartenders in the Back Bay, and the Friends of the Eliot treasury was born. Then he started to collect from the patrons at the Eliot. Dr. Charles Tifft recalls that everyone was happy to give to a cause if Tommy felt it was important. It was the one time they would all give willingly, unconcerned about any tax-deductibility they might be missing. "It just made you feel good to give to a cause that Tommy felt was important."

Tommy read about two blind men who were mugged in the subway two days before Christmas and had their social security checks stolen. The fund provided them with a check, and the gentlemen wrote a thank you to the Eliot.

One year a college student from Eritrea, an East African country, had his leg severed by a hit-and-run driver while trying to help someone push a car out of a snow bank on the Massachusetts Avenue bridge. The Eliot threw a benefit party and Friends of the Eliot provided close to $400 for his medical care. Tommy went to the hospital to present him with the check. Later, a group of people from Eritrea brought an award of gratitude to the Eliot.

The Villanova University band had their truck stolen along with $10,000 worth of equipment and uniforms. The Friends fund helped to defray some of that loss.

When Eddie heard about a Boston bartender who had been shot by a drunken customer in 1988, he raised $4,000 in three days from his patrons for a scholarship for the family.

When State Trooper Mark Charbonnier of Norwell was shot to death in the line of duty, Tommy helped to acquire donations for a benefit held for the officer's family.

At age thirty-three, Dick Bearsdley, who had been coached by Bill Squires to the famous duel with Alberto Salazar in the 1982 Boston Marathon, finishing second with 2:08:54, suffered a serious farm machinery accident. It left him with a broken wrist, broken ribs, damage to his calf muscles, and severe ligament damage to his left knee. Tommy and Eddie, together with Coach Squires, Billy and Charlie Rodgers, Patti Catalano Lyons, and others, began a "Boston Runs for Dick Beardsley" fund, soliciting money not only from runners but from anyone who had enjoyed the Boston Marathon over the years. Money came in from small businesses and large corporations, runners and many people who were total strangers to the sport of running as well. Eddie commented to Anne Driscoll of the *New York Times*, "You can't replace a limb, the hurt or suffering. It's the token, the feeling that someone says we care."

Eddie Doyle and his Barleyhoppers running club, established in 1978, met on Mondays for a run to a specific pub somewhere in the city, true to their motto, "We run for fun, we roam for foam." Word spread about the format of this club, and it grew from a handful of men and women to about 100 adventuresome souls who were interested in exercising their beer bellies away while still imbibing guilt-free. The culmination of their summer/fall runs was the Great Boston Beer Chase, in which each runner was required to stop at each bar on a designated map and consume a 5-ounce glass of beer (twelve bars was the most stops they had ever had). The last Beer Chase was held a few days after a huge hurricane blew through the city of Boston. They had a party planned under a tent adjacent to a North End waterfront restaurant. The storm had left the tent a pile of twisted remains, so the restaurant let the runners inside for their party. Eventually, in deference to liquor liability issues for the pubs and drunken driving awareness, they began to drink 5-ounce glasses of non-alcoholic Moussy beer at ten designated stops between the Eliot and Lewis Wharf. The Barleyhoppers continued their Monday night beer runs into the 1990s, and twenty-three couples who met through the Barleyhoppers are now married with families.

Tommy and Eddie spoke several times of creating a fun run between the Eliot and the Bull & Finch that could culminate in a big party at the finish-line pub. Proceeds of the run could go to charity, and they bounced around ideas of different groups they could help.

Before their idea crystallized into reality, a couple came into the Bull & Finch Pub who were in charge of Halcyon Place on the corner of Commonwealth Avenue and Berkley Street. Halcyon Place was similar in concept to the Ronald McDonald house. It was a place for families to stay who had children who were burn victims and were being treated at the Shriners Burns Center at Massachusetts General Hospital. The couple were discussing fundraising ideas for Halcyon Place, along the lines of cocktail parties or auctions. A light bulb went off in Eddie's head. He gave a quick call to Tommy, and the first "Eliot to the Bull" fundraiser was born.

Halcyon Place was thrilled with the concept and the exposure they would receive. One day Eddie went over to Halcyon Place to pick up their logo for promotion. He was introduced to a small young boy from Brazil whom someone had set on fire. The little boy begged Eddie to pick him up and carry him to the door. Looking at the faceless child who had two holes where his nose had once been and a tiny reconstructed mouth, Eddie called upon all his inner strength to maintain his composure. Lifting the boy up, they walked around Halcyon Place together. The boy's joy and happiness convinced Eddie that the run would definitely be worth the effort to organize. Although the management of Halcyon Place didn't really have a clue about how the event was to be organized, they agreed to have the patients and families out front as the runners went by.

Joe Fitzgerald gave the run a nice plug in the *Boston Herald*, which prompted a Boston Police sergeant to call Eddie and chew him out saying, "You guys know better. You need a permit to pull off something like this." Knowing it was too late, and admiring the good works of Doyle and Leonard, he then softened and said, "I'll send down a couple of cars and a few motorcycle units," much to Eddie's relief.

A miniature cannon that produced a thunderous blast, shaking the putty off the nearby windows, sent the runners across the starting line in front of the Eliot and down Commonwealth Avenue on the one-mile trek to the Bull & Finch Pub. Runners contributed $10 and were given a buffet meal and a free pint of Sam Adams beer at the end.

Each year a different athlete or celebrity would be the guest of honor. The first year of the run was 1988, when "Spaceman" Bill Lee of the Red Sox was running for president for the Rhinoceros Party. Lee was the guest of honor for the run. He rode in an open-air Cadillac while runners dressed in tuxedo jackets, running shorts and shoes, and "rhino noses" on their faces ran alongside the car like security guards. Eddie remembers Lee waving to all the imaginary people and thinking he looked like General Douglas MacArthur in a New York ticker-tape parade.

That first year Anne-Marie Carroll, Executive Director of Halcyon Place, wrote a thank-you letter to Eddie and Tommy. Her letter ended with a note of personal thanks: "Working with you was the highlight of my September activities. You helped me keep in focus the pleasure of working with people of such good will."

The second year of the run Gary Bell, pitcher for the Cleveland Indians, Boston Red Sox, and Chicago White Sox, was the guest of honor while Gary Waslewski (pitcher for the Red Sox, St. Louis Cardinals, Montreal Expos, and New York Yankees) together with Dick 'the Monster' Radadtz (pitcher for Boston Red Sox, Cleveland Indians, Chicago Cubs, Detroit Tigers, and Montreal Expos) lent their support.

Tommy and Eddie then changed the fundraiser to the Jimmy Fund (founded in 1948 when the Variety Club of New England teamed with the Boston Braves baseball team to raise money for young cancer victims). Gene Connolly, who played for both the Boston Red Sox and the Boston Celtics, was the guest of honor. Tommy and Eddie were told the Jimmy Fund could use some VCRs, so they contacted a distributor, who gave them five units at cost. They delivered them to the Jimmy Fund building and were given a nice tour. Kids in isolation could now watch movies and play video games. They both left the building with tears in their eyes but joy in their hearts that they were able to help kids in need. "We're just a couple of slobbering old fools," says Doyle.

The last "Bull to the Eliot" run had Joe Morgan, third base coach of the Boston Red Sox, as the guest of honor. Everyone found Joe to be a gracious honoree, a wonderful storyteller, and a terrific listener.

For a few years after that the run didn't happen. Then tragedy struck a young hockey goalie for Boston University, JP McKersie. JP was a doorman at the Bull & Finch and had just returned from working out with the Olympic team. One night after the pub closed, JP was riding his bicycle home at about 2 in the morning. A jeep came flying over the hill JP was climbing and struck him head on, sending him through the windshield. JP sustained massive head trauma. Eddie and Tommy resurrected the "Bull to the Eliot" run and created a lot of media and community attention. Politicians, pro hockey players, radio and TV personalities, and many runners by nature all participated in the run, with tremendous support from the Boston Police.

In 1990 the Dana-Farber Marathon Challenge became one of the inaugural organizations in the official BAA Boston Marathon Charity Program. Its primary goal is to achieve a world without cancer through its support of innovative cancer research. Runner-fundraisers who didn't qualify to run in the Boston Marathon or who simply want to run for a charitable cause can obtain entries by pledging to raise money for Dana-Farber. Like so many charitable organizations that raise enormous amounts of money through running, they provide their members with training support, exclusive race weekend activities, camaraderie, and general support. Thousands of people who otherwise would never complete a marathon have accepted the challenge in the name of the charity of their choice.

The Eliot Lounge became the unofficial headquarters of Boston's Dana-Farber Marathon Challenge members. JJ Larner, one of the Eliot's part-time bartenders and a marathon runner, had joined the DFMC in 1993. By 1994 JJ was a team captain responsible for group runs. The runners met on Thursdays at the Woodland "T" and ran the Newton hills. JJ suggested they meet at the Eliot, where they could deposit a change of clothes, take a train to Woodland, and then run the Boston Marathon course back to the Eliot. This conveniently provided him with the opportunity to get a workout in and still arrive to work in time for his shift. And it helped him provide his group with that "most important of all training ingredients...replenish your fluids," as he described in his history of the Eliot, written for his Dana-Farber co-runners before the Eliot closed. Since the Eliot epitomized the spirit of the challenge, it became the haunt of choice for the Dana-Farber runners.

One of the most enjoyable joint ventures for Tommy and Eddie was the "Bring Back Mack" campaign. Mack was one of eight bronze ducklings walking behind their mother near the Charles Street entrance to the Public Garden. Based on the beloved children's classic *Make Way for Ducklings* by Robert McCloskey, the bronze sculpture was created by Nancy Schon of West Newton.

The story is about a family of ducklings who wandered all over Beacon Hill before making their home in the Public Garden. The Bull & Finch/Cheers Pub is right across the street from the statue. Eddie could see schoolchildren with their teachers climbing all over Jack, Kack, Lack, Mack, Nack, Ouack, Pack, and Quack every day.

Mack went missing from the Boston Public Garden in December 1988. Eddie drew a likeness of Mack, which was printed on "Bring Back Mack' buttons that Tommy and Eddie sold to their customers for $1 apiece.

They also contacted Perrier, which helped them stage an ice skating party on the Public Garden pond. Guests were then invited to a dance at the Hampshire House, where they were served soup with "quackers." They held a mini-auction of books and prints in which a commemorative edition of *Make Way for Ducklings* signed by the author sold for $350.

Eddie got permission from the Friends of the Public Garden to tie yellow ribbons around the remaining ducklings to symbolize hope that Mack would return, saying, "The story tells how Mrs. Mallard was afraid to land in the Public Garden, as she was afraid of turtles and foxes. She never planned on some guy with an acetylene torch coming along."

Tommy admitted that some customers would ask him, "Are you quacking up?" when he'd approach them with buttons to buy, but everyone was happy to contribute. Doyle and Leonard recruited a number of other businesses to help sell the buttons, and they were able to raise the necessary $5,000 to have another Mack cast in bronze.

Sculptor Nancy Schon told Anne Driscoll of the *New York Times*, "I had sort of lost faith after Mack was stolen, but they (Eddie and Tommy) restored it....I couldn't believe there were two people who would care so much, who would be so thoughtful. I've had people call me, meet me, tell me how awful this thing was, but these two guys were moved to action."

The campaign received a lot of newspaper and TV news coverage. Gloria Negri's *Globe* article "Pushing Buttons to Bring Back Mack" prompted lots of letters from folks requesting buttons for their children. One mother sent a check to purchase buttons for her son's entire first-grade class. It seemed like every school child in Massachusetts was rooting for the return of Mack.

One second-grade class from the Raphael Hernandez School got involved with the letter writing campaign, sending Tommy and Eddie letters of thanks for bringing back Mack. The bartenders sent boxes of popcorn and newspaper articles about the ducklings to the children. Teacher Ginny Dunn sent letters of appreciation to the two kind-hearted bartenders who helped to bring joy to these inner-city kids. This was the beginning of a relationship that is ongoing today and has evolved into an annual event at the Bull & Finch/Cheers Pub, "Cheers for Kids."

Eddie had read about a child being killed in a drive-by shooting in the neighborhood of Ginny Dunn's school. Then he read about a young brother and sister who witnessed their father shoot their mother and then place the gun in his mouth and pull the trigger. Eddie contacted Ginny and invited the second-grade class to the Hampshire House for a meal and tour of the kitchen. Together they contacted four other inner-city schools and got them involved with the event as well. With the support of Hampshire House owner Tom Kershaw, Eddie solicited donations and wholesale items for the party. The children were thrilled with the Red Sox banners from Twins Enterprises and the Coca-Cola visors they were given.

The day I interviewed Eddie for this book in June 2004 happened to be "Cheers for Kids" day at the pub. Eddie was wearing his wizard hat: "The Wizard knows all….He has all the questions and all the answers." The kids were shouting answers to the quiz questions Eddie had made up about the city, the state, and the country, with a few involving SpongeBob Squarepants and other current cartoon characters. Once a kid gives a correct answer, he or she must let the others have a chance, and all are given prizes. Eddie's favorite question, "Who is buried in Grant's tomb?" has been answered enthusiastically and emphatically with a variety of names: "Elvis Presley!" "Whitney Houston!" "Bill Clinton!" "Johnny Damon!"

On that June day, a young girl was working in the "Cheers" gift shop. She had come to the pub as a second-grade guest of the "Cheers for Kids" program. Eddie estimates that over 2,000 kids have come to the pub through the program.

Three years after Mack was returned to the Public Garden, someone with either a blowtorch or a hacksaw confiscated Mack's sibling Ouack. Once again, Eddie drew a "Bring Back Ouack" button, and the two bartenders solicited a donation from the Poland Spring Company to make the buttons. They recruited the help of Johnson Paint on Newbury Street, Seven's Ale House on Charles Street, and the Charles Restaurant on Chestnut Street to help the Eliot and the Bull & Finch sell the buttons. Mo Vaughn of the Red Sox agreed to be the chairman of the campaign and affectionately became "Ouackman" to the kids hoping for the return of Ouack. Once again, the "duo with duende" raised enough money to replace the missing and beloved duckling.

In 1990 Tommy and Eddie began the annual Falmouth Walk, held the day before the Falmouth Road Race as a fundraiser. With thousands of people in Falmouth each year for the road race, they realized they could create a fun event for everyone, not just the runners, and raise money to help others at the same time. Walkers purchase tickets to walk a 3-mile course along Falmouth's beautiful neighborhoods and waterfront streets. They are given T-shirts (donated by such companies as Beck's, Sam Adams, and Reebok over the years) and a bag of goodies and coupons from the walk sponsors, which recently included Savings Bank Life Insurance, Sam Adams, Reebok, and the Quarterdeck Restaurant.

A couple of years ago a raffle was added to the walk, which more than doubled the funds raised and added an element of excitement to the post-walk party held behind Laureen's Restaurant. Tommy, Eddie, and friends solicit donations and gift certificates from businesses and restaurants in the village of Falmouth as well as all over New England. In 2003 Tommy solicited gift certificates for dinner for two in all fifty states based on his theory that we all enjoy commonality, and someone's "Uncle Fred" just might live in a state where a prize was won. He not only acquired a dinner for two in Frankfurt, Germany, but also a "Rod Dixon Running and Dinner Package" with dinner prepared by Rod Dixon in New Zealand. Tommy figured the lucky winner would easily work out the small detail of how to get to New Zealand.

In 2004, as the walkers enjoyed pounds of donated pasta salad, bananas, watermelon, and Smitty's ice cream, the walk committee raffled off such items as Reebok shoes and gift certificates, Red Sox tickets, Boston restaurant gift certificates, round-trip ferry tickets to the Vineyard combined with other island gift certificates, a beach motif lamp from the Lamplighter in the Berkshires, T-shirts, sweatshirts, hats, bottles of wine, and more. The businesses and restaurants of Falmouth are very supportive of this annual walk. When Tommy's friend, Holyoke Talking Turkey race director Billy Harbilas, asked his next-door neighbor and restaurant owner to donate to the cause, Michael Carduff generously gave six $50 gift certificates redeemable at his two places, the Log Cabin and the Delaney House in Holyoke.

Walkers have enjoyed and endured hot and sunny conditions as well as pelting rain over the years, but the weather never dampens the spirits of the walkers. Many of the road race entrants also look forward to participating in the walk, including Frank Shorter, Rod Dixon, and Steve Jones.

The year 2004 saw the largest crowd yet, with 490 walkers raising $12,000 for the Falmouth Free Clinic, which provides health care services to the uninsured and underinsured, as well as those with MassHealth and Medicare insurance on the Upper Cape.

The 2004 Falmouth Walk was dedicated to the memory of Eddie and Tommy's longtime friend and walk volunteer, Fran Coffey of Cohasset, who passed away suddenly in June 2004. Fran had annually devoted his time to helping with the organization of the walk and driving along the course to be sure everyone was okay.

The Walk Committee is composed of devoted volunteers such as Ed and Pat Pas, Ed and Pat Foristall, Bill and Sylvette McCabe, and Marj and Scott Williamson of East Falmouth; Rob and Rita Pacheco, Richard and Anne Prior, and Joan and Russ Pelletier of Falmouth; as well as Eddie and Marcia Doyle, Tommy, and others. Asked why he volunteers, Russ Pelletier told Joanna Briana-Gartner of the *Falmouth Enterprise*, "Tommy has done so much for so many people over the years, it's simply a great feeling to be able to help him help other people. He genuinely appreciates the efforts of all the volunteers." Tommy, when asked why he continues to do this sort of thing, simply responds, "I'll do whatever it takes to put a smile on someone's face."

As reported in the thirty-second *SBLI Falmouth Road Race Magazine*, over three dozen charities and organizations have benefited from the Falmouth Road Race, including the American Diabetes Foundation, American Liver Foundation, Angel Fund for ALS Research, Boston Children's Hospital, Cam Neely Foundation, Cape and Islands Special Olympics, Cape Cod Center for Women, Cystic Fibrosis Foundation, Dana-Farber Cancer Institute, Easter Seals, Falmouth Hospital, First Baptist Church of Hyannis, Gordon Heald ALS Fund, Gosnold Treatment Center, Help for Abused Women and Children, Hospice of South Shore, Lawrence Boys and Girls Club, Leukemia and Lymphoma Society, Lymphoma Research Foundation, Make-A-Wish Foundation, Multiple Sclerosis Society, Steppingstone Foundation, Team Cheryl for Lymphoma Research, United Way, and the Will McDonough Fund. In 2003 these groups received over $325,000 from the Falmouth Road Race. The following year $460,000 was raised and donated to sixty-seven nonprofit groups.

Locally, more than $33,000 was distributed in 2004 to Falmouth groups, including sports teams, youth and scout groups, scholarship funds, and community organizations such as Falmouth Hospital, Falmouth Free Clinic, Celebration 2004, Falmouth Teen Center, Falmouth Recreation Department, Falmouth Parent Teacher Organization, Falmouth Community TV, Falmouth Amateur Radio Club, Falmouth Parks Department, Falmouth Band Parents, and the Visiting Nurse Association.

SBLI President and CEO Robert K. Sheridan said, "It has been very gratifying to see the tremendous response to this program. Most of the participants have gone well beyond the minimum fund-raising requirement to earn their numbers. This has become a true labor of love for them. We are proud to be a part of this effort."

Tommy Leonard, who has spent an entire lifetime giving to others, gets his greatest satisfaction and pleasure from knowing that his little race from pub to pub that had ninety-eight runners in its 1973 inaugural run now touches the lives of so many, many people in such positive ways. Not only have people improved their own health by participating in the race, but they have also increased the joy in their hearts as they help the many causes that the race is involved with.

When Tommy established the Westfield Road Race in the 1990s, he asked that the money raised be split between the athletic programs at Westfield High, Westfield Vocational, and St. Mary's High. He wanted to give back to the community that had given him a chance in life.

Tommy has had several scholarships and awards established in his name to support runners and athletic programs. On the tenth anniversary of the Falmouth Road Race, a group of Tommy's friends established the Tommy Leonard Scholarship Fund to help defray college expenses for deserving runners at both Falmouth High and Westfield High. The "Falmouth in the Fall" road race, directed by Don Facey, is a quieter version of the Falmouth Road Race. It follows the same course in the month of November, when hordes of humanity no longer populate the Cape. Proceeds of the race benefit the Tom Leonard Awards Fund, which goes to deserving runners at Falmouth High and Westfield High as well as the Lupus Foundation of America–Massachusetts chapter.

During the Christmas holiday season of 1977, Billy Rodgers and his brother Charlie went for a group run with eleven other runners, singing Christmas carols as they ran to Boston Common. This gave birth to the annual Jingle Bell Run, a casual fun run whose proceeds benefit the Massachusetts Special Olympics. Thirteen years later, Billy helped to organize a Jingle Bell Run in Springfield, Massachusetts, to benefit the Pioneer Valley Special Olympics. Billy initiated the Tommy Leonard Award at that first run, to be given annually to someone who has helped promote the sport of running.

The first Tommy Leonard Award was given to Ed Carroll, Jr., of Longmeadow, who at the time owned Riverside Amusement Park. He was also president of the Sheriff's Track Club and subsidized the Riverside Park Twilight 5-miler.

Other recipients of the Tommy Leonard Award have included Michael Tierney, director of the Holyoke St. Patrick's Day 10K since 1975 and Tommy's foster brother; Billy Harbilas, director of the Holyoke Elks Talking

Turkey 10K; and Dick Osgood, director of the Great Paper Chase (a 10K sponsored by the Springfield newspapers) and writer of the "On the Run" column in the *Sunday Republican.*

Eddie Doyle and the staff at the Bull & Finch/Cheers Pub at the Hampshire House annually raise money from their loyal customers and the many tourists who come to see Cheers. Eddie remembers the first fundraiser for the *Globe* Santa Fund in 1978. The patrons got into a drunken bidding war up and down the bar over a $2.99 Yahtzee game that was being auctioned. The game sold for $250, and the auction brought in $600 that year. By 1984 the proceeds were $23,800, and in 1989 the Cheers effort donated $42,966 to the fund, which is a campaign by the *Boston Globe* to distribute gifts to needy children at Christmas.

When Boston Bruins hockey standout Cam Neely and his brother Scott began to raise money for the Neely House at Tufts–New England Medical Center, a bed-and-breakfast–style home away from home for cancer patients and their families, Eddie (a former hockey player himself) organized one of the first fund-raising events to support it. He created a "tongue-in-cheek award" for a worthy member of the Boston Bruins hockey team. Called the Eddie LeBec Memorial Cup, it was named after the character on the *Cheers* sitcom who was married to Carla, the feisty waitress. As it turned out, all the players who received this award over the years were traded, were sent to the minors, became injured, or retired. The award became the "kiss of death" for the players. One recipient, Dave Poulin (now the coach at Notre Dame), got food poisoning and couldn't appear to receive his award. His teammate Don Sweeney was supposed to drop it off at Poulin's house, but didn't want to touch it for fear of bad luck.

In 1991 this event was added to the *Globe* Santa Fund event, which evolved into a "Cheers for Children" grand auction and gala party sponsored by the Kershaw Foundation and Hampshire House. 2004 was the twenty-fifth anniversary of the auction, and the proceeds benefited the *Globe* Santa Fund, the Neely Cancer Fund, the Jimmy Fund, and Friends of Floating Hospital for Children. The *Globe* Santa Fund has received over $400,000 since the event began, and Eddie estimates that the other three groups have received over $170,000 each over the past fourteen years. As a volunteer for Friends of Floating Hospital for Children, Eddie is gratified by how he sees the money being spent.

As of December 2004, "Cheers for Children" reached the million-dollar mark in funds raised over the twenty-five-year life of the event!

Eddie and Tommy had another collaboration that wasn't exactly a charitable fundraiser, but took some dedication to accomplish. Tommy came up with the idea of painting Billy Rodgers's footprint on the half-mile markers along the Charles River Esplanade for a 10K distance, and got a permit from the city to do it. Although he had mentioned the idea to Billy, he never did get Billy's footprint on paper. So Eddie Doyle stuck his foot in a bucket of paint and created a stencil out of it.

One hot summer day, the duo set out in the early morning with a few footprint and number stencils and began painting the walkway with "Billy Rodgers's footprint." Eddie was due at work at 10 AM, so Tommy went with him for a few brews and some chili before opening up the Eliot.

When Eddie's shift ended, he joined T.L. at the Eliot for a few pints of Bass Ale and they then took their measuring wheel back to Memorial Drive to finish the job. It was now beastly hot, and swarms of gnats and mosquitoes were clinging to the sweat on their faces. The dark and the drink and the dogged insects had the duo dazed, but once they located the spot where they'd left off in the morning, they were able to complete the job, going all the way around the old MDC Police Station. For several years, many a runner measured their workout by "Billy's footprints," until the paint ran thin and disappeared.

Tommy and Eddie were featured on the cover of the April 6, 1995, issue of the *Boston Globe Calendar* along with Boston bartenders Jim (Lockers) Loughlin of Paddy Burke's, Janet Bernazzi of Frogg Lane, and Martin Berry of 8 Holyoke for an article by Kevin Cullen titled "Boston Bartenders—What It Takes to Be the Best." Tommy and Eddie were cited not only for their personable skills with their customers but for their avid community service as well.

Tommy Leonard and Eddie Doyle have chests of memorabilia containing countless letters of thanks from individuals, churches, schools and school children, athletic teams and organizations, corporations, newspapers, radio stations, magazine editors and writers, road race directors, and others. All have been helped in some way, whether with food or prize donations, road race help, travel and accommodation help during road race and marathon weekends, or fund-raising efforts. Every letter thanks them for their kindness, generosity, loyalty, support, enthusiasm, and spirit of goodwill.

Despite the hard work and dedication that has gone into their efforts, they are quick to credit their philanthropic success to their bars' management, staff, and loyal customers and friends who have supported them throughout the years.

Today, Eddie continues to manage and tend bar at the Hampshire House and Cheers in Boston. Tommy has found a home, a job, and a very satisfying life in the village of Falmouth. People continue to flock to the Quarterdeck Restaurant to enjoy his wit and humor and his ability to lift one's spirits.

Tommy now works part-time, so the bartenders at the Quarterdeck are often barraged with the question "Where's Tommy?" to which the usual response is something along the lines of "Well, there have been a lot of spottings…"

12

Cape Cod

The Finish Line

"I'm not doing too bad for an over-the-hill bartender. Now it's time for a cold pop"

—Tommy Leonard

When the Eliot Lounge closed in September 1996, many patrons went through a sort of period of mourning. According to Dr. Charles Tifft, a regular in Coach's Corner with Coach Squires, Joe Concannon, Jack Kearney, Bernie Corbett, Charlie Pierce, Leigh Montville, and others, "We were now a bunch of men without a club. We used to meet for a beer and to see if anyone needed anything. We had our own private parking on the bridge and the meter maids ignored us. We'd have a drink or two, say hello to Tommy, talk to our friends, and then the evening band would start to set up and that would drive us out. It kept us well behaved and out of trouble."

Eddie Doyle reflected to Lisa Amand of the *Herald*, "The Eliot was an institution. Somebody can't just say I'm going to take over where the Eliot left off. I don't think anything can ever replace the Eliot. It was more than just a friendly neighborhood bar." Doyle recalled how its absence really hit home after the running of the Tufts 10K in Boston. "We stood there like refugees trying to figure out where to go."

Nine years after the Eliot closed, *Sports Illustrated* ran an article during Super Bowl week 2005 on the "25 Best Sports Bars in America," which had a sidebar article titled "Requiem for a Beloved Bar," written by Charlie Pierce (one of many writers who were daily bolted to the stools of the bar after work), that lamented the demise of the Eliot as "one of the best sports bars ever." Pierce wrote how he had just finished writing a book in 2000 and "was halfway to my car on my way to toast the occasion before I remembered that the place wasn't there anymore. All of the celebration went out of me and into the air because there didn't seem to be any real place for it to go."

For a few years after the closing of the Eliot, Tommy was hired by the Back Bay Brewing Company on Boylston Street, near the marathon's old finish line, to continue his role as "Official Greeter." The Back Bay created a Tommy Leonard Room with lots of the photos and memorabilia from the walls of the Eliot.

Although the Eliot was gone and left a gaping hole in many runners' plans for marathon weekend, finding Tommy's smiling face at the Back Bay gave comfort to these lost souls looking for their "Good Shepherd of Running" to pontificate with about their running experiences. Tommy was in his element, saying, "I'll be greeting people and making them feel welcome in the City of Boston. I thrive on that."

One week before the 1998 Boston Marathon, Tommy was treated for melanoma at the Boston Evening Medical Clinic. Shaken by the experience, Tommy said, "I can deal with this because if anything, this experience has intensified my appreciation for the aesthetics in life.

"It changed my perspective, but I don't know if I'm going to the checkout counter....There are a hell of a lot of people worse off than I am. I don't know too many bartenders who've had the experiences I've enjoyed. I've had the best customers, the best friends. I don't want to get down about this."

In April 2000 Tommy arrived at the Back Bay Brewing Company with his arms full of shamrocks to honor his beloved friend and *Globe* sportswriter for thirty-three years, Joe Concannon. Joe had passed away in February that year at the age of sixty, two years to the day after his mother, Mary Concannon, died in Litchfield, Connecticut.

"I don't want to see black armbands," said Leonard. "Joe loved Ireland and this would be a good way of honoring him. He did so much for the running community." Green shamrocks were seen on many runners, marathon officials, volunteers, friends, and members of the media in 2000 to honor their friend.

Tommy went into a kind of limbo when the Eliot first closed, not knowing what to do with himself after twenty-four years as one of Boston's most personable and genuine bartenders. At the time, my husband and I owned the Cork 'n Hearth Restaurant in the Berkshires of Western Massachusetts. We invited Tommy to live with us and work the bar for the holiday season.

Tommy joined us enthusiastically and helped us through the holidays, despite his change making and drink mixing deficiencies. His good humor and jovial personality kept the customers happy regardless of whether their soup or salad happened to be delivered after their entrée or dessert. After the holiday season, he made plans to go visit his Westfield buddies Don Foley and John O'Connor in California while he pondered his future.

Upon returning to the East Coast, he gravitated back to his beloved village of Falmouth and found a job as a bartender at Rob and Rita Pacheco's Quarterdeck Restaurant on Main Street His longtime friend Don Facey gave Tommy a room at his house for a while, and T.L. settled into a new life on Cape Cod, making new friends and enjoying old ones.

This was 1997 and the year of the twenty-fifth anniversary of the Falmouth Road Race, which provided Tommy with endless activities to plan for the festivities of that event. Rob and Rita discovered in no time that their new employee was good for business, as hordes of runners and other friends began to descend on the restaurant.

Tommy became friendly with QD bartender Marjorie Mitchell, who was quite friendly with QD regulars Richard and Anne Prior. The Priors are second-home owners in Falmouth as well as owners of investment real estate. Along with Margie, the Priors kept their eyes open for an appropriate apartment for Tommy. When the Priors purchased a small commercial building on Palmer Avenue, they realized the bungalow in the rear of the property could be an ideal home for Tommy.

Located less than a mile from the QD, the one-bedroom bungalow offered a spacious open living/dining/kitchen area and a private backyard perfect for gardening and bird-watching, one of Tommy's favorite activities.

So, at age sixty-seven, after a lifetime of living in other people's homes and apartments, Thomas Francis Leonard moved into the first home he could truly call his own. In exchange for a few maintenance jobs on the property, the Priors offered Tommy a very reasonable rent and the happiness of enjoying his own space in the autumn of his life.

In 2000 Richard and Ed Pas of East Falmouth built an outdoor shower for Tommy in his backyard so that he could enjoy one of the Cape's greatest pleasures—standing *au naturel* under an open sky, washing away the sea's salt from the skin. It was dedicated with a well-attended "shower party." Attendees sported "Tommy's shower" T-shirts designed by Sally Rohan, and they all piled into the new shower stall for the "memorial pictures." The T-shirt depicts a mustachioed and eyeglassed image of Tommy under a baseball cap running in the buff into the shower with a couple of female runners "towel-whipping" his butt while a small bird sings atop the shower stall.

The Quarterdeck Restaurant has been sold to the Jarvis family, and Tommy continues as part-time bartender, truly enjoying the generosity and care the Jarvises extend to him. They have created Holy Cow Ale, with T.L.'s photo in the center of the logo on the stick for those who want to enjoy some "Tommy" suds.

QD bartender Jeff Fumorala first met Tommy in the 1990s, when he would travel from his hometown of Troy, New York to run the Boston Marathon and make an annual visit to the Eliot and his friend, Tommy. Jeff happened to be in Boston on the last day the Eliot was open, so he stopped in for a beer with Tommy. That was the last Jeff saw of Tommy.

Then, in 1999, Jeff decided to make a change in his life and he moved to Falmouth. He picked up a job as a bartender at Liam Maguire's, and within his first two weeks on the job he won the Friday night 5-miler held weekly in Falmouth (an informal race that Tommy helped Courtney Bird and Kenny Gartner to get started). Liam's wife noticed in the paper that Jeff had won and said, "I see you are a runner. Do you know Tommy Leonard?" "Yeah," Jeff replied, "I know Tommy." She then astonished Jeff by saying that Tommy worked down the street at the Quarterdeck Restaurant.

As Jeff walked into the QD, Tommy looked up from behind the bar, exclaiming, "Jeff! Holy Cow! What are you doing here?" "I live here, Tommy," he said. "I live here too!" exclaimed Tommy. "You've got to work here, Jeff!" Owner Rob Pacheco came down that night to meet Jeff and hired him on the spot. Jeff and Tommy have worked together for the past six years. When the Pachecos sold to the Jarvises, the bartending duo weren't sure if the new owners would be bringing in their own staff. The Jarvis family has owned the Chart Room in Cataumet, Massachusetts, for the past thirty-five years, so their keen assessment told them that their bartenders were assets and it would be foolish to replace them.

Tommy's ability to remember people's names and facts about them continues to charm his customers and friends alike. Recently, however, there were a couple of incidents in which his friends worried that he might be losing it.

One such event occurred in May 2004, when Tommy traveled with Billy Harbilas and his fiancée Sally Rohan to the Boulder-to-Boulder Race in Colorado as guests of Steve Jones.

Tommy was approached by a gentleman saying, "Tommy Leonard!" Tommy responded, "Hi, how are you?" with no recognition on his face. It was the first time in over thirty years that Billy witnessed Tommy not knowing someone who approached him. Tommy asked, "Where are you from?" and the gentleman said, "Tommy, you don't recognize me?" "Well, what's your name?" Tommy asked. "Jimmy Fitzgibbons," the man replied. "Jimmy Fitzgibbons! Holy Cow! Where the hell did the rest of you go?" Tommy exclaimed. "Well, I lost 120 pounds," Jimmy said. "No wonder I didn't recognize you. Someone give this guy a sandwich. He needs it!" Tommy cried.

Russ Pelletier of Falmouth had a similar experience with Tommy when they went to the Peoples Beach to Beacon 10K road race in Cape Elizabeth, Maine, guests of Joan Benoit Samuelson. During the awards ceremony, Russ and Tommy were sitting on a park bench listening to the proceedings when a group of runners approached them. One of them took a look at Tommy and said, "I know you. You're Tommy Leonard! We finished the Boston Marathon together in the early '80s." Although Tommy did not recognize him at first, he carried on a lengthy conversation with him. Suddenly, Tommy looked at him and said, "You're a teacher, aren't you?" "Yes, I just retired this year," the runner replied.

While driving home, Russ, who'd been stunned by the exchange said to Tommy, "I have to ask you. The only time you ever spoke to that guy was twenty-three years ago while you were finishing a marathon. How the hell did you remember that he was a teacher?" Thinking for a moment, Tommy said, "Well, I remembered that we were talking about it as we ran."

There is a lifetime of food stories connected to Tommy, as he somehow manages to leave a trail of crumbs, ice cream drippings, or fried rice all over the floors, walls, or bathtubs he passes or falls into. One Monday after the Falmouth Road Race, Billy Harbilas was in the QD with Steve Jones while Tommy worked the bar. Steve was laughing his head off, so Tommy came over saying, "Okay, Billy. I can see you are telling stories. What are you talking about now?"

Billy said, "Well, it's not the most complimentary story. It's about you and food." Looking at Billy, Tommy said, "The mashed potatoes in Minnesota?" "No." "The spaghetti in Syracuse?" "No." "The baked Alaska in Malibu?" "No." "The chocolate chip cookies in Peoria?" "No." "The swordfish in Westfield?" "No." "The steak and potatoes in Holyoke?" "No." "The clams in Chicago?" "No." "The chicken fried rice in Westfield?" "No, Tommy, it wasn't that either. I guess it wasn't the first food problem you ever had." Tommy said, "Billy, I've had trouble with food all my life."

Even Neil Cusack, the only Irishman to win the Boston Marathon, recalled a gastrointestinal anecdote from when Tommy stayed with the Cusacks for the Dublin Marathon in the 1980s. Tommy came down distraught one morning because he had swallowed a very expensive false tooth. Not knowing what to say, Neil suggested he let nature take its course. A couple of days later, an elated Tommy announced that he had retrieved his false tooth!

"Falmouth Chatterbox" Kitty Baker wrote of Tommy in the October 10, 2004, *Cape Cod Times*. "Seeing him pictured with children who need a helping hand pulls at the heartstrings and makes one happy to know him….He could easily rest on his laurels, but not Tom, he continues to organize, give of his time and be as affable as he can to all who know him."

As Tommy goes about his days on Cape Cod, many people are looking out for him. He manages to get rides to the market and other places he needs to go. The Jarvises are generous with the "full scholarship" Tommy enjoys at the QD. Richard Prior and Ed Pas make sure the bungalow is well maintained and cared for. Many of the people I interviewed for this book said that Tommy always seems to have a guardian angel looking out for him. But as Leigh Montville so poignantly pointed out while recalling when the regulars would occasionally pitch in and get him a room for the night at the Eliot Hotel so he wouldn't sleep on top of the beer cases in the basement, "Tommy created his guardian angels with the way he treated people and cared about them."

Tommy's friends have planted a wall of impatiens along his backyard fence, birdhouses fill his yard, and the Marine Corps flag hangs daily by his front door. Tommy enjoys his little piece of heaven and literally feeds the birds with his bare hands. While he sits with his birds and flowers and thinks over his lifetime of accomplishments and experiences, perhaps he ponders the words on the plaque of the well in Grandmother's Garden in Westfield, where he used to walk the girls while skipping high school track practice:

> The Kiss of the Sun for Pardon
>
> The Song of the Birds for Mirth
>
> One Is Nearer God's Heart in a Garden
>
> Than Anywhere Else on Earth

One of Tommy's favorite books is *Tuesdays with Morrie* by Mitch Albom. The lessons that Mitch learned from Morrie are lessons that Tommy seems to have known his whole life: "The way you get meaning into your life is to devote yourself to loving others, devote yourself to your community around you, and devote yourself to creating something that gives you purpose and meaning....Do the kinds of things that come from the heart. When you do, you won't be dissatisfied, you won't be envious, you won't be longing for someone else's things. On the contrary, you'll be overwhelmed with what comes back."

The little boy whose father left him at the mission at age six had a poet's soul and the tenacity to follow his dreams. Despite the fact that his bank account has never been one of his largest assets, he has traveled to several countries, attended several Olympics, and seen much of the United States by virtue of the friendships he has developed while caring for and about others. He is the first to say his life has been filled with joys and blessings. The assets in Tommy's Leonard's portfolio are intangible, and he wouldn't trade them for all the money in the world. Many friends interviewed for this book commented that if the measure of your life is how many friends you have, then, just like George Bailey in *It's a Wonderful Life*, "Tommy is the richest guy I know."

No amount of abuse, beatings, or disappointments could make young Tommy Leonard view the glass as half empty. To him, the glass (or, in his case, pint) is always half full, and with a little bit of effort the suds of life's joys will be brimming to a blissful cascade over the top.

Wanting a family to call his own, he created the largest family one could ever have. The crowd assembled at the Tommy Leonard Wicked Awesome Hampshire House Happening in 1996 represented a vast cross-section of that "Tommy Leonard family." As he gazed out at the crowd that night and exclaimed to this family of his, "If this is Heaven, I am going to be a good boy," Tommy Leonard knew that Heaven on earth had already found him.

The Answering Machine at the Bungalow

September 28, 2000

"There's a touch of fall in the air as I speak. The best season is yet to come....Tom Leonard here. I will return your call."

October 11, 2000

Phone answers to harmonica music playing the Marine Corps Hymn followed by: "Corporal Thomas Francis Leonard; I'll get back to you! *Semper Fi!*"

November 23, 2000

"It's my all-time favorite holiday of the year. Happy Thanksgiving! I'll get back to you as soon as possible. Bye-byyeeee!"

October 21, 2002

"Happy Fall to one and all. I shall return your important call. Tom Leonard here at the Bungalow"

November 22, 2002

"Over the hills and through the woods to Grandmother's house we go [sung by T.L.]. Happy Thanksgiving. I'll return your call as soon as I get back. Bye-byyeeee!"

February 6, 2003

"This is Tom Leonard emanating from the quaint little village of Falmouth-by-the-Sea. Spring is in the air! [while snow was on the ground] Bye-byyyeee!"

March 26, 2003

"Good Morning. You have reached the bungalow of Thomas Francis Leonard. I'm not here but I *will* be and I will return your call. Happy Spring! Bye-byyeee!"

February 6, 2004

"Good Morning, Mr. And Mrs. America and all the ships at sea! I will return your call when I get back from my walk around the block. Happy Spring….It is just around the corner!"

March 23, 2004

"Good Morning, World! Tom Leonard emanating from the Bungalow in the quaint little village of Falmouth-by-the-Sea. I will return your call as soon as I get back from the old QD! Until then, Cheerio!"

July 20, 2004

"By the sea, by the sea, by the beautiful sea

You and me, You and me

Oh how happy we will be! [sung by Tommy]

Tom Leonard in Falmouth. Will return your call as soon as I get back. So there! Bye-byeeee!"

August 6, 2004

[Paraphrased:] "I don't care if your name is George W. Bush, Laura Bush, John F. Kerry, Ted Kennedy, Arnold Schwarzenegger, Mitt Romney, Sally, Sarah, Billy, Bud, Randy, Bobby, Jimmy, Glenn, Michael, Joanie, Grete, Lynn, Frank, Bernie, Jackie, Jeff, Dave, Scott, or Mr. Magoo. I have no more numbers for the Falmouth Road Race!"

September 12, 2004

"I've never felt better in my life and I hope you feel the same. Have a great afternoon. I'll call you back. Bye-byeeeee!"

October 6, 2004

'Tis the season to go leaf peeping

And inhale that crisp autumn air

And await the World Series between the Boston Red Stockings and the St. Louis Red Birds. So there! And I will return your call, by the way!"

October 19, 2004

"Good Morning! Good Morning! Happy Almost Halloween! Looks like it's the Red Birds. I'm a little suspect about the Red Stockings. They may be down but they're not out. So hang in, baby! Bye-bye pumpkin pie!"

October 26, 2004

"Happy Red October! Congratulations Red Stockings and Red Birds. Not sure who I'm going to cheer for but I like living in New England so you can make that decision. I'll return your call. Happy Halloween! Bye-byeeee!"

October 31, 2004

"Good Morning! Good Morning! I think the Cardinals flew the coop. Outside of that, life is good! I'll return your call."

January 9, 2005

"Good Morning, Mr. And Mrs. America and all the ships at sea. This is Tom Leonard emanating from the Bungalow in the quaint village of Falmouth-by-the-Sea. I want to wish everyone the happiest New Year ever! Bye-byeeee!"

March 17, 2005

"Good Morning! Happy Almost Spring! But more importantly, Happy St. Patrick's Day! Just be patient. Spring is just around the corner. The little bluebirds and chickadees will soon be returning from Ft. Lauderdale-by-the-Sea to Falmouth-by-the-snow bank [after one of Cape Cod's snowiest winters]. Till then, I will return your call! Bye-byeeeeee!"

April 7, 2005

"Good Morning, All! After this drab and dreary winter, spring is HERE! The grass will be greener than green and the little songbirds will return. So, lighten up! I will return your call. Bye-Byeee!"

April 17, 2005

"Good Morning, All! The little songbirds have returned from Ft. Lauderdale. It's gonna be a great day Monday for the Marathon so I'll see ya there! I will return your message. Bye-Byeeee!"

Bibliography

The Boston Globe

Bauer, Nancy. "80 Beer Chasers Drink and Run," August 30, 1981.

Bickelhaupt, Susan. "Shorter, Rodgers Face Off," August 14, 1998.

———. "No Run of the Mill Race, Falmouth Can Be called an Event," August 15, 1999.

Bickelhaupt, Susan, and Dezell, Maureen. "Tommy Leonard Room at Back Bay," September 30, 1997.

Buchanan, William. "Marathon is His Baby," April 18, 1975.

Burris, Joe. "Feats Commemorated by Running Stars' Feet," July 17, 1993.

Chamberlain, Tony. "Still the Scenic Route after 28 Years, Falmouth Race Has Not Lost Its Appeal," August 20, 2000.

Cobb, Nathan. "Over-rated," July 13, 1983.

Concannon, Joe. "How Many Starting Line Crashers Tomorrow?" July 16, 1976.

———. "Leonard Gets His Just Due," November 1977.

———. "Falmouth's Finest Hour," August 23, 1980.

———. "Fukuoka Loses Runners, Appeal," November 28, 1980.

———. "Fukuoka Was for the Fastest," December 25, 1980.

———. "Falmouth Place to Be," August 16, 1981.

———. "Last Chance for Falmouth," May 1, 1982.

———. "Scholarship Tribute to Leonard," June 26, 1982.

———. "BAA Plans on Troika to Direct Marathon," July 17, 1982.

———. "Beardsley Still Savors Boston," August 7, 1982.

———. "Falmouth Ten Years Running," August 14, 1982.

———. "New Year's Resolutions," January 1, 1983.

———. "Falmouth Has Makings of 4300 Carat Gem," August 20, 1983.

———. "Boston at Crossroads," April 13, 1983.

———. "I Doubt I'll Make It," May 19, 1984.

———. "A Vastly Changed Face at Falmouth," August 25, 1984.

———. "Hodge and Falmouth Grow Together," August 26, 1984.

———. "How Boston's Running Class Views Boston," April 12, 1985.

———. "A Fast Formidable Field for Riverside 5-Miler," May 26, 1985.

———. "Falmouth Star-Riddled Tommy Leonard's Dream True as Ever," August 17, 1985.

———. "Hancock Puts 10 M on Marathon," September 5, 1985.

———. "Marathon Follows Green Line: Boston's 90 Year Tradition Is Now a Run for the Money," April 18, 1986.

———. "Leonard Legacy, Falmouth's Unique Flavor," August 16, 1986.

———. "Homeward Bound Tommy Leonard Follows His Heart Back to Boston," February 17, 1987.

———. "A Glorious Field Day for Boston," April 19, 1987.

———. "Leonard, Falmouth: A Winning Combination," July 13, 1987.

———. "It's a Coming of Age for Falmouth Road Race: 15-Year-Old Road Race Grows to International Prominence," August 16, 1987.

———. "BAA Starts Early," October 30, 1987.

———. "Hyannis Marathon Strictly for Fun," February 20, 1988.

———. "A Test for Samuelson," August 20, 1988.

———. "Falmouth Can Still Get Leonard's Heart Racing," August 19, 1989.

———. "Falmouth Just Keeps Going: Last Year's Champs Set to Defend," August 18, 1990.

———. "It's a First for Falmouth: Treacy at Starting Line," August 19, 1991.

———. "In her 10th Race, Joan Benoit Samuelson Reigns as Queen of Falmouth," August 17, 1991.

———. "Their Marathon Imprints 15 Years Ago," April 17, 1992.

———. "Tommy Leonard Had a Burst of Inspiration 20 Years Ago," August 16, 1992.

———. "Falmouth Gets Set for Another Field Day," August 24, 1994.

———. "Meyers, Somers Are on Collision Course: Johnny on the Spot," April 15, 1995.

———. "Falmouth Sweetens Pot for Top US Finishers," May 5, 1995.

———. "Leonard's Dream Marks Anniversary in Falmouth," August 19, 1995.

———. "Leonard's Spirits Get a Boost: Greeter Savors Week Despite Illness," April 17, 1998.

———. "Out from the Shadows," April 19, 1998.

Concannon, Joe, and Barbara Huebner. "Samuelson at 40 Just May Master Boston," April 18, 1997.

Collins, Bud. "Tommy Leonard, Marathoner," April 18, 1981.

Cullen, Kevin. "What It Takes to Be the Best Boston Bartenders," April 6, 1995.

Globe staff. "Marathon Notebook," April 17, 1977.

Griffith, Bill. "The Long Run Flynn Plan to Spur BAA to Action," July 11, 1985.

Huebner, Barbara, Marvin Pave, Michael Madden, Bill Griffith, and Don MacAuley. "Number Crunching Brings Total to 17,813," April 17, 2000.

Indrisano, Ron. "Greetings," April 18, 1986.

Lord, Ken, and Bob Monahan. "Great Non-Beer Chase," October 18, 1985.

Madden, Michael. "Paying Their Bill: Today's Event at BC a Tribute to Squires," April 16, 1989.

———. "It's Last Call at the Eliot Lounge," September 27, 1996.

Martins, Gus. "Litchfield Race Loaded with Talent, Charm," June 11, 1989.

Negri, Gloria. "Pushing Buttons to Bring Mack Back," February 24, 1989.

———. "Friendship Pact over Mack is New Twirl in Duck Tale," June 15, 1989.

———. "Again Boston Duo Make a Way to Replace Duckling," March 22, 1992.

Powers, John. "Fastest Drinkers on Two Feet," April 1977.

———. "Where Runners Can Be Sociable," April 1979.

———. "The Shore Thing: Falmouth Guarantees Starry Field," August 11, 2002.

————. "Falmouth Five Appear to Be in It for the Long Run," August 8, 2003.

Roberts, Ernie. "Road Racing Has a Convert," April 17, 1975.

Shaughnessy, Dan. "Wallowing in Their Footsteps," July 11, 1993.

Thomas, Jack. "Running a Tab at Eliot Lounge for Marathon Runners," August 20, 1993.

"Wetzel, Sally. "Stolen Duckling Replaced," April 17, 1989.

The Boston Herald

Armand, Lisa. "Where Will the Thirsty Run?" April 18, 1997.

Connolly, John. "Tom Will Win This Race," January 3, 1988.

————. "Running Classic Is a Real Love Affair," August 17, 1997.

————. "Falmouth Road Race, Thrive at 25, Falmouth Hits Milestone in Stride," August 17, 1997.

————. "Leonard Keeps Eye on Sunny Side," August 16, 1999.

Dew, Dick. "It's a World Series of Distance Running," April 16, 1979.

Dornbusch, Jane. "Run for Their Money: Restaurants Race to Prepare for Marathon," April 14, 1998.

Gee, Michael. Boston Marathon, Runners Have Spring in their Step, April 19, 1999.

Harris, Steve, "BAA Is Next Test for New Mom," April 16, 1978.

————. "Rodgers, Rodgers, Rodgers," April 17, 1979.

Herald staff. "Marathon Magic," April 16, 1978.

————. "Strongest International Field," April 17, 1978.

————. "Front Runners Predictions," April 16, 1979.

————. "Beautiful Run in the Sun," August 19,1985.

Kimball, George. "Tommy Leonard Gears up for Grind," April 6, 1980.

————. "Lounge Act Nears Finish," April 8, 1996.

————. "101st Marathon: Guru the Best Guest, Bar None," April 22, 1997.

Reavis, Toni. "A Fitting Farewell: This Falmouth May Be Leonard's Last," August 10, 1986.

Vaughan, Robin. "A Piece of Ireland Leaves the Eliot," September 27, 1996.

Periodicals

Angelo, Holly. "First Westfield Road Race Gets Started on Right Foot," *Springfield Union News*, May 10, 1993.

Balf, Todd. "Midnight at the Eliot Lounge," *Yankee Magazine*

Bennett, Elizabeth. "Boston's Tommy Leonard Gives Houston a Run for Its Money," *Houston Post*, October 22, 1986.

Bisson, Kristin. "Requiem for the Eliot, BAA 101st Boston Marathon Program," April 1997.

Bogen, Mike. "Tommy Puts Bite into Talking Turkey 10K," *Springfield Union News*, November 16, 1995.

Burfoot, Amby. "The Race to Decide the King of the Road," *Runner's World*, November 1978.

————. "Tommy Leonard, Eliot Lounge Barkeeper Extraordinaire," *Runner's World*, April 1983.

Bruce, Allan. "26 Miles and Nary a Bucket of Suds," *NH Sunday News*, February 25, 1973.

"Dedicate Heights Bench to Road Race Founder," *Falmouth Enterprise*, August 5, 1985.

Denison, Jim. "Thirstiness of the Long Distance Runner: The Natural Affinity of Running and Beer," *All About Beer*, July 2002.

Driscoll, Anne. "Two Boston Bartenders Try to Do Something about Tale of Woe," *New York Times*, April 16, 1989.

Duca, Rob. "Denmark Award Recognizes Courageous Firefighter," *Falmouth Road Race Official Magazine*, August 1998.

———. "Denmark Award Recognizes Special Achievement," *Falmouth Road Race Official Magazine*, August 1999.

———. "He Went to Lofty Heights," *Cape Cod Times*, August 9, 2004.

"Economic Impact Survey Concludes Runners Are Big Spenders," *32nd SBLI Falmouth Road Race Official Magazine*, August 8, 2004.Falmouth Enterprise Road Race Supplement, August 15, 1980.

Falmouth Road Race. Enterprise Publishing, August 1999.

Falmouth Road Race. Enterprise Publishing, August 2000.

Gartner, Ken. "Tommy Leonard Recalls the Early Years," *Falmouth Enterprise*, August 1997.

Giera, Theresa Mett. "Dr. Tommy Leonard," *Springfield Sunday Republican*, May 26, 1985.

Hawkins, Brent. "Running Guru Visits Uniontown," *Greensburg Tribune-Review*, August 21, 1983.

———. "History of the Litchfield Road Race," *27th Litchfield Hills 2003 Road Race Program*, June 2003.

Higgins, Bill. "Denmark Award Honors Courageous Achievement," *Falmouth Road Race Official Magazine*, August 1992.

———. "Falmouth's 25th Reunion—One for the Ages," *Falmouth Road Race Official Magazine*, August 16, 1998.

————. "Ron Pokraka: Staying the Course, Somehow, Some Way," *30th SBLI Falmouth Road Race Official Magazine*, August 11, 2002.

————. "Fleet Feat," *Cape Cod Times*, August 9, 2004.

Jacobson, Murray. "Road Race Adopts Polish Theme: Kielbasa Spices up Polkas," *Springfield Union News*, May 16, 1994.

Kenney, Paul. "A Run for the Eliot," *Patriot Ledger*, April 17, 2000.

Kimball, George. "Footloose 'n Frenetic in Falmouth," *Boston Phoenix Sporting Eye*, August 24, 1976.

————. "Guru on Tap," *Official Program, NYC Marathon*, October 1977.

Lajoie, Rick. "Westfield 5K Race Popular, Fun Event," *Springfield Union News,* September 14, 2000.

Loth, Renee. "Why I Drink Where I Drink," *New England Monthly*, October 1985.

Lussier, Mark. "She Made the Race Work," *Springfield Union News*, May 16, 1994.

Maclone, Rich. "SBLI CEO Plans to Be Around for Long Haul," *Falmouth Enterprise*, August 14, 2001.

Matheson, Kathy. "It's Been Quite a Run," *Middlesex News*, April 13, 1996.

Montville, Leigh. "A Road Well Traveled," *Sports Illustrated*, April 20, 1987.

Osgood, Dick. "Talking Turkey Had Quite a Start," *Springfield Sunday Republican*, November 18, 1990.

————. "Holyoke's Numbers Add Up," *Springfield Sunday Republican*, March 15, 1992.

————. "Holyoke Tradition Grows," *Springfield Sunday Republican*, March 14, 1993.

————. "Road Racing Committee Honors 'Quiet Man' Tierney," *Springfield Union News*, December 5, 1994.

————. "Irish Road Race Becomes Major Event at 20 Years," *Springfield Union News*, March 15, 1994.

————. "Runners Can Pick Two Gems," *Springfield Union News*, September 18, 1997.

Pedlosky, Dove Helena "Families Host Elite Runners," *Falmouth Road Race Program*, Enterprise Publications, August 1999.

Pelletier, Russ. "Holy Cow!" *New England Runner*, July/August 2003.

————. "Road Trip," *The Road Record*, Falmouth Track Club, Summer 2004.

Perry, Jack. "Tommy Leonard's Dream," *Cape Cod Times*, August 17, 1997.

Peters, Paula. "First Person View Shows Why This Race Is So Special," *Cape Cod Times*, August 12, 2002.

————. "Working on the Pee Patrol," *32nd SBLI Falmouth Road Race Official Magazine*, August 8, 2004.

Pierce, Charles. "Watch on the Brine," *Boston Phoenix*, August 12, 1980.

————. "The Last Sports Bar," *GQ*, October 1996.

————. "Requiem for a Beloved Bar," *Sports Illustrated*, February 7, 2005.

Reynolds, Dorothy. "10th Annual Denmark Award Goes to Frank Shephard," *29th SBLI Falmouth Road Race Official Magazine*, August 12, 2001.

Ross, Ken. "Hundreds Race to Help Scholars," *Springfield Union News*, September 17, 1997.

Schulian, John. "Marathon's Ale Fellow, Well Met," *Chicago Sun-Times*, April 19, 1982.

Seto, Rick. "A Runner's Day," *Springfield Union News*, May 10, 1993.

Shea, Jim. "Boston Marathon Has Bar of Its Own," *Hartford Courant*, April 16, 1989.

Sherman, Elizabeth. "Mt. Rushmore Flag Inspires Many," *29th SBLI Falmouth Road Race Official Magazine*, August 12, 2001.

———. "Denmark Award Winners Provide Inspiration to Many," *32nd SBLI Falmouth Road Race*, August 8, 2004.

Simeson, C. "Westfield's Adopted Son Gives 5K Gift," *Springfield Union News*, May 3, 1993.

———. "Westfield Race Earns Some Notoriety," *Springfield Sunday Republican*, February 6, 1994.

———. "Westfield Race Pays Tribute to Its Polish Citizens," *Springfield Union News*, May 10, 1994.

———. "Westfield Race a Day of Fun," *Springfield Union News*, April 27, 1995.

"650 May Run Sunday," *Falmouth Enterprise*, August 15, 1975.

Springfield Union News staff. "Harbilis Credits Volunteers," November 24, 1994.

Springfield Union News staff, "Billy Harbilis," November 26, 1998.

Stewart, Phil. "Rodgers Sets Falmouth Record," *Running Times*, October 1978.

Tempesta, Mike. "Leonard Ponders Goodbye," *Middlesex News*, August 14, 1986.

Tetreault, Kate. "Friendship Forged by Road Race," *Falmouth Enterprise*, August 9, 2002.

———. "Determination Spurs Longtime Falmouth Road Race Runner," *Falmouth Enterprise*, August 9, 2002.

25th Harvard Pilgrim Health Falmouth Road Race Official Magazine, August 17, 1997.

29th SBLI Falmouth Road Race Official Magazine, August 12, 2001.

31st SBLI Falmouth Road Race Official Magazine, August 10, 2003.

Wagner, Kellie. "Brisk Pace Established for 5K Registration," *Springfield Union News*, March 9, 1996.

————. "Westfield Race Has Special Flavor," *Springfield Sunday Republican*, March 12, 1996.

————. "Road Race Crowd Brightens Wet Day," *Springfield Sunday Republican*, May 19, 1996.

Wagenheim, Jeff. "A Guide to the Falmouth Road—As Time Goes By," *Boston Phoenix*, August 21, 1984.

Waterbury Sunday Republican. Sportester cartoon, July 6, 1980.

Wilson, Craig. "A Final Toast to the Keeper of the Boston Marathon Suds," *USA Today*, April 8, 1996.

Zemek, Susan. "Beantown Bar's Regulars Follow Their Race Favorite," *Olympian Newspaper*, May 12, 1984.

Other Documents

Ackerman, Joan B., and Patricia Cramer. *Images of America: Westfield.* Westfield Atheneum, Arcadia Publishing, 1996.

Bulger, William M., President of Massachusetts Senate, State Senate Official Citation, June 15, 1989.

City of Westfield, 1946 Annual Report.

Congressional Record, "The Eliot Lounge," *Proceedings and Debates of the 104th Congress, 2nd Session*, September 19, 1996.

Connecticut Valley Historical Museum, 1930 census.

Flynn, Ray, Mayor of Boston. Certificate of Recognition, October 8, 1992.

Flynn, Ray, Ambassador to the Vatican. Letter to the Tommy Leonard Wicked Awesome Hampshire House Happening, September 18, 1996

Grandmother's Garden Plaque, Westfield, MA

Images of America, Vintage Postcards, Westfield Atheneum, Arcadia Publishing

Kearney, Jack, The Ballad of the Eliot Lounge

Kearney, Jack, Leonard Vs. Clemens, It's no Contest

Larner, JJ, Eliot Lounge Appreciation Party for all you Little Farber Heads Out There, September 14, 1996

Melconian, Linda, State Senator, MA Senate Letter of Commendation, May 23, 1985

Shurtleff Mission records at Westfield Atheneum

Springfield Daily News, Obituaries, November 17, 1951

St. Michael's Cemetery Records, Springfield, MA Report 5290, Pg 5

Scott, Jane and Roscoe Scott, eds., Westfield, MA 1669–1969—The First 300 Years, The Authors Tea, Westfield Women's Club, December 1, 1968, Westfield Tri-Centennial Association

Times and Newsletter, Opening of Children's Home, December 13, 1899

Proclamations

City of New London, Tommy Leonard Day, August 3, 1979, Carl Stoner, Mayor

City of Boston, Tommy Leonard Day, July 2, 1982, Kevin White, Mayor

City of Houston, Houstonian Goodwill Ambassador, April 22, 1983, Russell Harris, President

City of Houston, Honorary Citizen Appointment, April 23, 1983, Kathryn J Whitmore, Mayor

Commonwealth of Massachusetts, Tommy Leonard Day, August 2, 1995, William F. Weld, Governor

City of Boston, Tommy Leonard Day, September 18, 1996, Thomas M. Menino, Mayor

City of Newton, Tommy Leonard Day, September 18, 1996, Thomas B. Concannon, Mayor

Commonwealth of Massachusetts, Tommy Leonard Day, September 18, 1996, William F. Weld, Governor

Books

Albom, Mitch, Tuesdays with Morrie, New York: Doubleday, August, 1997

Falls, Joe, The Boston Marathon, New York: Collier Books, 1977

Higdon, Hal, A Century of Running Boston, PA: Rodale Press, 1995

McCloskey, Robert, Make Way for Ducklings, New York: The Viking Press, 1941

Rodgers, Bill with Joe Concannon, Marathoning, New York: Simon and Schuster 1980

Interviews

Tommy Leonard—October 2000, November 2000, March 2003, November 2003, numerous phone calls and visits, 2004, 2005

Francis X Tierney—October 16, 2000

Susan Tierney Oslin—e-mails, 2003, 2004, 2005

Billy Neller—April 8, 2003

Brent "Hawk" Hawkins—e-mails, 2003, 2004

George Kelleher—September 23, 2003

Kenny Balducci—October 6, 2003

Don Foley—November, 2003

Peter Butler—November, 2003

Michael "Champ" and Ann "Pinky" Morris—December 9, 2003

John "Jiggs" Morrissey—December 9, 2003

Barbara Benhardt—January 29, 2004

Fred "Moe" Placzek—May 5, 2004

Dick "Blizzard" Barry—May 5, 2004

Coach Bill Squires—May 6, 2004

Eddie Doyle—May 13, 2004, and numerous e-mails

Sharpless Jones—May 13, 2004

Fran and Kit Coffey—May 13, 2004

Doug Brown—May 15, 2004

Don Aiken—May 14, 2004

Jackie Pierce—May 16, 2004

Carol Bannon Flynn—June 18, 2004

Neal Hansen I—June 18, 2004

Dante Malta—June 18, 2004

Yoichi Furukawa—e-mails, 2004, 2005

Del Wynn—July 11, 2004

Billy Rodgers—August 2, 2004

Ron Pokraka—August 9, 2004

Brian Salzberg—August 9, 2004

Michael Bennett—August 9, 2004

Don Delinks—August 9, 2004

Jimmy Tierney—August 29, 2004

Billy Harbilas—August 29, 2004

Sally Rohan—August 29, 2004, and numerous e-mails, 2004, 2005

Toni Reavis—e-mails, September 21, 2004, and 2005

Russ Pelletier—e-mails, 2004, 2005

Jack Kearney—October 1, 2004

Bill "Spaceman" Lee—October 5, 2004

Rich Sherman—October 5, 2004, and numerous e-mails, 2004, 2005

Eddie Burke—October 7, 2004

George Robbat—October 7, 2004

JJ Lerner—Fall 2004

Grace Leonard—October 12, 2004

Kenny Gartner—October 12, 2004

Joan Benoit Samuelson—October 13, 2004

Peter Sheehan—December 2004

Frank Beatty—January 11, 2005

Ron Della Chiesa—January 12, 2005

Jay Fiandella—January 17, 2005

Dr. Charles Tifft—January 18, 2005

Bernie Corbett—March 8, 2005

Jeff Fumorala—March 11, 2005

Craig Virgin—March 14, 2005

Glenn McKinnon—March 20, 2005

Greg Meyer—March 22, 2005

Dick Hoyt—March 28, 2005

John Connolly—March 29, 2005

Senator John Kerry—e-mail, March 2005

Richard and Anne Prior—2000–2005

Scott and Marj Williamson—2000–2005

Ed and Pat Pas—2000–2005

Bill and Sylvette McCabe—2000–2005

Michael Cleary—1978 to present

Web sites

www.BAA.com

www.bartender.com/2specials/halloffame-1.html

www.Boston.com/sports

www.Chezjays.co/folklore.htlm

www.coolrunning.com

www.digitalcity.com/losangeles.dining/venue

www.2cs.cmu.edu/afs/cs.smu

www.harvardclub.com

www.la.com

www.library.bowdoin.edu/arch/subject/bowdoin/prize.html

www.marines.com/history

www.medievalmanor.com

www.SBLIFalmouthroadrace.com

www.sportfilm.com

www.usmc.mil/HD/Historicalcustoms

www.vernonwhite.com

www.wentforth-by-the-sea.com

www.wikipedia.org/Duffy'sTavern

978-0-595-35698-0
0-595-35698-2

Printed in the United States
37011LVS00003B/286-288